# HOW TO THINK LIKE
# AN ANTHROPOLOGIST

# How to Think Like an Anthropologist

PRINCETON UNIVERSITY PRESS

PRINCETON AND OXFORD

# CONTENTS

# HOW TO THINK LIKE
# AN ANTHROPOLOGIST

# INTRODUCTION

In the summer of 1879, Frank Hamilton Cushing set off from his desk at the Smithsonian Institution to undertake three months of research in New Mexico. Under the auspices of the federal Bureau of Ethnology, his task was to find out everything he could "about some typical tribe of Pueblo Indians."[1]

Cushing ended up in Zuni, one of the pueblos. He was captivated by the Zuni's methods of farming and irrigation, animal husbandry, skill at pottery, and elaborate ceremonial dances. He stayed longer than three months—a lot longer, as it happens, nearly five years. By the time he returned to Washington, D.C., in 1884, he spoke the language fluently, was a decent enough potter, and bore a new title, alongside that of U.S. assistant ethnologist: "First War Chief of Zuni."

Cushing published several essays on his time in Zuni, among them a series with the rather prosaic title "Zuni Breadstuffs." Yet the Zuni attitudes toward their food, and toward raising crops, were anything but dull and mundane. What we learn via Cushing is not only how the Zuni till the land or bake cornmeal bread. This is also the series of essays in which he sets out the importance of hospitality, explains how grandparents instill the values of patience, respect, and hard work in young children, and interprets how the rich symbolism of the Kâ'-Kâ festivals underscores the importance of the practice of uxorilocal marriage (the technical term for when a man goes to live in the homestead of his wife).[2] What emerges from this treatment of Zuni foodways is something of the culture writ large, of how a society in this often harsh and unrelenting environment flourishes through communal ties and mutuality. "Patient reader, forgive me for having lingered so long in the Zuni cornfields," he writes at one point. "However closely we may have scrutinized these crops growing green, golden grown as they may have been, we have but barely glanced at them according to the rules and practices of their dusky owners."[3]

In 2000, Caitlin Zaloom set off from Berkeley, California, to London to undertake research on futures trading. Zaloom had already spent six months in 1998 working as a runner at the Chicago Board of Trade. The value of runners had been tested by time; these were the people who literally ran across trading floors, scraps of paper in their hands with orders placed by customers on the other end of a phone. The Chicago pit was a "financial melee," Zaloom writes, "runners often elbowed each other out of the way," and "the noise was deafening."[4] It wasn't the chaos of the floor that bothered these ambitious capitalists, however. It was the dawning of the electronic age. Electronic trading was on its way, and it would radically transform the nature of their work within a few years. As in Chicago, in London Zaloom was up at the crack of dawn every day and off to the City. There, though, she didn't throw on a trader's coat and exchange elbows with her peers in the pit: "I spent nine hours a day with eyes fixed on my screen and fingers lying lightly on the mouse, poised to click the second an opportunity for profit appeared."[5]

German treasury bond futures might well be recognized as closer to the workings of power than a Zuni cornfield, but they are hardly a riveting topic. For Zaloom, however, futures trading was a window onto the larger world of markets, morality, and conceptions of rationality. It was also a window onto the processes of globalization, itself furthered by new technologies, market regimes, and culturally specific systems of exchange. What made electronic trading particularly interesting to her was the extent to which it promised to deliver a truly "free" market—one based on the rationality of electronic, disembodied transactions rather than humans literally fumbling over each other. Get out of the trading pits, the promise of e-trading held, and it's almost as if you step out of culture; you free yourself from the biases and background factors that might hamper your profits. As Zaloom makes clear, the promise wasn't delivered, in large part because you can't step out of culture—you can't trade futures in a culture-free zone.

Cushing in Zuni; Zaloom in London: this is anthropology. Over the past 150 years, the discipline of anthropology has been driven by a curiosity with humankind's cultural expressions, institutions, and commitments. What is it that makes us human? What is it that we all share, and what is it that we inherit from the circumstances of society and history? What can seemingly small details, like the cultural significance of maize or our use of computers, tell us about who we are?

Anthropology has always worked at the intersection of nature and culture, the universal and the particular, patterns and diversity, similarities and differences. Exactly how that work takes place has changed over time. Back in Cushing's day, theories of social evolution, modeled on the findings of Charles Darwin in biology, drove the ways in which the newly emerging field of anthropology approached cultural diversity; back then, the Zuni were thought to occupy a different, earlier stage of human-kind's development. Today, an anthropologist such as Zaloom would be much more likely to argue that the truck and barter of small-scale societies should be treated in the same frame as e-trading in cyberspace. Still other approaches have been dominant, and even today there are distinct ones: there are cognitive anthropologists and postmodern ones too; Marxists and structuralists; most—including me—would subscribe to no such labels, preferring to draw from their own handmade portmanteau. But what binds them all is the stitch of the cultural.

This book focuses in the main on the kind of work that Cushing and Zaloom have done, which is often called social or cultural anthropology. It's the kind of anthropology that I do as well—hence my slant. But not all anthropologists work with living, breathing people, situated in a particular place or community. In several national traditions, the biological and evolutionary aspects of humans are looked at alongside the cultural ones. Archaeology and linguistics are often important areas of anthropology too. Some anthropologists, in other words, focus on teeth and hip bones; others on what prehistorical settlement patterns can tell us about the emergence of agriculture, iron smelting, and state formation; still others on technical aspects of Bantu noun classes and phonology (the study of the organization of sound use in language). When it comes to archaeology and linguistics, the links with culture are pretty obvious: archaeology, after all, is concerned with what we often call "material culture"; language and culture are two sides of the same coin. (And besides, most linguistic anthropologists study language use rather than its abstracted formalities. That means studying it in particular places and particular times, much like cultural anthropologists.) Yet even for anthropological specialists in anatomy and evolution, the building blocks of culture are a central interest. The size of our brains, our dental makeup, and the strength of our thighbones are studied by biological anthropologists for what they can tell us about the origins of language, tool use, and the rise of bipedalism. In a word, culture.

## FIRST CONTACT: A PERSONAL TALE

I remember very well the first piece of anthropology I read. I was a first-year student at university, holed up in the library on a cold Chicago night. I remember it so well because it threw me. It challenged the way I thought about the world. You might say it induced a small culture shock. It was an essay titled "The Original Affluent Society" by Marshall Sahlins, one of the discipline's most significant figures. In this essay, Sahlins details the assumptions behind modern, Western understandings of economic rationality and behavior, as depicted, for example, in economics textbooks. In doing so, he exposes a prejudice toward and misunderstanding of hunter-gatherers: the small bands of people in the Kalahari Desert, the forests of the Congo, Australia, and elsewhere who lead a nomadic lifestyle, all with very few possessions and no elaborate material culture. These people hunt for wildlife, gather berries, and move on as necessary.

As Sahlins shows, the textbook assumption is that these people must be miserable, hungry, and fighting each day just to survive. Just look at them: they wear loincloths at most; they have no settlements; they have almost no possessions. This assumption of lack follows on from a more basic one: that human beings always want more than they have. Limited means to meet unlimited desires. According to this way of thinking, it must be the case that hunters and gatherers can do no better; surely they live that way not out of choice but of necessity. In this Western view, the hunter-gatherer is "equipped with bourgeois impulses and paleolithic tools," so "we judge his situation hopeless in advance."[6] Drawing on a number of anthropological studies, however, Sahlins demonstrates that "want" has very little to do with how hunter-gatherers approach life. In many of these groups in Australia and Africa, for example, adults had to work no more than three to five hours per day in order to meet their needs. What the anthropologists studying these societies realized is that the people could have worked more but *did not want to*. They did not have bourgeois impulses. They had different values than ours. "The world's most primitive people have few possessions," Sahlins concludes, "but they are not poor.... Poverty is a social status. As such it is the invention of civilization."[7]

After reading Sahlins, I could never hear talk about "affluence" in quite the same way. I could never rest easy with my own assumptions about what it means and how my assumptions often took on the rather dangerous garb of common sense. This lesson from Sahlins was only the first of many when it came to words I thought I knew how to use, how to think with. As a student, I quickly learned that anthropology is very good at questioning concepts, at questioning "common sense." One of the discipline's trademark clichés is that we make the familiar strange and the strange familiar. It is a cliché, but it's no less true for being so. And that process of questioning, that process of turning things upside down, is one of lasting value.

In the chapters to follow, I take a page from Sahlins's book—from every good anthropologist's book—and set about exploring and questioning concepts. They are not technical concepts, and they are all ones with which you will be familiar. They are, in fact, everyday words, and purposefully so. As a rule, anthropologists are interested in everyday things. I begin with anthropology's foundational concern itself—culture—and then go on to consider a small number of others: civilization, values, value, blood, identity, authority, reason, and nature. It is a barebones list; I am all too aware of what's being left out. What about "society"? What about "power"? But there is no point in trying to be exhaustive; there would always be another term to add. This book is a map with some points of orientation. It is meant to be a useful guide to a larger territory—the territory of our lives—which is and always will be defined by the importance of taking account of the lives of others.

Anthropology doesn't just level critiques. It doesn't just point to the ways in which our understandings of "affluence," "civilization," and "blood" are culturally specific, or even handicapped by the blind spots of our common sense. Anthropology also explains. Above all, it explains both how and why culture is central to our makeup as human beings. We are not automatons. We are not governed by a strong "human nature," and we are not simple products of our genes. We make choices. The hunter-gatherers have had choices, and they have often chosen, historically speaking, to cultivate the value of egalitarianism, while downplaying that of property, in order to maintain their ways of life. The nomadic existence of hunting and gathering is dependent upon both of these things: the sharing of resources and the discouragement of status and accumulation (stuff, after all, only weighs you down). Up until the 1960s, for example, the Hadza, a group of hunter-gatherers who live in Tanzania, chose not to adopt the ways of nearby pastoralists.

Our "choices" of course are often constrained. The environment plays a role, cultural traditions play a role (we can't make them up out of whole cloth), and the broader currents of politics and society play a role too. Sahlins published "The Original Affluent Society" in 1972. By that point in time, the ability to live a nomadic lifestyle had been seriously curtailed. Colonial expansion often led to seizure or redeployment of the land that nomadic groups had relied upon. So we *do* find impoverished hunters and gatherers, Sahlins notes, but this has to be seen as a result of "colonial duress"—of being dragged into the orbit of "civilization."[8] That's what he means by saying that poverty is an invention of civilization. This duress has continued into the present day, although more often now under the auspices of globalization. Over the past fifty years, the Hadza have lost access to 90 percent of the land they traditionally relied upon to hunt game.[9] Similar stories can be found around the globe, from the Kalahari Desert in Namibia to the forests of Malaysia. Hunters and gatherers don't have nearly as many choices these days. Another thing I learned from "The Original Affluent Society" then is just this: no culture exists in isolation. No culture is ever really original; every culture is, we might say, always on a nomadic path.

## ANTHROPOLOGY PROPER

Before embarking on our more focused discussions, it will be helpful to provide a bit more background on anthropology as a discipline. This book is not a history of anthropology. But throughout, I will highlight some of the key figures, trajectories, and trends because the story of anthropology's emergence and development tells us important things about the modern academic disciplines more generally. Some background is also helpful given the emphasis here on the subfields of social and cultural anthropology. These are not as well-known as archaeology and biological anthropology. I am a cultural anthropologist, yet I still have some blood relatives who think I dig potshards out of the ground or measure skulls. Also, if people are aware of the sociocultural traditions, they often think anthropology's remit is Zuni, not London— that London, being in the West, and perhaps even "modern," is the preserve of sociologists. While it's true that anthropologists traditionally tended to focus on the non-Western world, there have long been exceptions—there is a great anthropological study of Hollywood published in 1950, for instance.[10] It's never just been jungles and drums.

Anthropology as we know it is just over 150 years old. The Royal Anthropological Institute of Great Britain and Ireland was formed in 1848. In 1851, Lewis Henry Morgan, a lawyer from upstate New York, published *League of the Iroquois* and went on to produce a series of seminal studies on kinship based on work with Native American peoples. In France, the first chair in anthropology was established in 1855 at the Musée d'histoire naturelle,

Paris.[11] This is about as far back in the modern genealogy as we can reasonably get. It is not unusual for anthropologists to claim earlier figures as ancestors: Michel de Montaigne (1533–92), for instance; Herodotus (484–426 BC) is also a favorite. Both had what has come to be known as an anthropological sensibility. Herodotus traveled to far-flung lands and provides us with rich descriptions of "Others" to the Greeks. Montaigne did not travel in this way, but for his important essay "Of Cannibals" he took pains to speak with three Tupinambá Indians (from what is today Brazil), brought to France, whom he met in Rouen. In the essay, he implores his readers not to be too swift to judge their supposed savagery (the Tupinambá were said to have eaten their Portuguese captives), urging us to understand the more holistic picture of their practices and ways of life.

In each of these prototype cases, as in the fully-fledged anthropological ones we've considered briefly, two key features stand out: (1) the importance of fieldwork; and (2) the principle of cultural relativism. You can't understand anthropology without understanding these things.

Fieldwork has long been the central rite of passage for the anthropologist. While some founding figures are better described as "armchair anthropologists" (because they relied primarily on the work and reports of others), and while some traditions have clearer and longer-standing divisions of labor between empirical research and theory building (the French, for instance), you generally can't be taken seriously without spending a year or more among the people you're studying. Some anthropologists begin their careers this way, off in the field, and don't end up returning a lot, or ever; they carry on doing anthropology by turning to more theoretical or conceptual concerns. In-

deed, some of the most important anthropological thinkers are not die-hard fieldworkers. But in nearly all cases,
they did it to start with and it confirms their bona fides.

The main aspect of fieldwork is participant observation. Exactly what this means can differ. If you are in
Zuni, or some hamlet in Chhattisgarh, India, it should
mean almost total immersion. You should live with the
locals, eat with them, learn their language, and take part
in as full a range of their activities as possible. In short,
and to put it in decidedly unscientific terms, you should
be *hanging out* and *doing stuff*. If you are in London,
total immersion can be slightly more challenging. Not all
futures traders, of course, live in something akin to a
pueblo, and they may well not invite you into their homes
on a regular basis to break bread. Not that hospitality
counts for nothing in England, but still, it's not the Zuni
of 1879. As Zaloom did, though, you should get into the
thick of things at work (or church, or gambling shops, or
whatever you happen to be focusing on): you should be
seeking those profits yourself because what you need to
appreciate is how the people you're studying think, act,
and live. One thing I always tell my PhD students is that
being a fieldworker is kind of like being that kid in school
who always wanted to play with everyone. "Hey, what's
going on!? Can I join in?" That's the life of an anthropologist in the field.

There can be a fine line between participant observation and going native. Anthropologists should not "go
native."* Going native can rob you of the critical distance

---

* Unless they *are* "native." The Japanese anthropologist Emiko Ohnuki-
Tierney (1984), for instance, studied "her people" in Kobe. The category of
native anthropologist is a fraught one, though, and has occasioned a lot of
debate. It usually only comes up if being "native" means being non-white and

you need to make an analysis; it can also prompt ethical challenges. During his fieldwork, Cushing came close on several occasions (actually, he went over the line): shooting at Navajo ponies (which, he claimed, had been wrongly brought onto Zuni lands), leading a raid on horse thieves (resulting in the death of two men), and even claiming an Apache scalp. Cushing had been inducted by his hosts as a war chief; claiming scalps is what was required of a man of his standing. Cushing also sent one U.S. senator into near apoplexy by exposing the fraudulent land claim of the senator's son-in-law, an action that led to Cushing's recall by the Bureau of Ethnology. "If a civilized white man can now get only 160 acres of land as a homestead by paying for it, and an Indian can get over 1,000 acres without paying for it," the angry senator wrote, "had not the white man better adopt the Cushing plan and become one of the Zuni Indians?"[12]

Cushing may have championed the Zuni's case against the shady dealings of the political elite, but it should not be forgotten that he was in the employ of the U.S. government and that he arrived not long after some of the most brutal and bloody chapters of America's westward expansion. In 1994, the Zuni artist Phil Hughte published a series of cartoons about Cushing, and it really captures the conflicted place of the anthropologist. Some of the cartoons express admiration for Cushing's dedication to the Zuni; others convey much more ambivalence, and

non-Western. So if you're Japanese and studying Japan, yes, that's "native." But if you're a white American studying, say, Hollywood, you probably won't be called a "native anthropologist." As we'll see, these debates tell us something important about anthropology's colonial history. In any case, the main point of the injunction against "going native" is that an anthropologist should not simply present the world in terms of the people being studied. At least for it to be anthropology, there has to be some kind of critical distance.

even anger, at what Hughte and many other Zunis have seen as betrayals and bullying—including reenacting parts of a secret rite for colleagues back in Washington. The final cartoon in Hughte's book is of Cushing's demise, in 1900, when he choked on a fish bone over dinner one night in Florida, where he was conducting an archaeological dig. The cartoon is called *The Last Supper* and Hughte tells us: "This was a fun drawing to do."[13]

Hughte's schadenfreude is not hard to understand. Anthropology has often been tagged as a handmaiden of colonialism. And in some respects, it was—and can be— in neocolonial and neo-imperial forms. In the United States, this has extended from "Indian affairs" in the nineteenth century to a series of controversial special operations and counterinsurgency programs in Latin America and Southeast Asia in the 1960s; from 2006 to 2014, the United States ran another controversial counterinsurgency program in Iraq and Afghanistan, engineered in large part by an anthropologist and staffed by many too.[14] In the United Kingdom, France, Germany, Belgium, the Netherlands, and Portugal, anthropologists often worked for the state or otherwise closely with colonial officials during the heydays of their empires, with many colonial officials in Britain being trained in anthropology themselves.

Yet even in the early generations, the commitment to anthropology and the ties anthropologists created with the people they studied often trumped colonial agendas— or even worked against their grain. In many ways, Cushing embodies the best and worst of what anthropologists can do. And we should not forget the worst. Today, though, to be sure, many anthropologists are active champions of the communities they study (and *not* by claiming enemy scalps). They promote group rights, are openly critical of detrimental or counterproductive government and NGO projects, and protest against the interests of mining companies and lumber mills in Papua New Guinea and the Amazon rainforests. Doctor and medical anthropologist Paul Farmer cofounded Partners in Health, a medical NGO, as well as the Institute for Justice and Democracy in Haiti. In the United Kingdom, dozens of anthropologists serve as witnesses in asylum tribunals, sharing their country expertise for cases pertaining to Afghanistan, Sri Lanka, Zimbabwe, and elsewhere.

If fieldwork is the hallmark method, cultural relativism is the hallmark mode. In one way or another, all anthropology is underpinned by it. Put simply, cultural relativism is a critical self-awareness that your own terms of analysis, understanding, and judgment are not universal and cannot be taken for granted. Yet putting this "simply" doesn't always do the trick; cultural relativism is one of the most misunderstood aspects of the anthropological sensibility—even, I would argue, by some anthropologists. Indeed, not all anthropologists are cultural relativists. But they all use cultural relativism to get their work done.

It's often helpful to explain what cultural relativism is by explaining what it's not. One of the most important essays on the topic, in fact, by Clifford Geertz, is called "Anti Anti-Relativism." Not even someone like him—he was a very gifted writer—could take a direct approach to such a delicate topic.

Cultural relativism does not require you to accept everything that other people do that you might otherwise find unjust or wrong. Cultural relativism does not mean you have no firm values or even that, as an academic (or poet or priest or judge), you can never say anything true or even general about the human condition or in a cross-cultural frame. Cultural relativism doesn't require you to condemn statistical data, scoff at the Universal Declaration of Human Rights, accept the practice of female circumcision, or declare yourself an unbelieving atheist. These are often the kinds of charges leveled against "relativists"—that they deny the existence of hard data or have no moral red lines, or maybe even moral standards. But none of this has anything to do with how anthropologists use relativism in their research and approach to understanding the human condition.

Another way to put this is that cultural relativism is the sensibility that colors the method. It is an approach, a styling. It is what helps anthropologists guard against the dangers of assuming that their common sense or even informed understanding—about justice or affluence or fatherhood or the elementary forms of religious life—is self-evident or universally applicable. For an anthropologist, it is vital to understand how justice, or affluence, or fatherhood, or religion gets understood locally—if at all. Indeed, it is not uncommon for the people an anthropologist studies to confound the terms of analysis offered up. *Art? What's that? Religion? Huh? Oedipus? Who cares? Freedom? That doesn't look like freedom to us.* We already had a hint of this in Sahlins's treatment of the original affluent society. At its most basic, relativism should provide an appreciation of what Bronislaw Malinowski, to whom we'll presently turn, called "the native's point of view, his relation to life"; the goal is "to realize *his* vision of *his* world." *[15]

---

* The term "native" has come up twice now. It is a term that can sound jarring. And so it should. In many ways it conjures up the image of colonial times made famous by such writers as Rudyard Kipling and Joseph Conrad—

## THE BIRTH OF A DISCIPLINE

It took a couple of generations for anthropology to professionalize what had originally been an amateur or "gentlemanly" pursuit of knowledge. When Cushing went to Zuni, there were no departments of anthropology in American universities; the modern university system itself, in which the social sciences came to occupy a distinct wing, was still in development. Cushing attended Cornell University but did not receive a degree. In Britain, Edward Burnett Tylor, who eventually occupied a personal chair in anthropology at Oxford University, never went to university himself and became an "anthropologist" partly because he was a sickly young man whose middle-class Quaker parents could afford to send him to the Caribbean, in the hope that the climate might do him some good. There, he met a true gentleman-explorer, Henry Christy; they went off to Mexico together and Tylor tried his hand at a popular literary genre of the Victorian era: the exotic adventure. His book on their travels in Latin America met with some success and led to a more systematic and ambitious study, *Primitive Culture* (1871). At Cambridge University, the first major "anthropological" expedition, in 1898, was undertaken by a

---

"the natives are getting restless" and that sort of thing. Up until World War II, and even somewhat later, "native" was used freely by anthropologists to refer to colonial subjects and it references an unequal power relation; it never meant "native of Berlin" or "native of San Francisco." Over the past several decades, however, many anthropologists have reappropriated the term, lacing it with irony and (self) critique, by applying it precisely to the natives of Berlin and San Francisco. The point such anthropologists are trying to make is that everyone is a "native" in one way or another—that anthropology's remit is the whole of humanity.

small group of men trained in psychiatry, biology, and medicine.

Early champions fought hard for anthropology's incorporation into the university system. Bronislaw Malinowski, regularly acknowledged as the founding figure of British social anthropology (though neither he nor many of his students were British), wrote a passionate critique of amateurism and a manifesto for "the law and order of method." Malinowski had no time for the kind of gentleman-explorers one found in Victorian Britain, or even any well-intentioned colonial officers or missionaries, whose observations were "strongly repulsive to a mind striving after the objective, scientific view of things."[16] He made an institution of what Cushing had been doing thirty years earlier: fieldwork by participant observation. In his classic study, *Argonauts of the Western Pacific* (1922), based on his two years of fieldwork in the Trobriand Islands, Malinowski made much of his tent, pitched in medias res on the Nu'agasi beach. Not for him the colonial district officer's veranda. In the 1920s and 1930s, at the London School of Economics (LSE), he trained or otherwise influenced almost all of the leading lights of the next generation: figures such as E. E. Evans-Pritchard and Edmund Leach (they were very English, actually), Raymond Firth (a New Zealander), and Isaac Schapera and Meyer Fortes (both South African). Firth and Schapera carried on at the LSE; Evans-Pritchard went to Oxford and Leach and Fortes to Cambridge, where in each university important departments grew up.

In the United States, the German émigré Franz Boas did at Columbia University what Malinowski had done at the LSE—and this was over a much longer period of time, 1896 to 1942. His students included Margaret

Mead, Ruth Benedict, Melville Herskovits, Zora Neale Hurston, Edward Sapir, Robert Lowie, and Alfred Kroeber, some of whom—especially Mead—became household names and were very widely read. Others went on to establish new centers of anthropology, including, for instance, the department at the University of California, Berkeley. Kroeber taught at Berkeley for over forty years; Lowie for over thirty years. Herskovits had a similarly long career at Northwestern University.*

For these early generations, especially in the United States, the task of "salvage ethnography" was often a major motivation: recording the ways of life of disappearing peoples, through either destruction or assimilation into the workings of modernity. One of Kroeber's main research interests captures this particularly well; for a time in the 1910s, he worked closely with a man named Ishi, the last surviving member of the Yahi people of California. Kroeber and some of his colleagues at Berkeley took pains to record as much as they could from this last "wild man," as he was referred to at the time. Boas himself is often noted for the prodigious amount of documentation he produced. Aficionados of anthropology's history will refer to Boas's "five-foot shelf"—the five feet worth of books and papers he wrote, that is. Some of these were classic studies of exchange systems among Native Americans of the Northwest Coast; some were their recipes for blueberry muffins. Although Boas lacked the flair of Cushing on similar topics, he is the canonical figure. For not only did he train so many of the first

---

* Like women in other academic fields and professions, women in anthropology, especially in these early periods, often came up against the glass ceiling. Neither Mead nor Benedict got top university positions, despite their formidable accomplishments and reputations.

few generations of anthropologists, he also shaped the paradigm of anthropology with which we still work—or grapple—today.

## CAVEAT EMPTOR!

Introducing anthropology is not easy—you simply can't cover it all. So you need to beware, reader, of what you have before you. I have already stressed that in what follows I'll be focusing in the main on social and cultural anthropology rather than other subfields. And as the scope of the last section implies, I am also going to be concentrating by and large on traditions that grew up in the United Kingdom and the United States. Yet a few points need to be kept in mind.

The first is that, while the British and American branches did start out as fairly well-defined traditions, they both changed and opened up over time. Malinowski and Boas were strong personalities; they had strong programs and that carried their work pretty far and pretty diffusely. Both are still read today, especially Malinowski (although it is probably Boas's legacy that has gained wider purchase). But they were never the only dominant figures, and it would now be impossible to find any such coherence, given the range of ways in which the discipline has unfolded. There are still ways in which "American cultural anthropology" and "British social anthropology" differ, but a lot of Americans teach in the UK and a lot of Britons teach in the United States; training of PhD students in the best departments is also thoroughly multinational and cosmopolitan (and well beyond the Anglo-American world). And, of course, remember that the founder of British social anthropology was Polish and the founder of American cultural anthropology was German. That leads us to the second point: there has always been a lot of international exchange. Another key figure in this was A. R. Radcliffe-Brown, an Englishman, who was something of an heir to Malinowski in Britain (not that Malinowski would have had it that way) but also extremely influential in the United States, where he taught at the University of Chicago in the 1930s. Chicago has been a leading department since then and has always aimed to include prominent figures on the faculty roster from outside the American tradition. Radcliffe-Brown also taught in Australia and South Africa. The other country with a dominant tradition of anthropology—France—also had links with both Britain and America, especially America via the wartime exile of Claude Lévi-Strauss, who spent some of the 1940s in New York City and whose seminal work on structuralism was partly made possible by the richly ethnographic case studies of Boas and his students. The affinity between Boas and Lévi-Strauss, despite the very different kinds of anthropology they produced, is captured in symbolism you could not top. Lévi-Strauss was at the luncheon in 1942 when Boas died; according to the Frenchman, Boas died in his arms. Many years later, though, it was British social anthropologist Edmund Leach who became Lévi-Strauss's main exponent and advocate in the English-speaking world. Mary Douglas, another British major figure, also drew heavily on structuralism.

Finally, it is worth noting the importance of other traditions altogether, with those in Brazil, the Netherlands, Belgium, Canada, South Africa, Australia, India, and each

of the Scandinavian countries playing notable roles. (The
Scandinavians punch well above their weight, actually,
and have done for several decades.) Indeed, a contemporary Brazilian anthropologist, Eduardo Viveiros de Castro, is one of the most influential figures at the moment;
we'll consider some of his ideas later on. And then there
are even more layered identifications and connections,
with, say, renowned Germans in Dutch universities, or the
fact that a Briton, an American, a Belgian, and a Dutch-
man direct the various prestigious Max Planck Institutes
in Germany that are dedicated to anthropology. Another
eminent contemporary anthropologist, Talal Asad, was
born in Saudi Arabia, raised in India and Pakistan, educated in the United Kingdom, and rose to prominence in
the United States. In short, you should not come away
from this introduction thinking the story of anthropology's positioning in the world of nation-states is a straightforward one.

Anthropology is also more than an academic discipline; we have seen this in the various brief examples
provided thus far—from taking scalps (again, not recom-
mended) to starting NGOs in Haiti. More broadly, however, what is often called "applied anthropology" can be
found in most sectors and levels of operation. There are,
as I noted earlier, anthropologists who put their skills to
use for the U.S. military; there are others who become
professional consultants and start their own businesses
to provide "ethnographic solutions" to various problems,
which might include anything from helping a housing association recognize the signs of domestic violence among
tenants to providing advice on how a French cosmetics
company might best market its products in Jordan. At the

University of Copenhagen, you can even now study for a master's degree in "business and organizational anthropology" and then maybe go on to work for ReD Associates, a Danish anthropology consulting firm. ReD knows that culture matters, and that it can be sold. They publish thoughtful articles like "Why Culture Matters for Pharma Strategy." In an online interview for the *Harvard Business Review*, Christian Madsbjerg, ReD's director of client relations, says that the problem with so much marketing (a $15 billion-a-year industry, he informs us) is that it too often doesn't understand the product "in its cultural context, in its average, everyday situation." This is Anthropology 101.[17]

And then there are the leavers; to wrap up the introduction to this introduction, I might as well point out that some famous people, and some who have made their names in other professions, have anthropology in their backgrounds. It is a small discipline and we need all the publicity we can get. Prince Charles has a degree in anthropology. Gillian Tett, the prominent journalist and an editor at the *Financial Times*, did a PhD in anthropology at Cambridge. Film director Jane Campion studied anthropology in New Zealand, and Barack Obama's mother, Ann Dunham, was an anthropologist of Indonesia. Nick Clegg, former deputy prime minister of the United Kingdom, has a degree in anthropology. Kurt Vonnegut was kicked out of the PhD program at the University of Chicago, but that might have been for the best: while a lot of anthropology has made a difference in the world, it's nice to have *Slaughterhouse Five* and *Cat's Cradle* in the annals of literature. Jomo Kenyatta, the first president of an independent Kenya, got his PhD in anthropology at the LSE; alongside his involvement in politics, he managed to produce a classic anthropological study, *Facing Mount Kenya*, on the Kikuyu people. (So he was a "native anthropologist"—and pretty early on.) Ashraf Ghani, president of Afghanistan, got his PhD in anthropology at Columbia University and was a professor for some time at Johns Hopkins University.

Anthropology is a discipline that on the face of it might seem to have little practical or vocational value. In today's intellectual climate that's increasingly something that has to be explained or excused. And it brings on the occasional existential shudder. But the discipline of anthropology offers a profoundly useful way of thinking about the modern world. In an interview from 2008, Gillian Tett spoke of how her move into the world of financial journalism was informed by her anthropological training. It was just after the 2008 crash. "I happen to think that anthropology is a brilliant background for looking at finance," she said. "Firstly, you're trained to look at how societies or cultures operate holistically, so you look at how all the bits move together. And most people in the City don't do that.... But the other thing is, if you come from an anthropology background, you also try and put finance in a cultural context. Bankers like to imagine that money and the profit motive is as universal as gravity. They think it's basically a given and they think it's completely apersonal. And it's not. What they do in finance is all about culture and interaction."[18]

In the manner of the classic by Marshall Sahlins, and echoing in a more popular register what we can find in the work of Caitlin Zaloom, Tett is pushing for that anthropological sensibility. And whether you're concerned with the financial world of the City of London or whether it's something else that piques your interest—traditional life in the Trobriand Islands, perhaps, or Hindu rituals; or why some NGO development projects fail, and some succeed; or how to sell hamburgers in Hong Kong, or understand the use of social media in Turkey; or, for that matter, how best to reach and serve victims of domestic violence in a social housing project—going for that holistic view, and appreciating the cultural dynamics in play, will most likely do you good.

we come from. He wanted to hear about America and I wanted to hear about life in rural Zimbabwe.

At one point in one of these low-level, culturally motivated chitchats, Philip asked me if I liked cricket. Just like that: *Do you like cricket?* Being an attentive student of colonial and postcolonial history, and well aware of the popularity of the sport among Zimbabweans, an image popped into my mind of a bunch of men standing around in white sweaters with something that looked vaguely like a baseball bat held by one of them, while another pitched (or, as I'd recognize now, bowled). As an American, though, I knew absolutely nothing substantive about the game, other than that it made baseball look fast-paced and exciting. (I also had a vague sense that cricket matches were stopped when it got cloudy and that they lasted several days.) But like any reasonable and well-meaning person thrown in the deep end of a student-exchange program, I muttered a half-hearted, polite "yes" to Philip. Why not?

He immediately popped up. "Right!" he said and beckoned me to follow him back down the slope to his homestead. I assumed I was about to be handed a bat or a ball (if not a white sweater) and that we'd knock around a bit. Back in the homestead, he disappeared into the kitchen hut where his mother and grandmother were engaged in the seemingly endless cycle of preparing meals for the family. I didn't think much about that fact—that it was the kitchen hut; lots of Americans keep their sports equipment in the environs of the kitchen or at the back of the house, so to speak. But when he emerged, he wasn't carrying a bat or a ball. He was carrying a small metal bowl that contained, as I clearly saw, a cricket—an insect, that is. It had been fried in oil. He had a smile on his face.

# CULTURE

Culture is the most significant concept in anthropology. It is also the most difficult to sum up. I can't offer you a pithy definition. Let me try the next best thing, though, which is to tell you a story from my fieldwork that conveys something of how it should be understood.

My first fieldwork project was in Zimbabwe. While the majority of my research was in urban areas, I spent a lot of pleasant time in Chiweshe, first as an undergraduate exchange student. An hour's drive north of the capital city, Harare, Chiweshe is a beautiful part of the country, marked by rolling hills and rocky outcrops, dotted by small groups of thatched huts, each comprising a homestead (or *musha*, in the local Shona language). During that student exchange, I stayed with a family in Chiweshe for a week and quickly befriended my host brother, Philip. We stayed in regular contact after that, and I visited the *musha* many times over the course of the 1990s.

It wasn't a busy time of year for the farming work that Philip's family had to do, so we got to spend the days leisurely. We took several walks up into the hills behind his homestead, where we could look out across the lower-lying areas and watch the troupes of baboons lounging around. His English wasn't great; my Shona, at the time, was even worse, and so conversations were quite basic. We would do what two people from radically different places often do, which is talk about what it's like where

I had *really* messed up. Total category mistake. Customs of hospitality are common enough around the world that, had I been offered the cricket otherwise, I probably would have accepted it. Of course, it all made sense now. I knew that caterpillars were a local delicacy—why not crickets? Indeed, crickets come even higher on the list of delicacies because they are extremely difficult to catch. I was being honored.

As I picked up the creature and brought it to my mouth, a year and a half of anthropology courses came rushing into my head: *Food is a cultural construct. You know some people eat dog meat, and horse meat, and even monkey brains. You can handle this, you're an anthropology major.*

All the book learning in the world, though, can't undo twenty years of life—learning of another kind. As I put the cricket in my mouth, chewed (it was too big to swallow whole), and choked it down, my body shook, my chest folded in, and within what must have been a matter of three seconds, the cricket, and my breakfast, came back up and out.

This was not a definition of culture but an example of it—an example that touched on most of what's important in anthropological understandings of the term. Culture is a way of seeing things, a way of thinking. Culture is a way of making sense. Culture is what prevents some people from ever thinking that crickets could be classed as "food." Culture is also what fills our head in the process of thinking in a particular way: the details of colonial history, of *British* colonial history (as opposed to French, say, or Portuguese), of the pursuits of peasant farmers in Africa during certain periods of the agricultural cycle.

Culture is a thing in itself. Or, if not a single thing, a range of things, and often certain types of things: houses, kilns, paintings, books of poetry, flags, tortillas, English breakfast tea, samurai swords, cricket bats, and, yes, even crickets. There is a materiality to culture. It is embodied and enacted. I threw up the cricket. But I didn't throw up because I had a stomach virus. It wasn't a "natural" or "biological" reaction in this sense. I threw up because my body is cultural, or enculturated, itself. And in my culture we don't eat crickets.

I'd like to think that this is all you need to know for an introduction to the anthropological understanding of culture. And I'd bet that none of it comes as a surprise or requires much mental exercise. Some combination of these ideas informs most everyday understandings, from Kansas City to Kolkata. We're used to thinking of culture as a point of view, or as objectified in things, or even tied to visceral reactions that make us think of the power of nature.

But anthropologists don't leave it here. "Culture" is in the paradoxical position of being the most commonly used and commonly contested term in anthropology.

## CULTURAL GLASSES

*Points of view on points of view*

The longest-lasting anthropological approach to culture promotes it as a kind of perception. For Bronislaw Malinowski, remember, the whole point of anthropology is to capture "the native's point of view, his relation to life … *his* vision of *his* world." Having a "point of view" in this sense doesn't mean simply having an opinion. This is not about the native's preference for taro over yams or for convertible cars, or a commitment to the Democratic Party. In this context, a point of view is much more comprehensive, reflected in what we take to be common sense or the proper order of things. Like not thinking of crickets as food.

The most important figure in developing this area of culture theory was Franz Boas. Boas was born and raised in Germany, before making his career in anthropology in the United States. Often called "Papa Franz" by his students, and much beloved, he was also an enigma to many, especially to any journalists who took an interest in his work. Joseph Mitchell, one of the greatest journalists and chroniclers of life in mid-twentieth-century New York, was granted an interview after Boas's retirement, in the late 1930s. Mitchell describes him as a man with "piercing eyes and a thinning shock of scraggy white hair" who was "hard to interview" but nevertheless delighted journalists "by muttering in a thick German accent such words as 'nonsense' or 'preposterous' when asked to comment on some statement or another by a Nazi propagandist."[1]

Boas originally trained in physics at Kiel University, Germany, but this was during an era in which distinctions between the natural and human sciences could be hard to hold. Boas was well-read in a variety of fields, but one important influence was the work of Wilhelm von Humboldt, a key architect of early modern culture theory. In German thought, culture (*Kultur*) became an especially important concept in the early nineteenth century among those who were arguing against what they saw as the excesses of Enlightenment discourse. This countertradition was skeptical of the universal and totalizing approach to reason and history; Humboldt and others were figures for whom any given nation should be celebrated and understood in terms of its specific genius. For Humboldt, or, say, Johan Gottfried Herder, *Kultur* became an organizing concept with which to express this commitment to particularity. It is no coincidence that Humboldt was a great linguist too; he studied Basque, several Native American languages, Sanskrit, and Kawi (a Javanese literary language), all of which both expressed and fostered his interest in humankind's diversities. Over time he came to see language and culture as intimately linked. "Language is the external representation of the genius of peoples," he wrote.[2]

Boas's 1881 dissertation at Kiel was on the distillation of light through seawater. In 1883, as part of further research, he traveled to Baffin Land, where he became more interested in the local Inuit people than the polar waters. It marked his conversion to the nascent field of anthropology.

Rather like Malinowski's pitching of the tent on Nu'agasi beach, the story of Boas's moment of realization in the Arctic has two core elements. The first has to do with the importance of fieldwork, of getting out of the lab in order to understand the workings of things: "in conditions as they actually exist in human experience," as Boas put it in his doctoral thesis.[3] I want to emphasize that this first point is not only a methodological one. It tells us something about the nature of anthropology's key analytical concept. In the early days of the professionalization of anthropology, fieldwork also served to underscore the importance of "being there" because culture had to be observed in situ: culture and place were two sides of the same coin.

The second element, intimately related to the first, is the primacy of perception, of vision. Boas didn't have the writerly flourish of Malinowski; he didn't popularize nearly as many turns of phrase. But what he offered was a more prosaic and diffuse rendering of Malinowski's commitment to capturing the native's point of view. Boas himself never really offered a very memorable or influential definition of culture (though neither did Malinowski). His approach to culture emerged out of the many works on his famous five-foot shelf, as well as in the distillations of the work of his numerous students. But even if diffuse, a strong emphasis in his approach was on what he called the "cultural glasses" (*Kulturbrille*) we all wear. It is through these glasses that we make sense of and order the world. In the Boasian rendering, culture is about meaning. "Perception" has to do with the world's ordering in some set of localized terms. You don't just see the world, you see the world as a young woman from the Solomon Islands, or even more specifically, a young woman in the Anglican Church from the island of Makira.

At least until the 1960s, this was most often expressed in just such particular terms: anthropologists wrote of Kwakiutl culture, Balinese culture, and Dobuan culture. They also wrote in more general terms, referring to Mediterranean culture, Melanesian culture, Islamic culture, or even primitive culture. In doing so, the unspoken understanding was that such generalities referenced a variety of more specific cultures, linked in that they had similar cultural glasses—ones with similar prescriptions, if you will. In reference to Mediterranean culture, for instance, any good student of anthropology from this period would be on the lookout for discussions of honor and shame, which were often argued to be organizing values.

Boas had dozens of students, many of them extremely influential in their own right. But in terms of culture as we're discussing it here, after Boas the next most influential figure was Clifford Geertz.

Geertz was active from the 1950s onward, but it was the publication of a collection of essays in 1973 that marked a new watershed. Geertz famously referred to culture as a "text" that anthropologists read over the shoulders of the natives. Here you can see the ways in which anthropologists treated culture like an object too. We'll be coming to that soon. Yet above all it is perception that matters in his metaphor, because what we do with those texts (and what the natives do, too) is *interpret* them. Geertz called his approach to culture a "semiotic one" and argued that anthropology is "not an experimental science in search of law but an interpretive one in search of meaning."[4]

Geertz's connection to Boas was not as direct as that of some others of his generation, but he drew on many of the same traditions of thought and analytical approaches. Above all for Geertz, as for Boas, if you wanted to understand what a culture "meant," if you wanted to understand what was important about it, what made it tick, what gave it significance and (inasmuch as this is possible) order, you have to focus on the particular, not the general.

This approach to culture still informs a good deal of contemporary anthropological work. And it is culture in this respect that anthropologists are often particularly keen on underscoring. In the area of medical anthropology, for instance, a lot of research has been done on how cultural factors can influence the prevalence, diagnosis, treatment, and even presentation of certain conditions or diseases. In China, for example, medical anthropologist Arthur Kleinman notes that people suffering from depression may be more likely to experience it through physical, rather than psychological, symptoms; and it is often boredom, not sadness, that best captures the disorder in Chinese eyes.[5] But it isn't even necessarily seen as such in the first place. In China, there is nothing like the idiom of depression that is to be found in the United States. The Chinese characters for depression are confined in the main to medical contexts. As one would expect, this can lead to problems for migrants; Chinese migrants to the United States, for instance, might well find a diagnosis of depression by an American doctor "experientially meaningless." "Culture influences the experience of symptoms, the idioms used to report them, decisions about treatment, doctor-patient interactions, the likelihood of outcomes such as suicide, and the practices of professionals," Kleinman explains. "As a result, some conditions are universal and some culturally distinct, but all are meaningful within particular contexts."[6]

### The objects of culture

Culture has long been linked to things in the anthropological project. "Material culture" is almost as common a term as "culture" itself. And although the *material* can be treated as an adjective, qualifying the noun, it's helpful to think of the words as symbiotic; that's certainly how they're often understood.

Inasmuch as anthropologists are observers, it would be impossible not to consider the materiality of culture. You would certainly be hard-pressed to find a society in which the literal and figurative objectification of culture didn't matter. Humans use material culture and other things (trees, rocks, and oceans) to make sense of, express, and sum up who they are. One of my favorite examples of this comes from a study of Québécois nationalism. At the height of the independence movement, in the 1970s, it was crucial for the nationalists to foster strong attachments to an especially Québécois culture. One of the ways in which this was done was to foster the idea of a national patrimony (*le patrimoine*), a lengthy list of "cultural property" owned by the people and expressing who they are. "Old things" had pride of place on the list, be they well-known historic buildings or, more simply, antique chairs and plows. But the list included animals too—the Canadian horse (descended from the stables of Louis XIV)—and even language. "In the same way as our history and the men who have made it," wrote one partisan, "to the same degree as buildings, furniture, tools, works of art, songs and tales ... *language is an important part of our patrimoine*, of the common property of the Québécois."[7] We even make words into things. We objectify language in projects of nationalism by trying to fix the meaning of particular words or phrases; we also objectify language in ritual, especially in statements that are repeated over and over (which has the social effect of making the statements seem "truer" than we might otherwise take them to be).

You don't have to be a nationalist to get animated by the objectification of culture in these ways, of course. You could just be an English (or possibly British) lover of

Stilton, let's say; someone for whom this delicious crumbly, salty cheese captures something of your character. In Georgia, one anthropologist even found that, after the fall of the Soviet Union, the Orthodox Church's campaign of church building met with great skepticism by local people because they thought for a church to be a proper church, it had to be *very old*.[8] These qualities matter.

It's clear that meaning, or value, is a link between the two aspects of culture discussed thus far. In some ways we could even conclude that the materiality of culture follows on from our discussion of *Kulturbrille*: you're not going to feel that that antique chair in a Quebec City market stall expresses *le patrimoine* unless you are a native with a certain point of view.

But this is not the only way in which anthropological culture theory has been elaborated with respect to things. There are more basic ways in which the materiality of culture has mattered. One is best explored in archaeology. Archaeologists have done more than most anthropologists to underscore the centrality of material culture to the course of human history.

One leading figure has referred to archaeology as "the study of past peoples based on the things they left behind and the ways they left their imprint on the world."[9] It is the study, in his words, of *small things forgotten*: the remnants of cooking pots, house foundations, clay pipes, roads, wells, burial mounds, and even rubbish pits (really good for figuring out ancient diets), all dug up, brushed off, and, where possible, pieced back together—usually by a small group of deeply tanned fieldworkers. (Archaeology can claim "fieldwork" as its method in a perfectly literal sense.) Whether cast in a folksy or colloquial register of "things" or whether articulated in the more academic register of "material culture" or "artifacts," the point is clear: it's important. And it's an invaluable resource for uncovering our past.

The focus on material culture by archaeologists helps us trace the development of human societies. From small, nomadic bands of hunter-gatherers to the origins of agriculture and settlements, archaeologists have looked at everything from carved bones (clusters of which can indicate seasonally based aggregations of nomadic groups) to the distribution of charcoal deposits (which can be helpful in determining a population density) to help illuminate the course of prehistory. And this extends beyond digging things up. One approach, used by Fiona Coward in her research in the Levant, for example, incorporates Geographic Information Systems (GIS) modeling to calculate the reach of social networks in the Epipalaeolithic and Early Neolithic periods. Using GIS, she tracks the extent to which similar material culture inventories can be found across an area. Her early findings suggest that these networks did not necessarily expand the larger the social groupings became; once again, hunter-gatherers defy modern common sense, which is that a "civilization" has a broader horizon than a "primitive" band.[10]

The focus and findings of archaeology contain an important lesson. It isn't just that material culture is a vehicle for meaning, the ways in which Québécois nationalists can harness sentiments for their cause. It's that culture itself—the ability to be a native and have a point of view in the first place—isn't possible without this material infrastructure. It's *stuff* that helps create the conditions of possibility for meaning. That stuff is part of the meaning-making complex.

In the generation before Boas and Malinowski, the anthropological project was much more closely tied to an interest in the long sweep of history (and prehistory). Archaeology helped meet this interest. But there is another important strand of early anthropological theory guided by material culture: social evolutionism.

Social evolutionism was the first major approach in anthropology. It was inspired by the theory of evolution by natural selection. Charles Darwin's *On the Origin of Species* (1859) had a profound impact on the emerging discipline of anthropology. As Darwin had done with barnacles and moths, the thinking went, so others could do with respect to social life. Social history was like natural history. The Zuni and the English could be understood according to a Darwinian Tree of Life not only in terms of physiology and anatomy but also through kinship systems, forms of political organization, and technological achievements. Culture, like biology, was understood to be subject to laws and classifiable according to a universally applicable system.[*]

American Lewis Henry Morgan and Britons Herbert Spencer and Edward Burnett Tylor became particularly influential proponents of social evolutionism within anthropology from the 1860s up through the first decades of the twentieth century. Many other figures in the emerging fields of anthropology and sociology were evolutionists too; it was the idiom of the late nineteenth-century academy. But it was these men who made the most of the paradigm and worked hardest to underscore the equivalence of the natural organism and the social organism.

---

[*] Evolution was not Darwin's unique idea; it had long been gaining ground. Social theorist Herbert Spencer published an article on organic evolution, anonymously, seven years before the publication of *On the Origin of Species*.

Of these "materialists"—a phrase sometimes used to describe them, and a telling one at that—Spencer was particularly bent on driving this home. His work on "the evolution of society" is filled with biological analogies. He moves from a discussion of liver cells, exfoliation of the epidermis, spores, germs, and bones to systems of governance, group identification, religious ceremonies, and population density with ease, and often within the same sentence. Everything comes back to Mother Nature.

It was Tylor who homed in on culture the most in all of this; he used evolution to outline what he called "the stages of culture," stages that could be classified and known according to material measures. At the gross level, Tylor and the others spoke in terms of savagery, barbarism, and civilization—each a moniker that could be applied through a simple tallying up: loincloth, wooden tools, itinerant or inhabiting mud huts? Savage. Top hats, steam-powered engines, town houses? Civilized. Every aspect of "culture" in this approach was treated as if it were a bean to be counted.

There is one extremely serious flaw in social evolutionism. (There are several pretty serious flaws too, but those will have to wait.) Unlike with Darwin, in the works of these social scientists, evolution became teleological. It had a design and purpose—as well as a heavy dose of moral flavoring. Because the man in the top hat is not only more culturally evolved than the naked savage—he is not only a more "complex organism"; he is *better*. Social evolutionism is moral philosophy masquerading as science. Darwin never turned his nose up at the barnacle because it wasn't the blue whale.

In this respect, figures such as Tylor were drawing on another important and still current use of the culture concept, one captured by Tylor's contemporary, poet and essayist Matthew Arnold, as "the best that has been thought and known in the world current everywhere."[11] This is often glossed as the "opera house" definition of culture and is reflected in judgments of some people being "cultured" or "more cultured" than others. In a stereotypical rendering, culture in this usage means Mozart, not Madonna. The latter, if designated cultural at all, would be part of "pop culture." Tylor and others were interested in music, to be sure. But culture was, in Tylor's more capacious definition, "that complex whole which includes knowledge, belief, art, law, morals, custom, and any other capabilities and habits acquired by man as a member of society."[12]

Boas was a vocal critic of social evolutionism. And by the 1920s it had been relegated to the margins of academic anthropology. Evolutionism in a more diffuse sense survived—and can still be found implicitly in some work. But the overt moralism, and the fervent insistence that a Frenchman and a bivalve mollusk really *could* be understood in the same sense, faded away.

Social evolutionism never lost all of its proponents. It enjoyed a renaissance in 1950s and 1960s, for example, in the work of Leslie White and Julian Steward. White and Steward had major disagreements with one another, but neither shied away from the general idioms developed by Tylor, Morgan, and others in the nineteenth century. They also both thought that, after Boas, anthropology had become too mired in the details of culture. All those recipes for muffins.... For White and Steward, too, "science" continued to have an authoritative ring; many of Boas's students had more humanistic sensibilities. It is notable that the social evolutionists worked more closely

with archaeologists and with a concern for the archaeological record; over time, Boasian and related approaches
moved away from an interest in the *longue durée*. In archaeology itself, social evolutionism remained part of the
backdrop: figures such as V. Gordon Childe in the UK
and Gordon Willey in the United States, both of whom
shaped debates and interests in the field, always worked
with evolutionism in mind, albeit not with the same air
of superiority that hung around their Victorian forebears.

### Culture and/as nature

There are several ways in which an overall approach to
culture can combine different aspects of what we've
considered. To think primarily in terms of *Kulturbrille* is
not to disavow culture's material aspects, and vice versa.
Yet there are tensions between different theories of culture. Boas, as I have noted, had serious reservations about
Tylor's approach and social evolutionism more generally.
Leslie White was often deeply critical of Boas; he thought
he was a poor theoretician (because he was so focused
on the particular) and not a very good fieldworker either
(calling into question, with a tinge of the personal, the
esteem with which his ethnography was held).

But the most significant area of tension and source of
debate in culture theory is not connected to whether you
think we ought to be focusing on the symbolic meaning
of pottery, or any given pot itself. Much more, it has to
do with where your overall approach sits with respect
to the third strand of culture theory I've identified, that
which touches on the age-old question of whether we are
creatures of nature or nurture. Is it biological drives that

shape us, our mental hardwiring, our genes? Or is it how we're raised, the conditions in which we live, and the dominant values of our society?

Biology and nature have nearly always played a secondary role in anthropological conceptions of culture. Even White, who wanted to talk about calories and the satisfaction of needs (which he identified as both "material" and "spiritual"), emphasized the primacy of culture. "The biological factor of man is irrelevant to various problems of cultural interpretation such as diversities among cultures," he wrote, "and processes of culture change in general and the evolution of culture in particular."[13]

It should come as little surprise that a discipline dedicated to the exploration and importance of culture—of humanity's diverse historical traditions and social expressions—would have this tilt. Still, not all culture theories are as cultural as others. The Boasian tradition, once again, has been the most influential at the culture end of the spectrum. In this tradition Ruth Benedict provided the most famous argument. In *Patterns of Culture* (1934), she mounted an all-out attack on biological determinism (some might even say biology, period). Drawing from a wealth of case studies, and consciously situating her remarks in relation both to the ethnographic record *and* to the contemporary American scene, Benedict worked to put all cultures in the same frame, to do away with an us-them divide and the Petri dish approach of some of her anthropological forebears: "Man is not committed in detail by his biological constitution to any particular variety of behaviour."[14]

Benedict's immediate target was racism. Boas and several of his students were very active in both academic and social terms in the fight against racism. (Long before

Boas called the Nazis preposterous he was denouncing racists and eugenicists in the United States.) In the United States, as elsewhere, the fledgling discipline of anthropology was often part and parcel of an effort to legitimize racial difference on a scientific basis. This is evident in an arc from the work of Daniel Brinton, an archaeologist and ethnologist who, during the 1890s, occupied prominent positions in a number of learned societies, to Carleton S. Coon, professor of physical anthropology at Harvard University who, in the 1960s, accepted the logic of segregation. Boas critiqued the work and ideas of both and played a crucial bridging role between his circle at Columbia University and the National Association for the Advancement of Colored People (NAACP). Boas also worked in various capacities with the likes of Booker T. Washington and W. E. B. Du Bois. As anthropologist Lee D. Baker argues, Boas's impact was not always immediate and direct. But over the first half of the twentieth century, his efforts and both academic and political alliances helped bring about two kinds of shifts on the American scene: a paradigmatic one within the academy and a juridical one with respect to the category of race itself.[15]

Of course, not all nature-heavy culture theories, if I can put it that way, turn on race. Indeed, probably the least cultural of all culture theorists, Claude Lévi-Strauss, was, like Boas, strongly anti-racist. Lévi-Strauss, the father of structuralist anthropology, had a very paradoxical position on culture. On the one hand, he was intensely interested in culture, if we take that to mean the minute details of Tlingit myths, Kuna shamanic practices, and even technological capabilities and achievements; he had a deep appreciation for the work of Boas and his students, precisely because of its encyclopedic detail. On the other hand, all of this cultural detail and cultural particularism was nothing more than data that could be used to underscore his true interest, which was the universal structure of the human mind.

For Lévi-Strauss, the proper unit of analysis was not a native's point of view but, we might say, *the native's state of mind*. At a core level this state of mind was both constant and universal. In this tradition of culture theory, the endpoint was not a celebration or recognition of difference for difference's sake but rather the uncovering of the mental architecture that linked all peoples to one another. "The savage mind is logical in the same sense and the same fashion as ours," he wrote.[16] In another text he drew on the imagery of material culture to make the same point, while turning the criteria of the nineteenth-century social evolutionists upside down. Think of a stone ax and a steel ax. We might be able to say that steel is stronger than stone—that it's "better" in that sense. But the task of anthropology is not to focus on *what* they are made of but *how* they are created. And if you look closely enough, he argued, what you see is that really they are the same.

It is the mind, rather than the body, that has in recent decades tended to interest more naturalistic proponents of culture theory. Much of this work is in an area known as cognitive anthropology. It has a diverse set of influences and interfaces: structuralism, various branches of psychology, linguistics, even philosophy. In general, though, approaches to cognition and culture wrestle with the extent to which the workings of the mind shape cultural expressions, values, and concepts. Are we natural dualists? That is to say, do all humans think in terms of opposites, binaries, or pairs? Are there other universals in perception or conceptualization—color terms, for instance, or kinship relations? How are cultural skills transmitted?

Tanya Luhrmann does work in this vein, at the intersection of anthropology and psychology. Indeed, over her career, she has studied everything from witches in England to psychologists themselves and how their training reflects and reinforces certain understandings of the mind. Her most recent book, on neo-Pentecostals in the United States, takes this focus on the mind to a new level by incorporating a series of laboratory-like experiments on how the practice of prayer affects these Christians' experiences of God. Working with over 120 participants, Luhrmann gave them iPods loaded with instructions on Ignatian-style prayer, set against the background of pleasant music. This focused attention, she found, increased the vividness with which her informants reported God's presence, a process she calls "absorption" (borrowing from the influential ideas of a psychologist). "The capacity to treat what the mind imagines as more real than the world one knows is the capacity at the heart of the experience of God."[17] Indeed, one of the things that most interests Luhrmann about these Christians is the extent to which they embrace the authority of science and secular logic of fact and fiction, real and unreal.

Cognitive anthropology raises important challenges for those who, like me, were raised on Benedictian nostrums about the primacy and power of culture. For too long, anthropologists have at best ignored, and at worst disavowed, findings and approaches in the cognitive sciences. That's beginning to change in some quarters. All the same, while many cognitive anthropologists want us to see cultural history in closer relation to natural history, it is important to recognize that most are not getting rid of culture altogether. The best cognitive anthropologists remain anthropologists; they remain committed to the value of long-term, qualitative data, to long-term engagement with particular people in particular places (even if they don't carry out this fieldwork themselves). They are not content with the lab or the isolated experiment. And so, in this sense, they stand behind culture just as their forebears did.

## CULTURE'S LIMITS

"Culture" is not a magic word. It's not a concept that solves all the problems posed by history and in society. And it can obscure as much as it can reveal. The anthropologists who use it most and promote it actively have always recognized this. Culture has its outright detractors too, and, even more, apathetic others. In the mid-1990s, at the end of a decade of particularly strong efforts to expunge the term—on the back of postcolonial and postmodern critiques—one professor documented no fewer than fourteen ways in which the culture concept was said to fall short.[18] I won't go over all of them, but this lengthy list could be broken down into three main concerns—all of which have been around a long time.

First of all, it's important not to take the connection between culture and place too literally. Here it's worth reflecting on the etymology of the word. In its earliest uses, according to the *Oxford English Dictionary*, the term "culture" referred to the tilling of the land; its roots (and excuse the pun) are expressed in terms such as *cul*tivation, agri*culture*, horti*culture*, and so on. For the culture theorists in nineteenth-century Germany, this was one of its attractions: a grounding in place and time in a manner that challenged the universalizing and abstracting logic of much Enlightenment thought. And this connection to place is central to the anthropological understanding. To have a point of view is to be situated, emplaced. And as both Malinowski and Boas insisted, to get culture you had to be there.

The problem with this is that it's not always easy to know where "there" ends and "another place" begins. Throughout *Argonauts of the Western Pacific*, Malinowski speaks of a number of peoples—"cultures"—as if they are discrete. Yet at the same time the most lasting contribution of the book is his exploration of the Kula Ring, a system of exchange that spreads over several islands and hundreds of miles. "Cultures," in other words, at the very least come into contact with one another. They borrow from one another, bleed into one another, and in some cases all this borrowing and bleeding can beg the question of whether we should really be talking about "culture" at all. And consider this: the Trobriand Islands in the 1910s is one thing. Okay, life there was shaped in part by the Kula Ring; there was some traffic "across cultures." Some fluidity and blurriness. But this traffic in "culture" is a far cry from what we can find in the Internet age, or even the radio age, or planes and trains and automobiles. What about Singapore in the 2010s? Or London? Or what if we want to get even more specific? Can we speak of "London's culture"? Or do we need to be more exact and speak of third-generation Bangladeshi Britons in Tower Hamlets, or Poles who moved to Ealing in 2005? Or the Smith family that has "always" lived in Catford? And yet further, can we necessarily call those whose grandparents came from Sylhet to East London in the 1970s "third-generation Bangladeshi Britons"? What if they couldn't care less about their ancestry? What if they consider themselves "native" Londoners? These are all fair and good questions about the work culture does.

So, culture is not bounded in place. That's the first main line of criticism. The second major line of criticism follows on naturally from the first: culture is not fixed in time. Cultures change. But it's true that anthropologists—often romantics (like many of their intellectual ancestors)—haven't always been good at acknowledging this. Indeed, one contemporary culture theorist argues that anthropologists still fall down on this point with regularity.[19]

This romanticism was often especially egregious in the colonial era. Consider the classic work of Victor Turner, one of my favorite anthropologists of all time (for his wonderful writing, his broad reading, and the fizz of his ideas). Turner spent the early 1950s with the Ndembu tribe, in what was then Northern Rhodesia, producing, with his wife, Edith, some of the most important studies of ritual we have in the anthropological record. The Ndembu are presented very pristinely, as if the huge political and economic changes and challenges taking place simply didn't register. We get natives out of time. Indeed, the Turners barely mention the colonial context in a lot of their classic work. This is all the more striking because Northern Rhodesia was something of an anthropological laboratory in the 1950s and 1960s, full of anthropologists studying culture change and the dynamics of sociality in emerging urban centers, especially on the Copperbelt, where mines sprung up and drew in labor from across the region. There was a close association for many of these anthropologists with a charismatic professor at the University of Manchester, Max Gluckman. He even inspired a "Manchester School," informed by Marxian approaches and much more committed to the study of social change and conflict than had been common in Britain to that point. Indeed, there were many excellent studies from the Manchester School in which colonialism and modernization figured prominently. But it is worth noting that of all this work, it is the Turners' that anthropology students read and that has had the biggest impact. And what the Turners gave us is a picture of the Ndembu in which macrolevel politics and change didn't really figure.

The third main line of criticism has to do with culture's coherence. What all of the flow, flux, and fragmentation of colonialism and globalization point to is a more basic issue, which is the assumption that culture, especially as understood in ideational, point-of-view terms, is in some way an ordered whole. It was certainly not unusual through the 1950s for anthropologists to write with very sweeping generalizations about what the people in any given "culture" believe, feel, or think. Such inferences and ascriptions came to be seen as increasingly difficult to justify—not only because of the impact of colonialism and globalization but because the ascriptions assumed that "culture" was both totalizing and holistic. Even within a remote island community, untouched by outside influences, we should not assume and do not necessarily find such coherence and uniformity. Sometimes, too, the official version of culture—what gets written up by the anthropologist—sits at odds with what's really going on. It's often a very bad idea to ask people about their culture, or to ask them what they "believe" or "think" or even what something (a ritual, fatherhood, the Omkara) "means." The problem is, they'll probably tell you something. But they might well be making it up or thinking off the tops of their heads; in some cases, it's even happened that the native will answer an anthropologist's question by referring to the book written by another anthropologist who lived in the village forty years ago. This can lead to an overly clean and tidy account—in short, a bad one.

Syncing up all three of lines of critique and concern—not bounded in place; not fixed in time; not very neat and tidy in any case—they tie together well into the knot of essentialism: "the belief in the real, true essence of things, the invariable and fixed properties which define the 'whatness' of a given entity."[20]

Essentialism can be very dangerous—and cultural essentialism often is. At a few points in later chapters, we'll have a chance to consider the dangers of culture talk. It does tend to invite—maybe even demand—a fixing of things, an appeal to stereotypes and even bald prejudices. This, at least, has often been the case when culture moves beyond the confines of the ivory tower and into the wider public. And it's infamously the case in at least one particularly reprehensive political ideology: apartheid. Indeed, within Apartheid South Africa, "culture" was a very important term in the nationalists' efforts at total separation: *Keep the African cultures intact! They need their homelands; we whites need our own spaces too.* It is no small irony, and a painful one, to think that less than a decade after Boas died (this anthropologist who had committed much of his energy to articulating a culture concept that was explicitly anti-racist) the architects of the National Party in South Africa could use culture to keep Africans "in their place."

I noted in passing that these concerns and others became particularly pronounced in the 1980s. At that point in time, some leading anthropologists, drawing from feminism, postcolonial studies, postmodernism, and certain traditions of sociology, started to move away from and even disavow the culture concept. It was often to do with one or another of the term's essentializing risks. The ideas of Michel Foucault and Pierre Bourdieu became influential alternatives. Foucault's interests in power and subjectivity, and his use of "discourse" as a heuristic framing device, fit well with these emerging approaches. So too did Bourdieu's "theory of practice," as encapsulated in his use of the term "habitus," which is a term like "culture" in many respects but understood to be more labile. In Bourdieu's rendering, habitus is a *disposition*: it refers to what people think, do, plan for, feel, say, and perceive within the context of a structure but is never wholly determined by that structure. In a now famous turn of phrase, he defined habitus as "structured structures predisposed to function as structuring structures." In other words, we are shaped by the world in which we live but are not always bound by custom and habit. As Bourdieu put it, what we do is neither a "mechanical reaction" nor the result of "some creative free will."[21]

Not all anthropologists who started to integrate more explicit concerns with power or write about habitus stopped using culture altogether. In fact even some of the most respected critics still use "culture" in what we might call a weaker sense—not as a major analytical term, that is, but in the processes of description or contextualization. Anthropologist Arjun Appadurai, for example—one of the most senior figures in the field, who has worked primarily in India—warned against the rigidity and objectivity of the culture concept. But that was in a book on "the cultural dynamics of globalization."[22] Lila Abu-

Lughod, another major figure and a leading expert on
Egypt, gender, and media, describes one of her main interests as "the relationship between cultural forms and
power."[23] But she is the author of a hugely influential
1991 essay titled, straightforwardly enough, "Writing
against Culture"; this is a piece that really crystallized
the appeal of Foucault and Bourdieu to many of my own
generation.[24] What Appadurai and Abu-Lughod are really
doing, then, is asking us to think more in terms of adjec-
tives than nouns. It is the move away from thing-like,
objective concepts that animates such approaches.

Much of the debate over culture was taking place in the
North American academy. In Britain, culture had actually
long since fallen into disuse, at least as an explicit, analytical term. Malinowski, as I have stressed, made some
contributions to culture theory, but he left the LSE for
Yale University in the late 1930s and died in New Haven
soon afterward. British-based interest in culture theory
pretty much died with him—at least within anthropology. However, it was taken up elsewhere, especially in the
work of such literary and social critics as Richard Hog-
gart, Raymond Williams, and, slightly later, Stuart Hall.
This work became known as "cultural studies"; its practitioners didn't go to the Trobriand Islands, though. They
asked how race, class, gender, sexuality, and youth shaped
contemporary Western society—and pushed against the
demands and expectations of the power holders and
agenda setters. Much of their work drew on Marx, Italian social critic Antonio Gramsci, and, later, Foucault.

After Malinowski left for America, A. R. Radcliffe-
Brown rose to prominence in Britain. Radcliffe-Brown
made his name with a series of papers in which "society"
rather than "culture" was the key term of analysis and

object of interest. He had an active dislike of the culture concept, calling it a "vague abstraction."[25] From that point on, really, British anthropology—often dubbed *social* anthropology, remember—never bothered much with theorizing culture, even if its practitioners did not abandon the word completely; indeed, you can flip through any of the key books in British social anthropology from the 1940s onward and find the terms "culture" and "cultural" deployed with regularity. But it is certainly true that some postwar British anthropologists found their American counterparts slightly obsessed with the "vague abstraction" and, after Geertz, with the attention to figurative language, symbolism, and semiotics it seemed to require. They focused more on what Radcliffe-Brown called social structures or social institutions, by which he meant kinship relations (how to treat one's mother-in-law; the specific nature of bonds between fathers and children); political structures and roles (dynamics between the commoner and chief in stateless societies); religious practices (the maintenance of taboos; the function of sacrifice); and other *grounded* things.

In general, though, most anthropologists trained in Britain didn't even bother to critique culture. They just got on with their commitments, which tended to draw on combinations of ideas derived from nineteenth- and early twentieth-century continental social theorists (Émile Durkheim, Marcel Mauss, and Karl Marx). Indeed, as early as 1951, Raymond Firth, Malinowski's heir at the LSE, could gently reprimand those colleagues of his who were "unnecessarily censorious" of "anthropologists who define their material and their major theoretical framework in terms of culture." For Firth it was clear that "'society' and 'culture' are concepts of which the significant elements phase into one another." Very sensible.[26]

## CULTURE ENVOI

In 1988, James Clifford, a historian of ideas who has given us some of the finest treatments of anthropological thought, wrote: "culture is a deeply compromised idea I cannot yet do without."[27] To my mind, and by the light of a lot of contemporary work, the discipline still can't do without it. Nor should it. Is it the be-all, end-all term? Of course not. Do all of my colleagues embrace it? Hardly. Some even still do it down. But by the turn of the twenty-first century, most who had devoted time to its dethroning started pursuing other agendas. Others saw it as a dead horse. So they stopped beating it. Still others have carried on, without much ado, with culture or something like it never far from their minds, even if it's not splashed across the page or flowing off the tongue. (There is a slight blush to the face any time an academic anthropologist uses a phrase like "Italian culture" or "Islamic cultures" or what have you. It feels so *simplistic*, even naive. When journalists ask us about such things, we sneer inside. When relatives do, we forgive them.)

One goal of the rest of this book is to showcase what culture is, warts and all. I stand with Appadurai and Abu-Lughod, who warned against culture's objectifying tendencies. But also with Malinowski, who recognized, in 1926, that "human cultural reality is not a consistent logical scheme but a seething mixture of conflicting principles."[28] And Robert Lowie, one of Boas's first students, who bluntly stated in 1935 that just "as there is no Simon-pure race, so there is no Simon-pure culture.... Aboriginal people have borrowed from one another for thousands of years, and the attempt to isolate one culture that is wholly indigenous is decidedly simple-minded."[29]

I duly note that, according to the two leading American deans of their time, 1952, the dominant trend of the day —again, 1952—was to recognize: "(1) the interrelations of cultural forms: and (2) variability and the individual."[30]

There is simply no other term that could serve as the canopy under which to consider the lessons of the anthropological record—or the diversity of approaches and perspectives displayed therein. Not all of the anthropologists I'll go on to discuss would or do share my stance. Far from it. And not all of the debates, analyses, and interests stem from, or revolve around, "culture theory." But all anthropologists share a commitment: to pay close attention, *very close attention*, to the social histories of humankind and to be wary of appeals to common sense, to human nature, and to reason. Even more than the culture concept itself, these others rile. Not always because they are inappropriate, or silly Western claptrap, or dangerously foolish. But because we know, from the ethnographic evidence, that they all have social histories of their own.

One of the reasons it is important to hammer culture home is because of the extent to which other disciplines make too much or too little of its central role in human life. At one extreme, there are political scientists who treat culture as primordial and unchanging. Reading some international relations theory can drive the anthropologist mad. It is as if the nation, or a national culture, is as well-defined and solid as a rock. At the other extreme, there are psychologists who do experiments on small groups of people and then extrapolate out to claims about cognition or human nature. But then when you look more closely, you see that the small group of people they studied happened to be students at the university where they teach. For any self-respecting anthropologist, one question immediately springs to mind: Can we really extrapolate from a group of college kids at Harvard University to the rest of humanity? In asking that question, the anthropologist is appealing to the culture concept. And it's a good thing too.

CHAPTER 2

# CIVILIZATION

Culture and civilization used to be closely linked in anthropological thinking. You couldn't have one without the other. For Edward Burnett Tylor, the terms were synonymous. Throughout the Victorian era they were at the very least necessarily connected. Arguably, in fact, anthropologists of this period were more interested in civilization than in culture.

And why not? Who wouldn't be interested in civilization?

When we think of civilization, we think of great monuments (ancient and modern), of libraries (in ancient Alexandria and contemporary London), of universities, courts of justice, hospitals, streetlights, and well-paved roads. To be civilized is to be morally upright—to be committed to the values that underpin the libraries and courts and hospitals: freedom of thought, justice, and care. Plus, if you're civilized, you have good table manners. The Victorians were interested in this all because they tied these signs of civilization to moral progress.

Sure, there are instances in which we recognize the flip side of this; some people had to *build* those great monuments, and they may not stand to benefit from the results. (Every schoolchild knows the Pharaohs weren't the ones lugging those huge stones into place for the pyramids.) Well-paved roads tend to jam with traffic. So we have inspirational figures who force us to question the trap-

relation to the wider world. They also allow us to explore one of anthropology's most as-yet unsuccessful missions, which is to move away from such language and thinking altogether. Because while you'd be hard-pressed to find many contemporary anthropologists championing the idea of "civilization," listening to the language of politicians, journalists, and commentators on the modern stage will confirm that the discourse of civilization is alive and well. So, too, unfortunately, is the logic behind it. After the attack on the Christmas market in Berlin in December 2016, Donald J. Trump tweeted: "The civilized world must change thinking!"[1] Trump says things that many other people don't say or wouldn't say, but this isn't one of them. This is run-of-the-mill for political talk.

"Civilization" is, or at least has become, a dangerous word—much more dangerous than "culture." To appreciate why, we have to go back again to the founding days of the discipline and consider civilization's place within the paradigm of social evolutionism.

## FROM SAVAGE TO CIVILIZED

After his time in the Caribbean and Mexico, Edward Burnett Tylor published a popular account of his travels; Victorians loved these adventure tales, which were often laced with ethnographically styled observations and accounts. It was in his later work, however, especially his magnum opus, *Primitive Culture* (1871), that Tylor secured his reputation as a leading figure in the newly emerging field of anthropology. Although as a young man from a Nonconformist background he could not attend Oxbridge, on the basis of his research he was appointed

pings and official storylines of civilization, figures such as
Henry David Thoreau, who retreated to the quiet shores
of Walden Pond; we also duly acknowledge the powerful
work of, say, Joseph Conrad, whose *Heart of Darkness*
challenged the atrocities of colonialism at the very same
time armchair anthropologists were collecting data from
its agents.

When Conrad published *Heart of Darkness* in 1899,
the pull of civilization was extremely powerful. It was
hardly stopped by his book. Like Conrad, however, a
small number of anthropologists of the time—above all,
Boas—began to question civilization as anthropology's
animating idea. It wasn't that they wanted to return forever to the shores of Walden Pond.* But they started to
recognize that the work of anthropology couldn't be
properly done with it. More than any of the other key
words in this book, the indelibly moral connotation of
"civilization" has vexed anthropology.

Vexed it, because it's never really gone away. To be sure,
with the notable exception of archaeologists (and I'll
come to that at the end of the chapter), you will not find
many contemporary anthropologists thinking or writing
in explicitly civilizational terms. But the grammar behind
the terms is often implicit or otherwise affects anthropology's framing or analysis.

Anthropology is now pretty consistently critical of
"civilization," yet there is no doubt that it has been a
central term in and for the field and that the discussions
surrounding it deserve attention. These debates allow us
to address important details of anthropology's past and

---

* Even Thoreau retreated to Walden Pond for just a finite period of time.
"At present I am a sojourner in civilized life again," he tells the reader on the
opening page (1897, 1).

to one of the first academic positions in anthropology, at Oxford University.

Tylor was not the only anthropological pioneer of his day. Herbert Spencer and Lewis Henry Morgan, both of whom were slightly older than Tylor, were also extremely influential. Morgan was a lawyer from upstate New York. He never went as far afield as the Caribbean but with a number of other young men formed a club, based on the members' shared fascination with Native Americans, called the New Order of the Iroquois. It was out of the need for a constitution for this club that Morgan looked into the political arrangements of the League of the Iroquois, the famous confederation of five nations spread across New York and into Canada that would go on to become a staple of anthropological interest.[2]

Tylor, Morgan, and others of this period worked in the age defined above all by Darwin, although it is important to reiterate that theories of social evolution (as indeed biological evolution) preceded the publication of *On the Origin of Species*. While the extent to which the Victorian-era figures were directly influenced by Darwin differs, all of them worked in the idiom of evolution and applied evolution as understood in the natural world (of mollusks and ferns) to the social world.

In *Primitive Culture*, Tylor acknowledges that placing plants and people in the same frame might trouble some of his more pious readers. "To many educated minds," he writes, "there seems something presumptuous and repulsive in the view that the history of mankind is part and parcel of the history of nature, that our thoughts, wills, and actions accord with laws as definite as those which govern the motion of waves, the combination of acids and bases, and the growth of plants and animals."[3] But for Tylor and these others, physics, chemistry, biology, and anthropology were all of a piece.

Spencer, as already noted, used to speak of liver cells and political institutions in the same breath; Tylor also borrowed heavily from the language of the natural sciences. He argued that the anthropologist should treat the bow and arrow as a "species," for instance, and stressed that any given culture should be "dissected" into its details. It was as if he was an eager student in the biology classroom, laying out a culture on the table, cutting it up, and labeling the parts. But the transplant of evolution into the social sphere did demand at least one new set of terms, organized around a concept of civilization.

One of the most important things to keep in mind about "civilization" is that it's a relational term. It really only makes sense if you have other conditions of life and outlooks to contrast with it. In the nineteenth century, the two most important were barbarism and savagery. Civilization itself was of fairly new coinage (it's often traced to the eighteenth century), but the other two were much older. The Greeks and Romans used them to distinguish themselves from other peoples. "Barbarian" was a derogatory term used to describe the language of other peoples as a kind of "babble"—not only unintelligible but undeveloped. "Savage" derives from the Latin *sylva*, or wood; people, in other words, who lived more like animals.[4]

This is the trio of terms that shaped the early social-evolutionary approach. Whereas the taxonomic rank of the biologist would account for kingdom, phylum, and class, that of the anthropologist worked at a gross level with the concern for differentiation between the savage, the barbaric, and the civilized.

Morgan had a particularly detailed approach to how one could determine where a society fit into one of seven stages. Savagery and barbarism each had lower, middle, and upper stages; civilization, on the other hand, was uniform (although this cannot account for the fact that these Anglo-Americans certainly thought themselves more civilized than, say, the peoples of southern Europe; an Italian Catholic was not quite the same as a British or American Protestant). Lower and middle statuses of savagery were differentiated by, for example, the use of fire; upper-status savages had such technologies as the bow and arrow. Upper-status barbarism was marked by the ability to smelt iron. Civilization began with a phonetic alphabet and the use of writing.[5] Within such bands, as we might expect, there were many minor differences. If you read Morgan's *Ancient Society*, for example, you'll come to appreciate the difference between pottery that is air-dried and pottery that is fired; the latter represents a step up the evolutionary scale.

In such a scheme, classification became a straightforward task. Loincloth and nomadic? Pretty savage. Wattle-and-daub huts, iron tools? Perfectly barbaric. Pasta, perhaps, or gunpowder, or a central political authority organized around written texts? Welcome to civilization. The scheme allowed figures such as Morgan to offer clear-cut pictures of the world: "while Africa was and is an ethnical chaos of savagery and barbarism," he notes in passing, "Australia and Polynesia were in savagery, pure and simple, with the arts and institutions belonging to that condition."[6]*

---

* It wasn't that Africa was inscrutable; it was an "ethnical chaos" because of the range of social formations found therein. The Hadza of East Africa, for instance, would be classed as savage hunter-gatherers, while the Nguni of

There is no doubt that social evolution and the discourse of civilization were shaped by moral sensibilities. While these early figures did not wholly denigrate the "ruder" peoples—Morgan had a genuine appreciation for Iroquois culture—there was little place for the Noble Savage à la Jean-Jacques Rousseau in this scheme.* This is evident not least in these men's commitment to a progressive view of history and even, as I've noted, a teleological one. The fact that, as Tylor put it, humankind was subject to laws in the same way as the motion of waves gave this paradigm a strongly deterministic bent.

At the center of this lawlike approach was the principle of "the psychic unity of mankind." Tylor and Morgan were champions of the view that the mental capabilities of the savage are the same as those of the civilized gentleman; humanity was one race and, at its core, of one mind.

This is a significant principle for two reasons. First, it gave the social evolutionists what scientists need, which is a constant. With psychic unity assumed, it became possible to construct a history and even prehistory of humankind through what came to be called "the comparative method." (Not a very original or specific term!) Second, it facilitated an approach that could rely on quantifiable, parts-based analysis. "If law is anywhere, it is everywhere," Tylor writes.[7] When Tylor argued that a culture

---

southern Africa would have been considered barbaric because of a clan-based political system and pastoral livelihood; barbarians, after all, have domesticated animals and political hierarchies.

* Tylor writes: "The Caribs are described as a cheerful, modest, courteous race, and so honest among themselves that if they missed anything out of a house they said quite naturally, 'There has been a Christian here.' Yet the malignant ferocity with which these estimable people tortured their prisoners of war with knife and fire-brand and red pepper, and then cooked and ate them in solid debauch, gave fair reason to the name of Carib (Cannibal) to become the generic name of man-eaters in European languages" (1871, 30).

could be dissected into its details, he meant it. The inventory of arts and institutions reproduced, on the microlevel, what the overarching scheme of savagery-barbarism-civilization did at the macrolevel.

For instance, if you're looking at a culture in this comparative method, one "detail" you'd need to consider is kinship. And the institution of kinship was, in this rendering, bound to be there; all you needed to do was calculate where it fell on the scale of evolution. Not all the details always matched up. But there were general rules (actually *assumptions*; we'll get to that). Thus a patrilineal system should be seen as more evolved than a matrilineal system, and this could be ticked off, like a box on a form, in the overall calculation of a society's evolved state. Why? Well, patrilineal descent is *clearly* more advanced, these Victorians would reason, because it relies on a certain moral rectitude, social stability, and social complexity. Since you can't know that a man is the biological father of a child with the same certainty as a woman is the biological mother, the patrilineal system indexes an evolved state of sexual and kin relations. Savages and barbarians, after all, do not control their sexual impulses. So a savage woman might have sexual intercourse with several different men and not know—or care—who the father is.

The principle of psychic unity also allowed for a play on time. Since we have this psychic unity, and since law is everywhere, and since we, like waves, ebb and flow in lawlike fashion, it was possible for the social evolutionists to treat the Iroquois and the Caribs and the Hadza as living fossils; we could observe them and take note of our own dark, rude past: "Our own remote forefathers passed through the same conditions, one after the other, and possessed, there can scarcely be a doubt, the same, or very similar institutions, with many of the same usages and customs."[8] Although in one sense informed by a concern with deep history—the development of humankind over tens of thousands of years—in another sense social evolutionism was profoundly ahistorical.

This ahistoricism was the root of Boas's discontent. In an article published in 1896, Boas criticized the work of the evolutionists for their assertion of laws governing humankind's social and cultural development. The problem, he argued, is that this ignores the significant extent to which we know, in fact, that culture traits and patterns of sociality are just as often borrowed and adapted. What's more, the emphasis on laws of evolution as developed by Tylor and others had produced a deductive approach. They worked from the general to the specific and this, Boas argued, is bad science. It's like starting with a conclusion and working backward. Anthropology has to be an inductive field of inquiry. It needs to build up from the specific to the general. This emphasis on history and specificity is, as we've already explored, the basis of the Boasian culture concept. Such a backstory allows us to appreciate how and why Boas found the social-evolutionary "dissection" of a culture into its "details" nonsensical. To dissect a culture is perforce to kill it. Boas was unsparing in his conclusion: "The comparative method, notwithstanding all that has been said and written in its praise, has been remarkably barren of definite results, and I believe it will not become fruitful until we denounce the vain endeavor to construct a uniform systematic history of the evolution of culture."[9]

There was another problem. Victorian social evolutionism was a moral philosophy masquerading as science. Yet before proceeding to expose and appreciate this further, it's important not to oversimplify the commitments of Tylor, Morgan, and others or read the record anachronistically. One point that often gets lost in the contemporary tut-tuts aimed at these Victorians is the progressiveness of their overarching principle. To say, in the 1870s, that a "bushman" in the Kalahari and a "gentleman" in London had psychic unity was to challenge a logic of racism and racialism that had long been (and still is) powerful: that white people and not-white people have qualitatively different mental capacities. On this point, indeed, Boas would have stood shoulder to shoulder with his Victorian forebears.

It was not at all unusual in this era to challenge the idea that Africans were mentally capable of achieving anything looking like "civilization." So when European colonial authorities and missionaries found statelike political systems in central Africa, they explained them away. The Tutsi, for instance, who stood at the center of a kingdom system in Rwanda, were not *really* Africans. Drawing heavily on the biblical story of Ham, many colonialists concluded the Tutsi had to be a lost tribe of Israel. Other and similar arguments were put forward with respect to the fallen Monomotapa kingdom in southern Africa; the magnificent ruins of Great Zimbabwe, it was argued (including by archaeologists), could not have been made by black people.

I say "*a* logic of racism" because there are many, and Victorian social evolutionism ended up promoting and legitimizing another. The Victorians' rationale was justified not by qualitative differences so much as quantitative ones. And this hinged on temporality rather than biology. The "others" in this evolutionary scheme were not different creatures altogether; they were us-as-before. Children, more like, who might become us some day but still had a long way to go.

This kind of paternalism served the purposes of empire extremely well. Just as the new anthropology professors were busy in their studies mapping out the trajectory of savagery, barbarism, and civilization, so a whole host of other nineteenth-century actors—British governors-general, French *troupes coloniales*, German Pietist missionaries— were harnessing the logic and grammar of civilization to justify imperialism.

The civilizing mission, or *mission civilisatrice*, is a ubiquitous feature of the colonial-era archive, the background against which it must be read. You cannot get far into any travelogue, mission report, or colonial circular without coming across its force. Any student of colonial history will be aware of the rhetorical flourishes employed by missionaries of the London Missionary Society or of the claims by politicians, such as the French prime minister, Jules Ferry, who declared the right and duty of France to spread "ideas of civilization in its highest sense."[10]

One study that captures the dynamics of the civilizing mission very well is by Jean Comaroff and John Comaroff.[11] Experts on the Tswana of Botswana and South Africa, they document in great detail how, over the course of the nineteenth century, the rhetoric of "Christianity, commerce, and civilization" shaped the colonial encounter and Western depiction of Africa as the "Dark Continent." Weaving together their own contemporary field research in the 1970s and 1980s with archival sources and readings of popular culture, the Comaroffs trace what they call "the long conversation" between missionaries (largely from Nonconformist backgrounds; men like Robert Moffat and David Livingstone) and their would-be flocks. That they focus on missionaries rather than colonial officials or merchants isn't to suggest these other figures were unimportant. But in fact it was often missionaries who got there first (wherever *there* was), stayed for longer, and figured things out better (until the government-sponsored anthropologists came along, of course).

An important part of what the Comaroffs show is how civilization had to be understood and worked out with respect to God and the market alike, as well as the attendant world of manners, ethics, and dispositions. A lot of what missionaries did in colonial Africa extended well beyond preaching the Gospel per se. Missionaries rearranged almost everything—not only obviously relevant things such as marriage practices (polygamy sent innumerable missionaries into moral fits) but even seemingly minor details such as the layout of a village or the use of utensils. To be civilized is also to be civil: to embody and enact the mores of polite society. The missionaries also often championed science, over and above what got cast as the irrationality and superstition of the natives. They established hospitals and schools to treat the body and train the mind.

"Colonization" was never one thing, never one unified project controlled by a bishop or a prime minister or an adventurous magnate. The Comaroffs and many other careful students of imperial and colonial history have demonstrated this much. What they also show, however, is just how powerful what we might call the grammar of civilization became.

The Comaroffs call this grammar the "colonization of consciousness" and it amounts to an argument that, wittingly or not, the subjects of empire and evangelization were drawn into a long conversation in which they had to accept the terms of discussion set by the Europeans and Americans. In an oft-cited chapter from one of their books, the Comaroffs illustrate this by discussing a passage from the work of David Livingstone, probably the greatest and most popular missionary-explorer of the Victorian era (his body is buried in Westminster Abbey; his heart, though, is buried in Africa, as he wished). In the passage, Livingstone recounts an exchange between himself and a Tswana man. Livingstone plays the part of the "medical doctor" (remember, these men of God were also often men of science in the service of God), while the Tswana man is referred to as a "rain doctor." In the exchange, Livingstone appeals to science, reason, and theology in an attempt to convince the rain doctor that his efforts are in vain—at best coincidence, at worst, cynically timed appeals (with clouds gathered on the horizon). The rain doctor actually holds his own in the exchange, refusing to succumb to many of the points that Livingstone makes—even pointing out the missionary's hypocrisy. Livingstone, then, presents an image of the resistant Other, not some passive, childlike primitive. Yet by the end of this conversation, it is taking place on the terms that Livingstone sets, with science, reason, and theology shaping the parameters of what's grammatical and ungrammatical. Civilization wins.

Did this conversation take place? Maybe. Did it take place exactly as Livingstone relates? Doubtful. He is telling his story, which would have been all the more compelling for its intended audience given the momentary retorts of the feisty native. As the Comaroffs argue, however, it is representative of a more diffuse, unfolding "confrontation between two cultures."[12] It is not that the

"Western culture" won. The very idea of there being such a thing is something the Comaroffs and most self-respecting anthropologists would dismiss—as I hope the last chapter made clear. Indeed, as the ethnographic record makes plain, such conversations, exchanges, and even confrontations are always two-way or more. A lot of what the Comaroffs document in their historical anthropology is, in fact, the Africanization of Western thought—of the extent, even, to which these designations only make sense in relation to one another.

But the ethnographic record also makes it clear that the grammar of civilization had a powerful and often pernicious effect on colonial and postcolonial social dynamics and cultural imaginings. Almost a century after this exchange in Livingstone's travelogue, another doctor offered a prescient diagnosis of the colonial condition. Frantz Fanon was a French-trained psychiatrist from Martinique who went on to practice at a hospital in Algeria and was latterly involved in the Algerian struggle for independence. In his 1952 classic, *Black Skin, White Masks*, Fanon provides a rallying cry for those who stand behind the Tswana rain doctor, a brisk slap in the face to the colonial master and colonial subject alike, calling foul on the assumption that "the Negro is a stage in the slow evolution of monkey into man" (so much for the progressiveness of the psychic unity principle). Fanon continues: "Every colonized people—in other words, every people in whose soul an inferiority complex has been created by the death and burial of its local cultural originality—finds itself face to face with the language of the civilizing nation; that is, with the culture of the mother country. The colonized is elevated above his jungle status in proportion to his adoption of the mother country's cultural standards. He becomes whiter as he renounces his blackness, his jungle."[13]

A different and more contemporary example of the "jungle status" effect comes from work on the Ese Ejja of northern Bolivia.[14] The Ese Ejja, whose language belongs to the Tacana family, number under 1,500 people, spread across parts of Bolivia and Peru; they hunt, fish, and practice swidden agriculture, and live in village settlements (which are today organized around football pitches). Like many small, indigenous groups, the Ese Ejja have often suffered at the hands of European settlers, remaining marginalized in remote villages or drawn into exploitative mine labor.

During fieldwork in 1999–2001, Isabella Lepri often heard the Ese Ejja say they were "not proper people," that they were still wild and savage, whereas the white and mestizo Bolivians of the cities were civilized. In the local language, white people are actually referred to as *dejja nei* (very beautiful/true/real/proper people). In many ways, Lepri tells us, the villagers she got to know wanted to be like the whites in the big towns. In the village, one woman she knew would cook with "white food" such as onions and cumin. She would have Lepri buy cheese when she went to town and always wanted to eat lunch at "noon" (though Lepri tells us this bore little relation to noon in clock time). There were some local cultural inflections; the young people who played football—the game is *huge* for the Ese Ejja—would mimic what they knew from popular culture about how to play, how to dress, and how to act on the pitch. But there was one notable difference: a goal never resulted in shows of bravado or even joy; to win or succeed over others is, in Ese Ejja tradition, to invite conflict and they do what they can to avoid conflict. (In an Ese Ejja match, the side that wins doesn't focus on the final score; they say how many goals the other side would have needed to tie.) Young people more generally were thought to be "almost *dejja*" anyway—further along the path to a civilized life.

The Ese Ejja have internalized the grammar of civilization. And yet they are not "abject savages" in any absolute sense. Other aspects of their attitudes toward white Bolivians reveal a more complicated picture. They may want to be "civilized," but they don't want to be white Bolivians or live in the towns, which they consider dirty, dangerous, and violent. In the village, they say, life is good and people care about one another. Food is plentiful and shared. The more the Ese Ejja come into direct contact with outsiders, the more this local pride seems to manifest itself, reversing the terms of understanding. Such shifts in self-identification and self-valuing are not unusual. But in the Amazonian context, a lot of recent work on local cultures has argued for a regional specificity to this dynamic, called "perspectivism." I'll come back to this anthropological approach in chapter 8, because it has garnered a good deal of attention in the past twenty years. The point here is simply to note that, coupled with the approach to football, we can see how the "Ese Ejja want to be *dejja*, but on their own terms and through selective imitation, excluding the kind of behaviour which contradicts their own ethics."[15]

Research on the Ese Ejja shows us how the language of savagery and civilization remains with us to this day. A central aspect of this is expressed not only in the explicit use of such terms but also in what I referred to earlier as the temporal hinge of evolutionary thinking. This hinge can often be well hidden and well oiled, but knowing it's there is crucial to understanding how the logic works. Much more often than awkward and uncomfortable remarks about not being "proper people," what we find people say about others (and sometimes themselves) is that they're *backward, behind the times, stuck in time,* and so forth.

This way of speaking is common not only in colonial and postcolonial situations but everywhere. If you live in rural Wales or rural Idaho, people from Cardiff or Seattle might well say you're behind the times. You might say it yourself and see it as a point of pride. These turns of phrase, while often used in innocent, cutesy jokes, express the logic of social evolutionism just as much as the Ese Ejja's self-denigration.

It's not only in jibes against rural Welsh folk, or anthropological analyses of indigenous Amazonians, that this same logic is at work. Take the "Global War on Terror," one view on which we considered at the start of the chapter in Trump's tweet. Immediately after the attacks on 9/11, the discourse of civilization came forth in full spate. Calls for the civilized world to stand firm against the barbaric acts of terrorists were made by politicians and pundits throughout the West and in some instances well beyond. There's nothing unique in this. The enemy other is always going to be barbaric or savage in some respect. Take a look at propaganda posters in America during World War I; the Germans—"Huns"—don't look very civilized. They're not even human in some images but scary apes. What does become especially relevant in the War on Terror, though, is the concept of civilization itself, especially as captured by a professor of political science at Harvard University, Samuel P. Huntington.

In 1993, Huntington published a hugely influential essay, "The Clash of Civilizations?" in which he set out his view of the future of world politics. With the Cold War over, he argued, geopolitics would no longer be defined by the ideological struggle between socialism and capitalism; indeed, the very language of First, Second, and Third worlds would fade into irrelevance. The Cold War order would be replaced by a clash of civilizations.

Huntington defines civilization as "the highest cultural grouping of people and the broadest level of cultural identity people have short of that which distinguishes humans from other species."[16] There is a great deal of slippage between Huntington's use of the terms "culture" and "civilization." The former is nested within the latter and has more mid- and microlevel specificities, but in many ways he uses these two terms interchangeably. In this respect, as well as the extent to which his definition relies upon the principle of psychic unity, Huntington's understanding is remarkably similar to Tylor's. For both men it is civilization, and the moral narrative behind it, that matters most.

To be sure, Huntington does not speak of "rude races" or even savages or barbarians. Civilization is the lowest common denominator of humankind—a "major civilization" might even exist in Africa, he tells us. (The Victorians wouldn't have said this.) Civilizations differ from one another "by history, language, culture, tradition and, most important, religion."[17] These differences are real and basic, and while they are not predestined to clash, or totally immune to change and blurring, they are a source of significant danger. And the biggest danger, Huntington felt, was a clash between the West and Islam. This was in

1993. By 1998, with attacks in East Africa on two American embassies linked to a certain Osama bin Laden, Huntington started to look insightful; after 9/11 he looked downright prophetic.

Not that "the coalition of the willing" endorsed Huntington's ideas wholesale. The War on Terror was never supposed to be a clash of civilizations in the official telling. It certainly wasn't expedient for George W. Bush to speak baldly in these terms. The message was always that the acts of the terrorists were a perversion of Islam. When Bush once did refer to the plan as a "crusade"—invoking a medieval image—his spin doctors reeled it back.[18]

Huntington had little time for the neoconservatives who engineered the campaigns in Afghanistan and Iraq. Like many catchphrases, however, Huntington's indicates a more widespread mind-set and mood. The War on Terror is an object lesson of social evolutionism's continuing appeal.

This is evident partly through the extent to which the wars, especially in Afghanistan, were linked to a civilizing mission. The campaign in Afghanistan always had especially strong moral force because of the Taliban; they were seen as barbaric, plain and simple, particularly in their treatment of girls and women. Afghanis had to be saved. In Iraq, though, it was about bringing democracy, which its advocates considered the most civilized, evolved political system. (Democracies, after all, are the political systems with *civil societies*, right?)

Once again, asserting the moral superiority of one's own side in a conflict is hardly new. The modern framing of civilization, though, has also drawn very heavily on the figurative language of time. Like Victorian anthropologists, key players in the War on Terror approached the

Other as living fossils, as stuck in the past. For me, one of the most telling remarks confirming this mind-set comes from a colonel in the U.S. Army: "In Western Iraq, it's like it was six centuries ago with the Bedouins in their goat hair tents."[19]

I'm no military strategist, but if I were, I'd certainly want to point out that this is a very bad way—a very *dangerous* way—to think about Bedouins. Thinking back over some of the less successful American wars in the recent past—Vietnam, Iraq, Afghanistan—it's not difficult to see how often confidence in the United States' technological superiority has been misplaced. Behind this is the culturally conditioned understanding that the power of a mighty civilization will always trump what a less developed society or enemy can do.

There is a term for this, coined by German anthropologist Johannes Fabian. It's called "the denial of coevalness," which means denying that you occupy the same time as someone else. Fabian came up with the phrase in the 1980s as a criticism of the way anthropologists often treated their subjects. By that point, of course, explicit commitments to social evolutionism had been almost universally dropped. Fabian's argument was that treatment of the Other as a kind of fossil or antique specimen still survived in other theoretical paradigms. Anthropology, he wrote, is treated like a "time machine."[20] When you leave your university study you are in the Time of Now. When you arrive in the field, you are in a Time Gone By.

Fabian was absolutely right. And while his book was instrumental in helping dispel such denial, the denial of coevalness is still an anthropological prejudice. It mostly comes across as a romantic sensibility—maybe harmless enough. But work in Africa, or lowland South America, or the Mongolian steppes often has more cachet than work in the United States or Germany.* This is because anthropology is still partly under the sway of the idea that to truly understand the human condition, we need to strip away the trappings of civilization and modernity.

There are softer sides to the legacies of social evolutionism. The mention of "modernity" might call to mind not projects of war but, rather, projects of development and peace. After World War II, some anthropologists became involved in the construction and implementation of "modernization theory." Early on in his career, for instance, Clifford Geertz directed the Committee for the Comparative Study of New Nations at the University of Chicago. Basically, this was a social-scientific effort to help understand how the former colonies (newly independent nations such as Ghana, Indonesia, Morocco, etc.) could and should modernize. What could bring these nations into the contemporary fold? How many roads and hospitals and trained architects did they need? Many modernization theorists were convinced that understanding culture was vital; hence the value of anthropologists being on board. It wasn't that they wanted to preserve other cultures—though a bit of local color and spice would be fine. Rather, it was about how to maximize the potential for advancement and integration into a world (i.e., Western) system. These theorists—economists such as Walt Rostow, sociologists such as Talcott Parsons and Schmuel Eisenstadt—put forward neo-evolutionary ideas in the language of development, achievement, and gross domestic product.

* Unless the work in the United States or France is on a marked Other: illegal Mexican migrants, perhaps, or the Turkish community in Berlin. Something that counts as exotic or marginal.

International development—the contemporary outgrowth of modernization—is now an important field of study. The range of approaches has grown, as has its moral purchase. No major transnational corporation these days exists without a "Corporate Social Responsibility" division or team; mining companies operating in South Africa and Papua New Guinea will build schools, support women's weaving cooperatives, and so forth in order to show that they are good citizens. Most of these initiatives are premised on local empowerment. As two of the leading figures in the anthropology of development have shown, old-school modernization assumed a trickle-down effect: work with local postcolonial elites and the new state institutions, and the benefits would flow to the peasant farmers below.[21] In fact, as anthropologists of development have argued, many such schemes either fell flat or made the situation on the ground worse, often because they were—despite the modernizers' stated commitments—completely oblivious to questions of culture.

If some development initiatives have gotten better and become more sensitive to questions of empowerment and local values, it is nevertheless notable just how ingrained the grammar of civilization and social evolutionism is now. Okay, so we find it in the work of hawkish political scientists and the theaters of war—just what we might expect, reason the lefty, progressive readers among you. But you need look no further than *The Guardian* newspaper—that venerable periodical of progressive journalism—to find it.

In 2008, *The Guardian* launched a three-year experiment in aid, in cooperation with Barclays Bank and the African Medical and Research Foundation (AMREF), an NGO based in Africa focused on health-care delivery.

The project was based in Katine, a village in northern Uganda. One of the distinguishing features of the project was its openness to the public, with *The Guardian* maintaining an extensive web-based collection of articles, videos, reports, seminar recordings, and reader commentaries as the project unfolded.[22] It is an amazing archive of material and reveals the complexity of development work, especially when it comes to building something sustainable. The archive shows us the cock-ups and hiccups as well as the successes. And there were successes—in the availability of clean drinking water, in the introduction of new crops, in child immunization rates, and in the building up of savings and loan associations. As Ben Jones, one of the anthropologists involved in its assessment, puts it, the project can help you see "why development is both difficult and necessary."[23]

The Katine project was a well-considered, innovative effort. Yet my own first impression of the project was a jarring one. On the day of its public launch—Saturday, 20 October 2007—I bought my *Guardian* as usual to see the headline story: "Can we, together, lift one village out of the Middle Ages?" This was followed by the strapline: "Launching an ambitious *Guardian* aid experiment, Alan Rusbridger travels a few hours from London—and 700 years back in time."[24] Rusbridger—then *The Guardian*'s editor—took the medieval metaphor from Paul Collier, an economist at the University of Oxford. In the article itself, he expands on the imagery, saying the project wanted to "help change lives still trapped in the 14th century."

This is even worse, and even more dangerous, than the American army colonel's remarks in Iraq. Is Rusbridger —or Collier, for that matter—simply a new incarnation of E. B. Tylor or some secularized version of David Livingstone? No. The project overall reveals a nuance of thought, self-reflexivity, and a much deeper awareness of the dangers of paternalism than the Victorians or modernizers ever did. But it is because of this, rather than in spite of it, that we should feel particularly disheartened by Rusbridger's rhetorical flourishes. A lot of people don't interpret these flourishes as metaphorical; they see them as literal. They think Africans in rural Uganda are trapped in the fourteenth century. The denial of coevalness is alive and well.

Why is this so dangerous? Because it prevents us from seeing that the lives of Katine villagers are not trapped in the fourteenth century but lived out in a twenty-first-century world shaped by a host of colonial and postcolonial economic and political dynamics. Katine is contemporary because it is shaped by the legacies of British colonial policies, by the regime of Idi Amin, by an ongoing regional insurgency, by the agricultural subsidies for farmers in the European Union, by the strategic plans of the International Monetary Fund, and more. If we can place the African Other in an earlier age, we don't have to face up fully to the reasons why their lives don't look like ours. To live in the twenty-first century isn't to have access to a functioning hospital, the Internet, and an untampered-with ballot box. That image of "now"— what constitutes the achievements of civilization—is mistaking a part for the whole; it's refusing to acknowledge that "now" is made up of more than a Euro-American imagining of modernity.

In the last chapter I defended the culture concept against some who would like to get rid of it, certainly as the term that frames anthropological analysis. Having done so, it would be unfair of me to banish another term altogether, perhaps especially one that has the closest links to culture. "Civilization" has run amok. It is used today in ways that often suggest superiority in nearly every sense—technological, moral, and ethical. Whether explicit or not, its use also often betrays a debt to the social-evolutionary schemes that animated the early days of anthropology and underwrote the case for European colonialism. But in concluding this chapter, it is worth considering what gets lost, or obscured, if we get rid of it altogether.

It is no small irony that it was in Iraq that our American army colonel evoked the image of medieval Bedouins in their goat-hair tents. As any archaeologist will tell you, goats were one of the first domesticated animals. In the big-picture view of prehistory, goats are evidence of civilization—not a sign of its absence. What is more, Iraq is, as schoolchildren often hear, "the birthplace of civilization." It was in ancient Mesopotamia, in the rich soils between the Tigris and Euphrates rivers, that what we call "civilization" began. Alongside ancient Egypt, we think of this Near Eastern swathe as the cradle of history, marked above all by the development of writing and urban settlements in the fourth millennium BC. In archaeology, "civilization" has long had this more descriptive function. It designates urbanization—not necessarily, or only, better manners and higher values.

David Wengrow, an archaeologist at University College London, has recently grappled with the complex history and possibilities of the term. "What makes civilization?" he asks.[25] Focusing on the ancient Near East, his answer is comprised of several parts. Above all, he argues, a civilization is not defined by its boundaries. Mesopotamia and Egypt have to be seen as separate and distinct, but it is a distinction marked in part by a history of significant interactions and exchanges across the region. For Wengrow, a civilization is what it is in no small part because of the quality and depth of its relationships. He bases this conclusion on a close reading of the ever-expanding archaeological record, tracing just how extensive the circulation and trade of raw materials and goods (from lapis lazuli to cereals) were in the third millennium BC. From Troy and the Mediterranean in the West to the Chagai Hills and Indus Valley in the East, it was a dense network. In making this point, he is taking particular aim at Samuel Huntington's suggestion that civilizations are so much like objects that they are prone to crash and clash.

Wengrow also wants to shift the focus of civilizational studies away from the monumental and the spectacular to the mundane and the everyday. Pyramids and ziggurats are impressive feats of engineering and writing is a breakthrough technology. But more than these, we should pay attention to the mundane practices of everyday life—cooking, body adornment, domestic arrangements—that archaeology can, with increasing accuracy, tell us about. This is another version of an archaeological catchphrase I invoked in the last chapter: looking in *small things forgotten.*

In the ancient Near East, one of the most striking conclusions to be drawn from this shift of focus is how it both reinforces and deepens an appreciation for the distinctiveness of Egyptian and Mesopotamian worldviews. Paradoxically, despite the extent of interactions in this, the "cauldron of civilization," a relatively distinct approach to the symbolic order of the world held sway for nearly four thousand years.[26] In Mesopotamia, this order was organized around the value of the house, whereas in the Nile Valley it revolved around the value of the body. The lesson here is to appreciate "the deep attachment of human societies to the concepts they live by."[27]

Wengrow's conclusion points to further questions for anthropology. If the disciplinary consensus is that the models of civilization and culture extending from Tylor to Huntington are both inaccurate and wrong, how can that be reconciled with the fact that the concepts we live by can be so distinct and long-lasting? Four thousand years is a pretty long time, even to an archaeologist. Equally pressing, if what we have seen over the past six thousand years and more of human history is not social evolution, what is it?

The answer to the second question is pretty easy. It's *change*. In some cases we might want to call this change "development" or maybe even employ awkward terms, like "complexification." But to call any such change social evolution is to mischaracterize the workings of culture. In terms of the first question, we've already got a good start on it, inasmuch as this chapter and the last have been animated by an important term that helps us understand it: values. And it's to values that we now turn.

---

## CHAPTER 3

# VALUES

Most of the aspects we've considered with regard to culture and civilization can be broken down further into a concern with values. This is blindingly obvious with respect to "civilization"—a term of evaluation if ever there was one. If you ask Americans to choose between their air-conditioning and their freedom, they'll choose freedom. "Live free or die," reads the state motto of New Hampshire. That would even be the case in Texas, where the air-conditioning is pretty handy.

In terms of culture, when anthropologists write about the Zuni, or futures traders in London, or indigenous footballers in Bolivia, a lot of what it boils down to is the analysis of values: hospitality, or success, or equality. In fact, anthropologists have often used values to gloss the types or kinds of cultures they study. Throughout the ethnographic record you'll find spirited discussions and debates about the nature of "egalitarian societies," "honor cultures," and so on.

We tend to think of values as enduring, fixed, and self-evident. What anthropology teaches us about values raises questions about this. Because when it comes to empirical studies, what we see is just how creative and flexible values can be. This isn't the same thing as saying that values are easily changeable, relative, flimsy, or even just cast off when inconvenient. But exactly what "freedom" means to an American, or anyone else, shouldn't be taken for granted.

We could explore this point in relation to almost any good ethnographic study. At one level or another, almost every study will tell us something about values—or even more precisely, values-in-action. In most cases, though, values aren't the explicit focus, and in very few instances do anthropologists operate with anything like a theory of them. But there are some notable exceptions to this state of affairs, two of which I'll use to frame our discussions in this chapter. The first is a body of work on the peoples and cultures of the Mediterranean, which explores the values of honor and shame, and which at least some anthropologists have treated as constitutive of a regional identity. The second is the even more theoretically explicit project of a French anthropologist, Louis Dumont, who saw the concept of values as a particularly anthropological one, deserving center stage.

## HONOR AND SHAME

One of the most important discussions of values has taken place among anthropologists working in the Mediterranean. In the late 1950s, these anthropologists started to think more broadly about the fact that the people they studied—be they highland Greek villagers, Algerian Berbers, or Andalusian peasants—seemed to organize their lives around the values of honor and shame. In some of the ethnographic accounts from this period, men and women (although often especially men) seem almost entirely preoccupied with promoting and protecting their honor. Sometimes it's personal honor, sometimes it's family honor; sometimes, even, it's the honor of the group. In a lot of cases, the concerns are sparked by threats to or transgressions by the womenfolk, especially sisters or daughters.

What many of these anthropologists working in Greece, Algeria, Sicily, Egypt, and Spain also found were communities in which social life seemed to revolve around a set of contradictory attitudes and dispositions: the people were incredibly hospitable, yet also deeply suspicious of outsiders; they championed an ethic of independence and equality, but lived according to strong social hierarchies and depended on patrons; men emphasized their piety and faithfulness, while simultaneously asserting their virility and machismo. So there were common elements to the social dynamics and relations, and many of these paradoxical relations seemed to turn on questions of honor and shame.

It's not difficult to conjure up a stereotypical image, and like most stereotypes it's problematic: the Sicilian man, maybe, chest puffed up, extremely hospitable and polite, very proud and self-assured, but whose charm and good grace can turn in a matter of seconds to a fit of anger over some slight; perhaps someone below him in the social hierarchy has spoken out of turn, perhaps his social better has demeaned him in some way, or perhaps a suitor has stood up his sister. Power, status, sex: these are the recurrent concerns of honor.

Hollywood has made a lot of money out of this stereotype. And of course that's the problem, really. It plays on much of what we discussed in the last chapter. You know, those southern Europeans ... those Arabs ... they're just not as in control of their emotions ... not as, well ... *civilized.*

I'll want to come back to some of these problems later on, especially in terms of how they were recognized and addressed by anthropologists of the region. By the late 1980s, the political and ethical risks of misrepresentation contributed to a shift away from work on honor and shame. But there is no doubt that this body of literature can help us understand the stuff of values, what it means to organize one's life and actions in accordance with certain ideas. In addition, this body of literature serves as an object lesson for two of anthropology's perennial challenges: first, how to balance general claims with particular findings; and second, how to be true to the people we study.

The really foundational moment for this work came in 1959, when a group of anthropologists got together in a castle in Austria to discuss what might unite their otherwise seemingly disparate projects.* They all worked in countries surrounding the Mediterranean Sea, but at first sight this might seem incidental. After all, the Mediterranean is a hugely diverse area, even given the longstanding trade routes and other connections crisscrossing the sea. We are talking about a region that encompasses major centers of the three Abrahamic faiths, that includes a longstanding mix of pastoral and agricultural societies in which we find a range of kinship structures, and whose

---

* The castle in Austria was owned by the New York–based Wenner-Gren Foundation for Anthropological Research, which is probably the most important funding body in the world devoted exclusively to the support of anthropology (all four subfields). They have since sold their castle, alas, but they still fund major workshops, among many other programs. In recent years, the papers developed in these workshops have been published in special issues of the journal *Current Anthropology*. These special issues are freely available to the general public online.

peoples speak the tongues of no fewer than three languages families (Indo-European, Afro-Asiatic, and Turkic). Even so, the convener of the workshop, J. G. Peristiany, was convinced of a connecting thread. For wherever you went in this region, the various participants observed, concerns with honor and shame were front and center in people's lives. These values, Peristiany argued, are constitutive to "Mediterranean modes of thought."[1]

The book that resulted from the Austrian workshop, *Honour and Shame: The Values of Mediterranean Society*, was published in 1965. With stand-alone chapters on Spain, Algeria, Egypt, Greece, and Cyprus, it's also one of those volumes in which the whole is greater than the sum of its parts. It certainly left an indelible mark on the anthropology of the Mediterranean.

One of the most influential chapters in the book is by Julian Pitt-Rivers. Trained at Oxford, and unusual in his day for his interest in Spain, his essay, "Honour and Social Status," is comprised of two main parts. The first is a thought-provoking mix of big-picture, broad-brush remarks on the history of the concept of honor—with entertaining references to Shakespeare's plays and tales of El Cid. The second is a more focused and grounded analysis of the situation in the Andalusian village where he conducted fieldwork. For those in the know, the essay is also interesting because Pitt-Rivers comes from one of the worlds he describes—and it's not that of the Spanish peasants.

Julian Alfred Lane Fox Pitt-Rivers was of aristocratic stock. His great-grandfather, also an Oxford man, was a gentleman archaeologist who founded the university's anthropology museum. (His father, unfortunately, was a eugenicist and Nazi sympathizer and spent part of World War II locked up in the Tower of London.) One of Pitt-Rivers's close associates once wondered why he bothered with a post as an academic; over the course of his career, he held positions in the United States, the UK, and France. Surely a *job* for someone of his rank and standing could only be a distraction from *one's real work*!

Pitt-Rivers seems to have had a classic version of the insider's ambivalence. In his broad-brush reflections on honor codes, one of the first parallels he draws is between the attitudes of aristocrats and the attitudes of gangsters. For each, of course, honor is paramount. But this is because they see themselves as the exception to the rule. Both aristocrats and gangsters think of themselves as beyond the law: in the former case, above it; in the latter, outside it. For each, codes of honor are incompatible with state-backed models of justice and right that are supposed to underpin the modern world.

The relative power of the state was often regarded as a key factor in the strength of an honor culture. The stronger the state—the stronger a system of centralized political authority, organized around an impersonal bureaucracy and model of justice—the less important honor would be as a central value. So the fact that the Mediterranean countries tended to have weak states was an important part of the equation in this values-related work. As many of the anthropologists working in these contexts stressed, authority resided above all in the strength of the family unit. Displays of power were exercised in and through individuals, even when they related to corporate identities. These displays of power and status were often made in the form of bravado and, on occasion, raw assertions of might—from sheep stealing (a fairly common practice among many Mediterranean pastoralists) to the settling of a disagreement or personal transgression by resorting to violence.

Pitt-Rivers also wanted to emphasize the strong connection between honor and the physical body. It's this link that makes violence such an important means of redress or a vindication for someone who has been dishonored. Take the rituals used to bestow or acknowledge honor. These often focus on the head, from the crowning of a monarch to the conferral of the Oxford degree (the graduates are touched on the head with the New Testament—although nowadays they can be touched by a secular alternative). In acknowledging someone else's honorable status, traditionally the cap is doffed or head bowed. For soldiers, think of the salute. Covering the head, for both men and women, is a way of maintaining and communicating one's honorable standing and disposition. We've come to associate headscarves with a certain kind of female piety among Muslims; but take a look some time at an old photograph of Catholic women in Sicily or Greek Orthodox women. Their heads will be covered with scarves. (And the men will likely be wearing caps, too.) On the flip side, Pitt-Rivers reminds us that for much of early modern European history, the most shameful form of execution was decapitation. "Off with their heads!" is not an arbitrary nastiness.

The more focused discussion on Andalusia in Pitt-Rivers's essay adds some wonderful detail and specificity to the big picture. In the town of Sierra de Cádiz, he tells us, honor is on everyone's lips. In this part of the world it functions as the social glue; in the absence of a strong and formal legal regime, concern for the standing of one's honor is what allows for smooth social and economic transactions. But there are limits to this arrangement. One must act honorably in dealings with others, especially those with whom one has or hopes to form close bonds: family, friends, or perhaps business associates. When it comes to dealing with more abstract others and authorities, however, such as the state, all bets are off. These Andalusians have no shame when it comes to cheating the state, he tells us, because the state doesn't allow for the kind of personal ties that an honor code demands.

The most important aspects of Pitt-Rivers's discussions, though, have to do with the sometimes contradictory dynamics of honor and shame—how a single "value" can make paradoxical demands or come to look like its opposite. Pitt-Rivers captures this in some scattered remarks he makes about a particular man he came to know, called Manuel.

Not to put too fine a point on it, Manuel was short, fat, and ugly—and married. Once, Pitt-Rivers tells us, at a fiesta in the valley, a beautiful young woman walked past Manuel without paying him any attention. Manuel turned to Pitt-Rivers and said, "If it were not for the ring upon this finger, I would not let that girl pass me by as she has."[2] As Pitt-Rivers explains, Manuel thus "eats his cake and has it": he can claim to be a manly man at heart, full of virile desires and energy, but a family man in practice, attentive to the honor of his wife. He saves himself from a certain kind of disgrace by saying something almost shameful (almost, because it's redeemed by his honorable fidelity). This is, apparently, a contradictory demand facing all the men of the village. They have to be revved up and puritan at the same time; the multivalent character of honor allows for this.

Short, fat, ugly, married—and poor. It gets worse for Manuel, it seems, for he was also of humble background and standing. But he did have one thing going for him: a knack for farming. Manuel knew a lot about agriculture and enjoyed his reputation as someone to whom others would turn when in need of advice. Manuel took this further than he ought to have had, though; Pitt-Rivers tells us he offered his opinions on a much broader range of subjects than agricultural advice, including when it wasn't sought. Honor cultures often tolerate high levels of boasting; it is one way of asserting and securing one's reputation. But even this has its limits and it seems Manuel stretched them too far. "I have not much fortune," we are told he liked to say, "but I have within me that which is worth more than fortune, my honour."[3] Here, the line between honor and shame becomes very thin indeed. And in the eyes of his community, Manuel seems to have erased it altogether.

Pitt-Rivers's observations here are exemplary; they're great anthropology. Because what he shows is that the values that matter most are stable and flexible at the same time. This is very important to recognize for understanding not only the honor cultures of the Mediterranean but the values of any culture or society. We shouldn't treat values like fixed points, even though we often assume they are. Values are more like weathervanes; they're "fixed" yet often move about or change direction on account of what's in the air. This is one of the lasting lessons from the anthropological study of values.

Not all contributors to the early honor cultures debate wanted to rest easy with an appreciation of the powers of ambiguity and fluidity behind the concepts that we use to organize our lives. For Jane Schneider, a well-known and respected expert on Sicily, what Pitt-Rivers and the other pioneers on honor and shame hadn't done was look behind it all to ask *why*? Why do we find such continuity across the Mediterranean area when it comes to the importance of these values?

Schneider offered a very simple answer: ecology. She argued that honor cultures tend to develop among pastoralists, and not just *any* pastoralists but those who are undermined over time by the influence of agriculturalists and thus face certain kinds of insecurity over access to resources. And not just any such squeezed pastoralists but those living in places and times where centralized political authority is nonexistent or relatively weak. (*Honour and Shame* did at least pick up on this.)

Pastoral life is tough. It requires a lot of movement, much of which is insecure because you don't know whether your sheep or goats are going to be given access to the fields they need to graze upon. Others may try to stop them or even steal the livestock for themselves. Theft in such contexts often becomes a virtue; in the right circumstances, it is even an honorable pursuit: "In Sardinia, the shepherd boy of nine or ten who has not yet stolen an animal is called a *chisnieri*, a sissy who clings to the ashes of the campfire."[4]

Pastoral life encourages a highly flexible social organization. The basic unit is the household, and these can expand or contract in line with the resources available to them. In times of plenty, households might grow; in times of strain, they can fragment and go their own way—or die out. Thinking in terms of households is a form of social insurance; you are only obliged to share what you have with others under your roof (or canopy, as the case may be). Your other relations are on their own.

A transhumant or nomadic existence, defined by the nimbleness of the group, also requires a good deal of political and economic autonomy. Among pastoral groups, adults (especially men) are their own authorities or must readily submit to the authority of others. Thus pastoral life is defined by a strong emphasis on the nuclear family, although in many ways this focus on the family is just a mask for hyperindividualism.

These pastoral dynamics can be found throughout much of the world. We find them in the Mongolian steppes, too, for instance. What made the Mediterranean different, Schneider argued, was the prevalence of a certain kind of agricultural community on either side of the sea, in the arid and mountainous zones. Basically, these agricultural communities were organized more or less like pastoral communities, in terms of kinship structure and political organization: highly fragmented and family centered, prone to infighting and concerns over food security. Schneider's hypothesis was that these particular agricultural communities were one-time pastoralists and had simply transferred their transient ways of life into more settled farms and villages. Trouble is, these ways of life were not well suited to the olive garden. A particular problem was brought on by the widespread custom in the Mediterranean area of what is known as partible inheritance (that is, allocating patrimony to all of one's heirs).* This can get tricky when it comes to dividing farmlands, leading to disputes among siblings over field boundaries, access to water, and so forth. (It can work better in a purely pastoral context: ten goats, five children = two goats each.)

So yes, it's tough being a pastoralist. And it's tough being a peasant farmer when you're a pastoralist at heart. Bang these communities up against one another, in lands

---

* Rather than, say, the eldest son, which is called primogeniture.

with poorly yielding soil and steep inclines, combine it with a strong ideological commitment to the family unit, but undercut by an even stronger commitment to oneself, and what you get, Schneider concludes, is a world of social relationships "much more complicated and conflict-laden" than in many other contexts.[5]

But they do not fall apart. They do not descend into chaos or unbridled violence, into a free-for-all over sheep and young women. Families actually cohere; cooperation exists; violence is not as common as one might think; some sheep and camels don't get stolen. This is because these societies have very strong codes of honor and shame, codes that regulate the tensions and risks of schism and dissolution.

In the end, I'm not sure Schneider's answer to the question *why* gets us much further. It begs another question: Why honor and shame? Is there something about this pairing of values that is especially fitting or natural among such fissiparous social groups?

Anthropology has a bad track record for explaining origins, with root causes and effects. This is not Schneider's fault, of course, and we have already seen the dangers and shortcomings of an approach based on lawlike analysis; it didn't work so well for Tylor and the social evolutionists, nor for many others. But it does leave us with the questions just posed.

One common answer to these and similar questions is well captured by another key figure in these discussions, Michael Herzfeld. In an essay published in 1980, he argued that the answer in part had to be that the question itself is a misleading one. This is because if you look at the range of terms glossed by the English-language word "honor," what you find is a great deal more variety, nuance, and distinction than you might have anticipated.[6] In other words, there is no such thing as an "honor and shame" culture in the Mediterranean, unless we take honor as an almost empty term. In essence, Herzfeld was taking what Pitt-Rivers did a step further. But where Pitt-Rivers saw virtue in recognizing the ambiguity and fluidity of honor and shame as ideas, Herzfeld saw vice—the vice of generalization.

To support his argument, Herzfeld drew on his fieldwork from two very different communities in Greece: Pefko on Rhodes and Glendi in western Crete. For both, a love of *timi, filotimo*, or "social worth" was of central importance. But its enactment and cultivation looked radically different in each of the settings. The Pefkiots, Herzfeld tells us, were law-abiding, sober citizens; the Glendiots, by contrast, made a virtue out of their lawlessness: they stole sheep, they gambled, they carried guns and generally flouted the authorities. In Pefko, then, *filotimo* was modeled by obedience to the state's diktats and concern for the community as a whole. During one drought, the mayor publicly scolded the few families who took too much water for their own crops; they needed to "show *filotimo*," and in being so selfish, they clearly weren't. In Pefko, too, *filotimo* stood at odds with *egoismos*, or "self-regard." These Greeks were quite well behaved and community oriented; this is what defined their culture of honor and shame.

In Glendi, on the other hand, *egoismos* was more or less a precondition for *filotimo*; you couldn't have social worth unless you expressed a very high opinion of yourself (evidenced through all of that gambling and sheep stealing). If there was ever a drought in Glendi, you wouldn't expect the mayor to get passive-aggressive over the public address system. You would watch your back and keep a close eye on your own water supplies. So in Glendi, the culture of honor and shame couldn't have looked more different from the way it did in Pefko. And this begs the question: Why bother calling these "honor and shame cultures" at all? On the face of it, it certainly doesn't seem to tell you all that much.

This move to be more specific became increasingly common among Mediterraneanists in the 1980s—from trying to think of a "culture area," defined by a certain set of values, they moved on to a finer-grained analysis, often committed to showing the diversity of expression of values even from *within* a given tradition or language group.* Work in the 1980s also became increasingly attentive to the gendered nature of the analyses and ethnography: in the earlier work, it often seemed to be the men maintaining and gaining honor; all the women seemed to be able to do was bring themselves and their families shame. In 1986, though, Lila Abu-Lughod published a stellar monograph, based on her work with Bedouins in Egypt, showing just how central honor was to the women, expressed in the idiom of modesty and explored by Abu-Lughod through a fine analysis of local traditions of poetry.[7]

The honor culture approach fizzled out in the late 1980s. There are three main reasons for this. First—and here we get back to the Hollywood point—because the stereotypes that it engendered were problematic. There

---

* Remember, 1980 was the heyday of interpretive anthropology. The concern with language, culture, and meaning—sometimes expressed as a "semiotic approach to culture"—was dominant, certainly in the United States where Herzfeld and Abu-Lughod were based. Geertz is also often referred to as a "particularist," meaning that he didn't like generalizations and thought that anthropology had to be the study of culture in context or it was nothing.

are ways in which an evolutionary logic takes hold here, as well as an androcentric one. Second, because of a more general change in the ambitions and agendas of many anthropologists; as I have just noted, by the 1980s it wasn't only that generalizing about cultures could invite caricatures of difference but rather that it constituted bad scholarship to generalize in the first place.

Like all pendulums, however, this one has continued to swing. Signs are that attitudes to the work on honor (or *filotimo*, or *egoisimo*, etc.) are softening and piquing new interest.[8] This is also seen in work in related areas, such as a major volume, published in 2012, on the anthropology of hospitality, another important value in the Mediterranean and one that often speaks to even stronger concerns with honor and shame.[9] But it's in an essay on "house politics" in Jordan that we find some particularly helpful arguments as to why honor and shame should be put back on the table.

Throughout his work in Jordan in the 1990s, Andrew Shryock was struck by the extent to which what he calls "house politics" defined the moral sensibilities of the people he got to know. In the Hashemite Kingdom, a strong house politics is in play. This is evident in the fact that social and political relations get framed in terms of family. The figurative language is one of kinship. So the king is a father figure and, to a certain extent, vice versa. This is hardly unique to Jordan, of course, or indeed to the Arab world, but it is combined here with a particular set of concerns around honor and shame that make it a powerful master register. In Jordan, "ideas of honour continually recreate a political culture in which families, tribes, and nation-states are answerable to the same kind of moral reasoning."[10]

Shryock argues that it would be impossible to think of politics in Jordan without paying attention to this register. To ignore it would be to disregard local concerns and commitments out of a sense of what he calls a lingering "intellectual embarrassment" over the whole idea of honor cultures in the first place. Once again, Hollywood-style trouble! But when you're an anthropologist doing fieldwork, and when ideas of honor, reputation, and dignity are applied by the people you're studying "in almost every conceivable context" (as Shryock characterizes it), the fear over intellectual embarrassment must be met with the steely resolve of a commitment to social facts.

The point here isn't just that anthropologists have to take account of the native's point of view; besides, we've already gone over that. Shryock makes another important point, which is that if we refuse to recognize house politics on its own terms and insist on sticking to the language and terms that fit Western academic sensibilities, we impoverish our analytical stance. The problem, in other words, isn't house politics or an honor code—even with all its Greek or Jordanian or Spanish particularities. It is an inability to appreciate their logic, force, and relevance as anything other than short of Euro-American standards.

I said there were three reasons why the honor culture idea fizzled out, and I've only mentioned two. The third might be the most important, which is that none of this literature ever benefited from a systematic structure. None of these anthropologists ever theorized values per se. In *Honour and Shame*, none of the contributors says what the attention to values can tell us about the nature of culture or society. For Pitt-Rivers and many others of his generation, values played a functional role in the maintenance of a culture; essentially they argued that in the Mediterranean honor and shame were release valves for the pressure that built up, pressure that couldn't be released or managed otherwise (for example, by a strong state). For Schneider, on the other hand, values are an index of all the various ecological, economic, and political factors that shape the life course of a social group. But actually, one could even ask whether Schneider is interested in values in the first place. In her seminal article on honor and shame, Schneider never uses the word "value": she refers to honor and shame as "ideology" and "ideas" and "rules" and "codes," never as values.

We learn a lot about values from this rich work on the Mediterranean, but still it doesn't offer us a "theory of values." That's not necessarily a problem, not least because it is almost always ethnography, rather than its theoretical packaging, that stands the test of time. And what we gain from the ethnographies of honor and shame in the Mediterranean is a rich and nuanced sense of the fixed yet flexible nature of the values (or ideas, or ideology) that help shape social life.

In the same period that all these honor culture discussions were taking place, a more systematic attempt to theorize value was underway. It's to this move, spearheaded by Louis Dumont from his base in Paris, that I'd now like to turn.

## HOLISM AND INDIVIDUALISM

Louis Dumont is best known for an important book he published in 1966 on the caste system in India, *Homo Hierarchicus*. As he sees it, "the caste system is above all a system of ideas and values."[11] Before getting into the details of his approach, though, let me say a bit about caste as it has been understood by anthropologists. (You might well get different explanations from Hindu priests.)

"Caste" is a word that in Spanish, Portuguese, English, and other Romance and Germanic languages originally meant race, exclusive group, tribe, or "something not mixed."[12] In most of the Indian languages (Hindi, Bengali, Tamil, Telugu), the term is *jati*, which often translates as "kind" or "species." There are thousands of castes, which are not always rigidly fixed.* At the same time, it is widely understood that you cannot move from one caste to another.

Caste is usually tied to a traditional occupation or skill. So throughout India there are castes of carpenters, leatherworkers, potters, brick makers, and so forth. These are important distinctions, and it is true that in some places it is only the leatherworkers who work leather. You will also find that lower-status castes, including Dalits (the people sometimes called "untouchables"), do the less salubrious jobs, like sweeping the streets and cleaning sewers. At the top of the caste hierarchy are the Brahmins, priests and teachers central to many of the rituals necessary for the coherence and purity of the overarching system. Brahmins are supposed to be the part of the whole system of Hinduism that best represents it.

Where caste can often be most palpable and concrete is in community organization and interaction. In a village

---

* Some anthropologists (e.g., Nicholas Dirks [2001]) have even argued that the British did more to fix the categories of caste than did the previous thousand years of Hindu thought and practice. Colonial governments like clear-cut social and legal identities; it makes running an empire much easier, especially with a colonial territory such as India, which was about ten times more complex, diverse, and intricate than that of Britain.

or small town in rural India, all the members of a given caste may live in the same relatively well-defined neighborhood, drink from the same well (and not others), and congregate in the same public spaces. It is also evident in terms of the people you eat with; commensality is very tightly controlled because it suggests certain forms of intimacy or connection.

Models, of course, are always neater than reality. Over the past two hundred years, we can trace a number of historical, social, and cultural factors that have reconfigured and sometimes challenged the caste system. Christian missionaries have long found particularly attentive listeners among the Dalits, for instance, because their messages provide new forms of self-empowerment based on individualism. Projects of social and political reform, spearheaded by such well-known figures as Gandhi and B. R. Ambedkar, have helped shaped popular perceptions and government legislation alike; there are now a raft of government measures meant to help the lower castes, and India's constitution makes provision for something akin to affirmative action (through the designation of "Scheduled Castes" and "Scheduled Tribes"). Western-style education (often provided by missionaries), as well as urbanization and globalization, has also affected caste-based distinctions. There are, at least, no *jatis* for computer programmers and airline pilots.

Anthropologists have studied most of these changes and more besides. In a now classic study, carried out in the 1950s, M. N. Srinivas traced the ways in which Peasants became the dominant caste in one South Indian village, largely through education and obtaining government jobs; this allowed them to buy up a lot of the local land, displacing the economic advantage of those above them in the caste hierarchy, including the Brahmins. So while the Brahmins were superior in the bigger, cosmological picture—only they could perform certain rituals, for instance, necessary for the proper functioning of social life—they always made sure to consult the Peasant patrons in the village because these Peasants called the shots.[13]

All the same, the general consensus is that caste, whatever else it may be—ancient Hindu theology; ideology propagated by the Brahmin elite; British imperial construct—is a postcolonial reality. "Caste," writes one expert, "is not an abstract, hidden principle of social organization; it is a visible dimension of everyday life in rural India, which is part of everyone's social and personal identity in a very real sense. Even now, when caste distinctions carry less weight than they used to, they show no sign of fading away completely. This is true in towns and cities as well, in spite of the fact that so much urban social activity involves anonymous strangers."[14]

Whether or not caste is a visible dimension of everyday life, Dumont's own interest lay elsewhere: in the values of the system. His approach to anthropology doesn't focus on whether the Brahmins in a particular Indian village own all the land or whether the Peasants have usurped it. Dumont was a structuralist. As such, he approached caste almost like an architect at the drafting table rather than a surveyor on the building site itself.

For Dumont, the interest in caste was as a set of values, and values are, above all, an attitude of mind, ideology, and ideas.[15] These values are social; he writes of "the presence of society in the mind of each man."[16] Such views, moreover, are remarkably durable. As a structure, caste is either there or not there. And for Dumont, caste wasn't going anywhere anytime soon. All of the seeming changes you might be able to document—landlord Peasants; landless Brahmins; born-again Christian Dalits—would be, in his terms, "change *in* the society and not change *of* the society."[17]

This approach earned Dumont many critics, from academics who felt it ignored the situation on the ground to political activists who saw it as an apology for a set of entrenched inequalities. Many anthropologists who work in India cannot stand Dumont's analysis. I was once at a dinner in Oslo with some colleagues and for some reason Dumont came up. My host practically choked on his venison in order to get out his objections to the man. For Dumont, though, such concerns—however legitimate they may be, and whatever place they may have in "political" terms—prevented one from seeing the bigger picture. And the bigger picture had to do with understanding the values of the caste system itself.

Hierarchy, of course, is a value in this system. So is purity, and it is in fact the concerns with purity that Dumont often emphasizes in his work: all of those strict rules about with whom one can eat or even interact, how to maintain a temple or shrine, and so on. But Dumont's interest in hierarchy operated at two levels, and he was more interested in the higher level than the lower level, what we might call the level of everyday life. Because hierarchy, he argued, should not be confused with social stratification, and this is what he believed Western critics of the caste system often did. Not least because, at a structural level, *every* system of values is hierarchical, including what we find in, say, the French Declaration of the Rights of Man or, on the other side of the Atlantic, the Declaration of Independence. At the theoretical level, hierarchy is just "the principle by which the elements of a whole are ranked in relation to the whole."[18] So for Dumont, some of the well-meaning Western critics of the caste system undercut themselves by not recognizing how their own value systems worked.

It might be helpful here to place Dumont's work on India in relation to his larger ambition of comparing Western values with non-Western values. Dumont wrote a lot on this subject—entire books and long articles dedicated to the rise of individualism, for instance, in Christian Europe. *Homo Hierarchicus* was just one part of a larger, comparative project.

In his treatments of Western values, Dumont was committed to deflating some of the more puffed-up claims we can find about the importance and seeming self-sufficiency of what he saw as the West's paramount value: individualism. Because, for one thing, individualism is clearly part of a hierarchy: it has a greater value than anything else in a "hierarchy of ideas."[19] In the West, Dumont notes, freedom is a precondition for individuality; this is partly why, he says, Westerners find the caste system unjust. It doesn't allow for free choices or social movement and thus it frustrates the realization of the individual. Let's consider this by returning to those Westerners who probably champion freedom more than any others, at least in their rhetoric: Americans.

"Live free or die" pretty much sums up what Dumont is talking about. Freedom is what you should die for—as opposed to, say, cooperation or respect. This represents a hierarchy of values. As Dumont points out, however, the imperative to be free—to be an individual—is marked by two paradoxical consequences. First, it means you *have* to be free, which isn't much of a free choice. Second, it means that we are really all the same; we are all individuals, after all, expressing our individuality, often in quite uniform ways—and probably only on the basis of cooperation and respect from all the other individuals who are also living free.

In a way, this takes us back to the fluid nature of what values can mean in particular places and particular times, as expressed in particular languages. We return, in other words, to some of the important points made by the anthropologists interested in honor and shame in Mediterranean cultures, those that Pitt-Rivers and Herzfeld were trying to stress. But what Dumont offers is a framework for thinking about value relations more systematically. And at the core of his approach is the argument that all societies have paramount values that "encompass" lesser or lower ones. This is what he means by a hierarchy of values, and it is the aspect of his theory that has had the biggest impact on other anthropologists.

Coming back to India and the caste system, Dumont says that its paramount value is holism. What matters is not any one part (be it a caste group or an individual) but the whole. This whole is made up not of competing or antagonistic parts but complementary ones that express a unity and harmony and that must all work together for a realization of the ultimate good: holism itself. It makes sense on its own terms, as a coherent symbolic system, expressing an order of the cosmos—a kind of order, moreover, that defines not only India but most of the non-Western world.

Very much in line with the metaphor of a structure, Dumont often refers to value systems in terms of their levels. In a system like caste, what this means is that social relations can be inverted or changed in certain contexts.

One common example of this is the traditional relationship between Brahmins and kings. (Indian societies used to be ruled by kings; while this is no longer the case, they are still a powerful symbol.) At the cosmological or religious level, Brahmins are a fuller and purer representation of humanity; they are part of the whole but also, in important respects, the part that best stands for the whole—at least at the religious level. In terms of political power, however, Brahmins are subservient to kings and must defer to them. So in a political context there is a disconnect between "status" (which the Brahmins have) and "power" (which the kings wield). In recent Indian history, we might say that economic power has overtaken monarchical power. Going back to the example from Srinivas, for example, we can note that the Peasants he studied in one South Indian village had the economic power, and it was a power that mattered in terms of village relations; Brahmins made sure to consult the local Peasant big shots. So again, this is a context in which status and power are not fully aligned. In each case, though, according to Dumont's model, Brahmins will always be considered superior because of their spiritual purity. The value of purity, then, "encompasses" those of political strength or economic success.

Similar dynamics take place in many Western contexts, and it is important to keep in mind that individualism doesn't always trump other values. Not even in New Hampshire. In fact some of these Americans to whom I keep referring, who want to live free or die as individuals, may well say: *okay, sure, freedom and the individual matter, but so does my family!* Family values get a lot of play in the United States, certainly. But this kind of "holism" often—and increasingly frequently—loses ground to the paramount value of individualism, as can be seen in a spectrum of examples, from the typical (rebellious teenagers), to the tragic (intervention by the state on behalf of a neglected child), to the as-yet still seemingly absurd (a thirteen-year-old boy in Rochester, New York, suing his parents for being born with red hair).*

Much of Dumont's interest lies in the differences between the Western and non-Western world. But he also argues that the differences have to do with being modern or non-modern. The course of Western individualism, he argues, emerges out of European history, especially via its religious (Christian) and economic (capitalist) currents. There was a time when red-headed boys couldn't sue their parents, even in the United States.

We don't have the space to trace the details of this history now. But if you're a fan of the hit television series *Downton Abbey*, created by the English writer Julian Fellowes, you'll be familiar with a condensed version of the story. Needless to say, there are major differences between Yorkshire (where the series is set) and India, and the organizing system is not caste but class. Still, it's a helpful comparison. (Caste and class may be different systems, but they do share some similarities.)

*Downton Abbey* traces the decline of the English aristocracy, in the period around World War I. The winds of change are sweeping Europe, with the Russian Revolution, women's suffrage, and the rise of the middle classes, who often have more business sense (and money) than the blue-blooded elites. Downton Abbey, home to the Earl of Grantham and his family, is an increasingly rare

---

*This last example is taken from a posting on the website of—wait for it!—the Virginia-based Center for Individual Freedom. See http://cfif.org/v /index.php/jesters-courtroom/3068-a-colorful-lawsuit.

thing: a working, aristocratic estate. But it is under pressure, in a number of ways, and really only survives because His Lordship married an American heiress. The earl actually loses all of her money, too, in a Canadian railroad scheme that goes wrong; Downton is then saved by the earl's middle-class, lawyer cousin from Manchester.

So Downton is living on borrowed time, during the course of which various members of the family and their servants play out and promote different versions of the social order. Some of the servants and even family members long for a new world of freedom and change; this is a modern world of individualism. Others find not only comfort but, it seems, some kind of peaceful justice in the old ways—in holism. Overall, a nostalgic image for the aristocratic estate usually wins out, in which everyone has their proper place and knows it, but it's all fine, it all works: the servants are respected and looked after, like part of the family—they get cheese and wine too, at their dinner table, and they are promised cottages upon retirement. They even get access to the family's London lawyer when it's needed. Most importantly, then, the aristocrats *care*, and they feel the call of duty to the whole ecosystem, which includes not only those "in service" (the cooks, maids, and footmen) but the tenant farmers and indeed the villagers nearby. Very much in a holist way, Lord Grantham often says he is only ever looking after Downton; he is a steward and not an owner in that crass sense of possessive individualism.

The drama of *Downton Abbey* is played out through the toss and turn of values in a changing world—duty, honor, freedom, loyalty—all of which turn on a kind of competition between the paramount values of holism and individualism. Slowly, over the course of six seasons, the holism of the aristocratic system loses ground to the individualism of the modern nation-state. But not without tears being shed for something lost.

*Downton Abbey* might be a more colorful example than Dumont's rendering of India to understand how values work in action. It certainly does a better job than *Homo Hierarchicus* of showing how the drama of life is colored by the values people hold. But there are anthropological studies that make good use of Dumont's theoretical ideas without sacrificing the details and drama of life. One of these concerns a small group in the highlands of Papua New Guinea that underwent a dramatic change of course in the late 1970s.

## A CASE OF MORAL TORMENT

The Urapmin are a group of some 390 people who live in the western reaches of Papua New Guinea. Most areas of Papua New Guinea are remote even today because of the mountains and dense forests. Throughout the colonial period, this meant that many Melanesian groups had very little firsthand contact with outsiders—certainly much less than other regions, such as South Asia, Africa, and most of South America (Amazonia being an exception).

Partly as a result, even as late as the 1970s the Urapmin had never felt the full force of the missionary effort. Nonetheless, a handful of Urapmin men had been educated at a regional mission school and, on returning home, their evangelizing led the community to a mass conversion. Nearly everyone became Christian.

When Joel Robbins set out to study the Urapmin in the early 1990s, he wasn't expecting to find such born-again fervor.[20] He had intended to study local traditions of ritual secrecy—a staple topic in the literature on Melanesia. But what he found were devoted Christians for whom many of the rituals no longer held purchase. It was a very charismatic form of Christianity, in which sin and salvation loomed large, and it was this that led the Urapmin to overthrow much of their traditional ritual system, as well the taboos associated with it. To be good Christians, they reasoned, they needed to overturn their heathen ways; they needed, as they put it, to be lawful—to follow the precepts of Christianity as they understood them.

This emphasis on Christian lawfulness and salvation demanded a new model of personhood. Because salvation (at least in this kind of conservative evangelical tradition) had to be personal, it had to be sincerely accepted in someone's heart. As one Urapmin man put it, "My wife can't break off part of her belief and give it to me."[21] Individualism became a paramount value. This worked well in many domains of life and the local church flourished. But as Robbins also observed, it sat at odds with the pre-Christian understanding of sociality, in which to be "an individual" made no sense at all.

As several prominent anthropologists of Melanesia have argued, the traditional paramount value is neither individualism nor holism—it is "relationalism." By this they mean that what Melanesians most value is establishing relations with other people. Relations in and of themselves are what make a good life—not, as in New Hampshire, being an individual or, as in Kerala, being part of some cosmic whole.

Like any value, relationalism has its challenges. The more relations one establishes, the more one puts existing relations in jeopardy. For any relation to be meaningful it needs work and attention. But there is only so much gardening or exchange one can engage in with new people before the old people feel neglected. For the Urapmin these challenges are understood as the tension between "willful" behavior (the desire to create new relationships) and "lawful" behavior (the recognition that existing relationships need regular maintenance and care). So willfulness and lawfulness are values nested under the paramount value of relationalism.

Christianity left very little room for willfulness—and required new kinds of lawfulness. Willful behavior in village affairs can often lead to tensions, anger, and jealousy—all of which are understood to be unchristian. So what had been an acceptable fact of life under the old system (at least in proper measure) became unconditionally sinful and, as a result, tormenting.

The situation in Urapmin was complicated further by the fact that while some areas of life could be given over to the Christian values, it was not so easy to do so when it came to many aspects of kinship and marriage, as well as food production and intervillage connections. In these key areas, then, relationalism still held sway and the Urapmin had to live with what Robbins calls a "two-sided" culture.

Robbins's work on values has gained a lot of traction. The Urapmin have become one of those case studies that many other anthropologists take up and debate with respect to not only theorizing values but also the more specific topics of Christianity, cultural change, and morality. What the Urapmin case can help us appreciate—almost feel, really, in some of the more detailed ethnographic descriptions that Robbins provides—is just how central "the contest of values" is to what we get up to as humans. Not everywhere in the world is as convicted or conflicted as the Urapmin community; such intensity is easier to spark, sustain, and see in a highland community of 390 people than it is in larger and more diverse societies. Neither is it always the case that we can speak of something like a two-sided culture. But what happens in this remote corner of Papua New Guinea is far from unusual or unique.

Values underscore the importance of humans as meaning-making animals. They are central to not only how we organize life but also how we measure its quality. Values play a functional role; while they're never fully determined or predictable, certain values suit certain forms of social organization more than others. An estate like Downton Abbey could never survive under the ethos of individualism. That's why it died and that's why it makes for good television. When we learn about people's values, we are also learning about the structures and contexts of their lives more generally: their political systems, religious sensibilities, family and social relations, economic networks, and so on. And yet values cannot be reduced to their social utility or "function." As the Urapmin case demonstrates, sometimes people uphold certain values even when they produce moral torment. Meaning is measured by more than one metric, and a smooth, uneventful life might not be the most important. In fact people often live their lives in a way that defies any reasonable definition of the path of least resistance. This is a point we can well explore by turning to our next topic.

## CHAPTER 4

# VALUE

In 1983, 40 percent of the cattle in the village of Mashai, Lesotho, died. The area had been suffering from a severe drought and the cattle had starved. The government had done what it could to forewarn people of this risk, not that the local people didn't appreciate the risk themselves— animal husbandry had long been central to Basotho livelihoods. A local official exhorted the villagers to sell off their herds before it was too late; at least they could get something in return for their assets. But in the harshest months of the drought—June and July—sales of cattle in many parts of Lesotho actually went down. The people were refusing to minimize their losses. As one man told anthropologist James Ferguson, this was because cattle "are the most important thing."[1]

Ferguson was conducting fieldwork in Mashai during the drought. As he came to understand it, this man was talking about what Ferguson was to label the "Bovine Mystique." This was not unquestioning acceptance of something sacred and untouchable. Cattle are special, yes, but the mystique has as much to do with how cattle affect social and household relations as it does with the cattle per se. Cattle are valuable for a host of reasons, especially to men. First of all, because most men in the village of a certain age worked as migrants in South African mines, ownership of cattle at home served as reminders of their authority. Second, cattle were central to the creation and maintenance of a range of social relationships. Perhaps above all, cattle were vital in this respect because of the Basotho custom of "bride wealth," whereby a man's family gives cattle to a woman's family as part of a marriage arrangement. More generally, a man with cattle could—indeed, was expected to—lend out his animals to others in the community. Such patron-client systems are common in many parts of Africa. Third, this system of social embeddedness took on added importance once a man returned from a career in the mines; cattle were, to him, a kind of pension fund over and above any other he might have. Finally, and relatedly, kinship and household rules dictate that, while cattle are part of the overall household wealth, it is the men who have the ultimate say in their use and fate. What Ferguson tells us is that if a man comes home with money, there are many in his family— not least his wife—who will have claim to it. The same is not the case if he converts that money into cattle.

Ferguson makes a number of points in his analysis. An important conclusion is that the mystique is obviously gendered; it serves men's interests above all. More generally, Ferguson wants to dispel the idea that African peasants are irrational and uneconomic. This is not a question of the villagers needing lessons in the basics of development, what happens when it doesn't rain, or the laws of supply and demand. There is a logic to their practice. Ferguson also wants to make clear that this "mystique" is not some ancient, traditional, sacred, and unquestioned custom. Quite clearly, it is part and parcel of the wider world in which the Basotho participate—a "modern" world of the wage-labor economy, organized around globally traded commodities.

What the Bovine Mystique also allows us to appreciate is the close connection between *values*, as discussed in the last chapter, and *value*, here examined in a more economic sense. For at the heart of the matter in Lesotho is an issue that has always intrigued anthropologists: the topic of exchange. And if we want to appreciate anthropological takes on value, the topic of exchange is a helpful place to begin.

The Bovine Mystique is a reminder of the sentiment (for those more familiar with rock and roll than cattle) well captured by the Beatles: "Can't Buy Me Love." Some things—the most important things—cannot be reduced to commodities bought and sold. Love is not like a can of beans; neither, in many parts of the world, are cattle. This is where "values" (love, trust, prestige, security) most inform "value."

The truth of the Beatles' song, or what the Basotho refuse to sell, is further reinforced by trends in the opposite direction in the contemporary world. In its simplest version, this is that everything has a price; in its most cynical version, it is that the commodification of everything is inevitable. We might not have monetized love yet, but we have certainly gone down this route with education, in which increasingly throughout the West university students are referred to with moral weight as "customers." (Part of this may be because they are charged a lot of money.) Such terminology, common in the kinds of papers circulated among university administrators, makes professors see red. Studying Shakespeare in the classroom is not like buying a car from the local dealer—not in any way, shape, or form!

The realm of "special things"—be it cattle, or love, or a student essay on *Hamlet*, or, for that matter, the silver brooch your grandmother bought in 1923—has long intrigued anthropologists. Special things allow us to test the rules that govern such important practices as exchange and, with them, the very constitution of social relations. In the case of cattle in Lesotho, the exchange of one's livestock for money is precisely what would ruin the fabric of social relations. As Ferguson argues, the social wealth provided by cattle (by lending them out or by using them to forge alliances between families through the bonds of marriage) is much more valuable than the economic wealth that a sale might produce—even if that social wealth gets decimated by a drought.

The Bovine Mystique is one kind of test case for these rules—by which people don't do something that outside observers often think they need to do. *Why would you not sell cattle in a drought, to cut your losses? It doesn't seem rational.* In the history of anthropology, though, it is often cases at the other end of the spectrum that have fueled interest and debate: when people do something that outside observers often think they really ought *not* do—or at least that seems to serve no "real purpose," has no "practical value," or looks "wasteful."

It's certainly true that throughout the world people do all sorts of things that apparently defy the logic of economic common sense—the kind of common sense that stood behind Lesotho government recommendations to the Mashai villagers in 1983. The path of least resistance may be the expectation in the realm of physics, but it is not always so in the realm of culture. Such seemingly counterintuitive practices range from the "potlatch"—the practice found in many Native American cultures along the Pacific Northwest Coast, in which a lineage group gives away or burns all of its possessions—to (returning to the love theme) the average cost of a modern British wedding, which, according to one popular magazine, was £30,111 in 2013.[2] Median salary for the same year was £27,000.[3]

## THE KULA

One of the most famous cases of seeming overelaboration stands at the heart of Bronislaw Malinowski's work in the Trobriand Islands. It concerns the exchange of red shell necklaces and white shell bracelets over islands stretching hundreds of miles off the eastern end of Papua New Guinea, known in the literature as the "Kula Ring."

Malinowski refers to Kula as a "system of trade," and yet "its main aim is to exchange articles which are of no practical use."[4] The necklaces (*soulava*) and bracelets (*mwali*) circulate around the ring in opposite directions, the former moving clockwise and the latter counterclockwise. As Malinowski notes, not only are these things of no "practical use," they also serve as poor ornamentation, inasmuch as they are never actually worn; many of the bracelets are in fact too small to wear, even for children. So, on the face of it they really do seem to be totally useless. But for the peoples who participate in Kula—the Trobrianders, Dobuans, Sinaketans, and others—they are so highly prized that men set off on lengthy and dangerous sea voyages to exchange some items of this jewelry for others. Even this seems curious at first glance, because the most sought-after necklaces and bracelets have distinctive histories and associations—even names—such that each is "an unfailing vehicle of important sentimental associations."[5] And why would you want to give away such a valuable? (Most are held for no longer than a year or two.)

Kula exchange is more intricate still. The actual exchange of necklaces for bracelets, and vice versa, is wrapped in ceremony and formality, including the rule that they should never be exchanged simultaneously—thus never, in a way, exchanged at all but rather *gifted*. This element of gifting is also underscored by the fact that a receiver (who has already given) will not openly question the equivalence of what he gets in return. And the trader is always a "he"; only men participate in the Kula exchange.

It is not difficult to get one's head around the idea of something having "sentimental value" that doesn't accord with its value in other respects. So we can speak easily of something having a lot of sentimental value but not "use value" or "exchange value." A tattered photograph of your grandmother, for instance, wearing her silver brooch, is not worth any money, but you might consider it priceless. It has "meaning." Yet the elaborateness of the Kula Ring does throw the whole question of value into relief, since there is obviously a lot going on here that has more to do with the general dynamics of sociality.

Malinowski offered what might seem like contradictory conclusions on the Kula, as they pertain to the nature of social relations. On the one hand, he said quite clearly that Kula exchange is "carried out for its own sake, in fulfillment of a deep desire to possess."[6] On the other hand, he says in a rather mystical way that "to possess is to give."[7] Likewise, his initial emphasis on the lack of the Kula valuables' practical use is betrayed by his conclusion that the cycle of exchange establishes important social bonds between men on different islands and in different communities; the necklaces and bracelets also build up their owners' renown. Okay, so a Kula bracelet isn't practical in the same way that a canoe or ax might be, but social bonds and even renown can come in pretty handy.

Malinowski's treatment of value in the Kula case set in train a series of debates about the nature of social relations that still command anthropologists' attention. At its core is the question: *Why* do human beings exchange things? Can it ever really be only "for its own sake," or is it always in expectation of gaining something in return? Another way of putting this is: Can humans ever be truly altruistic, or is everything they do really out of some self-interest?

## THE GIFT AND THE FREE GIFT

This question has particular purchase in the contemporary world, in which "the market" reigns supreme. It is why love songs by the Beatles and others are so common and so popular. But it may well be the economist Milton Friedman, rather than the Fab Four, who put it best when he said "there's no such thing as a free lunch."

Friedman's free-market principles, underpinned by a strong commitment to self-interest, capture more generally held ideas about exchange. For Friedman it's not a problem that no lunch is free. Self-interest is what makes the world go round and there's nothing to be ashamed of. I'm giving you sandwiches, yes—or maybe even lobster salad—but you're going to help me clear out my garden, or move house, or maybe offer advice to my son about how to get a job in advertising (like one in the firm where you hold a partnership). But why is that a bad thing? Can't we just be honest and realize this is the bedrock of social life? For a free marketeer like Friedman, the question of self-interest versus altruism is answered by suggesting that they are actually the same thing.

In the tradition of Western economic thought, this emphasis on self-interest has long held sway. It underpins early modern theories of the social contract and is often further elaborated into a theory of human nature in which our desire for more (sex, money, power, Pokemon cards, etc.) is endless. This is one place where Marshall Sahlins's argument about the "original affluent society" fits in, as discussed in the introduction. What he shows in his analysis of small-scale, hunter-gatherer societies in Australia and Africa is essentially that Malinowski's invocation of the Trobrianders' "deep desire to possess" has to be understood as a cultural elaboration. As Sahlins puts it elsewhere, this line of thinking is part of the "recurrent attempt to make individual need and greed the basis of sociability."[8] But the question then becomes: Whose cultural elaboration is it? Is it Malinowski's alone, or does it share something with the people of the Trobriands?

Three years after Malinowski wrote his major account of the Kula, French anthropologist Marcel Mauss published a long essay, *The Gift*, addressing just such questions. Drawing on a range of ethnographic studies, including Malinowski's, Mauss concluded that the very formulation of the problem—opposing self-interest and altruism—is wrong. It is not how people really "calculate" (or refuse to calculate) processes of exchange and the social relationships they create. And one of the best ways to understand and appreciate this fact is by turning to the seemingly exotic and quixotic kinds of "gift economies," as Mauss called them, found throughout Melanesia, Polynesia, and the Native American cultures of the Pacific Northwest.

Many anthropologists consider *The Gift* the single most important contribution to our understandings of reciprocity and exchange. Dozens of books and essays have been devoted to what Mauss was arguing—partly, as even his most appreciative readers admit, because it isn't always clear. In addition, much ink is spilled on the meanings of indigenous terms that were central to his analysis, especially the Maori term *hau*, which is often translated as "the spirit of the gift" and has developed a life of its own. (We'll come back to this.)

The central point of *The Gift* is that no gifts are free—ever, anywhere. We expect a return—indeed, the return is obligatory. On first impressions, this sounds about right. In our own lives, we all know there is an unwritten and often unspoken expectation to reciprocate. How many of you, readers, have felt the embarrassment of not having a present for your rarely seen cousin (because she lives in Hawaii and you live in Belgium), or her children, when she has one for you? The reason you're embarrassed is probably some combination of the following: (a) it shows (or you're worried that it shows) that you really don't care about her or her children; (b) it shows (or you're worried that it shows) that you don't care about your uncle (mother's brother), either, and therefore by extension your mother; or maybe (c) it shows that you are just some kind of lesser person because you can't afford to buy them gifts. (There is a reverse embarrassment here too—when your gift is too expensive or personal; for instance, you better not out-gift the boss.)*

At the same time, if we are the ones who give and don't receive, we will quickly say, "Oh, don't worry about it! Don't be silly, it's just a little something," as we work to help our cousin recover from her own embarrassment. We might even be sincere, and we will likely insist at the very least that it is *possible* to be sincere: that we can give and neither expect nor desire something in return.

It is important to clarify that Mauss is not thinking of "gifts" only in these terms, or of what one gets at Christmas, or Hanukkah, or a birthday, or a wedding. These most common kinds of gifts are only part of the picture: things given that indicate a personal relationship. The same point extends to the Kula Ring, which Mauss felt Malinowski approached as a particular kind of gift exchange because this is what it looked like from a Western perspective, in which there is a strong differentiation between gifts and commodities. (So much for the native's point of view.)

For Mauss, though, the seemingly unromantic and cold conclusion that no gifts are free has more to do with the modern Western insistence on trying to cordon off certain

---

* Social hierarchies play an important role in the kinds of reciprocity allowed. For instance, I often buy my PhD students coffee, and sometimes even cake, when we meet to discuss their work. I never expect them to buy me coffee, though, because I am the wage earner and I am their supervisor. (Not that I am a hierarchical supervisor or anything, but still. This is the way it should be.) Then again, my supervisors bought *me* coffee a long time ago, so there is still a kind of reciprocity going on. David Graeber, some of whose work I'll discuss later in this chapter, would refer to this as a relatively "open" form of reciprocity, which means the gift doesn't get returned within a set time frame, or even necessarily at all, or to the original other person. Rather it can go to someone else within a community—in this case, the ever-expanding community of anthropologists.

kinds of exchanges or relationships from others. Again, can't buy me love. The Maussian rejoinder to this might well be: *Can't buy me love. Sure. Can't buy me yams, either.* If we look at the evidence from the Trobriand Islanders, the Maori, or Kwakiutl, what we find is a completely different starting point. Both exchanges (love and yams, if we take the Trobriand case) have something in them that is personal and impersonal, free and constrained, interested and disinterested. What Mauss wants to recuperate out of the category of the gift is a model of economy and society that is based upon recognition of the ties that bind. At the core, he argues, exchange should always be about solidarity, about human connection.

This phrasing—*should always be*—is mine, but it speaks to the heart of what Mauss intended. More than most anthropologists he was committed to highlighting the moral conclusions arising from his work. Mauss was a socialist, and he has since inspired others in anthropology with strong political commitments—not only other socialists but also anarchists, devout Catholics, and even an inveterate gambler or two.

More than anything else, it is Mauss's analysis of the Maori term *hau* that has come to substantiate the point about solidarity and connection. As we noted, *hau* means something like the "spirit of the gift" or "spirit of the thing," and it is important for Mauss because it captures the extent to which the Maori understand any object given to include something of the person in it. "Hence it follows that to make a gift of something to someone is to make a present of some part of oneself."[9] Mauss said this is why we feel obliged to reciprocate; expressing it in a way that might seem strange to us, he spoke about the gift as longing to be returned to its giver, its owner. Mauss argues that we see a similar logic at work in the Kula Ring. Kula valuables, you recall, are closely associated with their owners, and are also understood to have biographies in themselves; it is these biographies that underscore their sentimental value.

If you stop and think about it, though, this is not entirely divorced from the history of the connection between persons and things in the West. The special things in our lives—whether they are cattle, or our grandmother's silver brooch, or, say, a scarf we have knitted by hand—carry something of us with them and in them. This is a large part of why we refuse to sell them, to treat them in the same way we treat a loaf of bread we buy in the store. Of course, the maker of that bread, especially if she is an artisan producer, making small batches by hand, might well feel that something of her is in the bread. In this case, though, we are paying a premium for the bread because we are, in essence, buying into someone's skill. That's what premium brands and premium goods are all about, in fact. And this is not really all that different, in principle, from what Mauss was referring to with respect to *hau* among the Maori.*

Although Mauss didn't frame it in these terms, the principle is related to what Karl Marx described in his work on the alienation of labor. In his observations on the Industrial Revolution, Marx argued that the workers in factories were, in essence, relinquishing their personal

---

* This point on the "spirit" of brands is made by the anthropologist William Mazzarella (2003) in his study of an advertising agency in Mumbai. He goes into a long and mentally stimulating discussion of how *hau* can be used to illuminate the allure of modern brands. Good brands blur the subject/object divide. Are you an Armani person or a Burberry person?

connections to the goods they produced. The owner of the factory was saying, "You're making this for me. I own it, and I'm going to sell it. In return, I'm giving you sixpence for it." This is the basics of alienation, and it is premised on the idea that something valuable is lost in terms of *who we are* when the fruits of our labor get monetized.

*The Gift*, indeed, is an open criticism of what Mauss sees as the "cold-hearted" and "cruel" workings of the modern, capitalist system—and the legal systems that underpin it, through which he traces out the separation of persons from things. He does not shy away from offering moral conclusions. And he does not think the cause is lost. "Fortunately, everything is still not wholly categorized in terms of buying and selling. Things still have sentimental as well as venal value, assuming values merely of this kind exist."[10] *Venal* is a strong word. While the immediate associations have to do with moral corruption, it can also mean something like "buyable" or "purchasable." This is where money comes in to discussions of value.

## MONEY, MONEY, MONEY

There is a longstanding anthropological interest in money. Caitlin Zaloom's study of futures traders is only the tip of the iceberg. If we reflect on the history of the discipline, as well as on the course of world affairs since its mid-nineteenth-century debut, this interest makes perfect sense. This is the era in which commerce spread at unprecedented rates, often along the lines and lineaments of colonial expansion in the first instance. In many places that meant introducing monetary systems where none had existed. In others, it meant effecting shifts from systems of trade based on shells, beads, or other currencies.

Take Lesotho, for instance. The great-great-great-great-grandparents of the Basotho people that James Ferguson got to know in the 1980s would have lived in a world without money, a world without jobs in South African mines or local shops with soap, tinned sardines, and Coca-Cola. The jobs and the sardines are part of the "modern world market" that has been made possible because of money. As such a significant catalyst for culture change, money is a natural focus for anthropology.

One of the most common anthropological observations about money is how it can radically alter social relations. Again, we get hints of this with Ferguson's example, given just how much the Bovine Mystique is tied up with the practice of migrant labor and negotiations between husbands and wives over household cash. In many cases, the reason is that money—as cash—is an impersonal medium of exchange and transaction. It is, we might say, devoid of spirit. No *hau*.

This can obviously be very useful. It allows for innumerable manners of transaction that are quick and efficient. When you buy that loaf of bread, you don't want to engage in a lengthy ritual, and you are not required to give up part of yourself for it. (We've already addressed what our artisan baker gives up, but that is part of the larger equation of value.) Moreover, you can use the same $5 bill to buy bread, jelly beans, aspirin, 13-amp fuses, grass seed, or a bus ticket (though of course exact change is preferred!). And while you are happy to use that $5 bill, the last thing you want to know is what the forty-seven people who possessed it before you did with it.* The note has nothing of these people in it. This is also exactly why someone buying something illegal, or paying "under the table," will use cash. The transaction is impersonal and anonymous in a very helpful way. One shouldn't buy one's cocaine with a credit card, and one shouldn't leave a paper trail of bank statements or receipts if one wants to cheat the tax authorities.

Other features of money also matter, in terms of how it structures exchange and social relations. It is, of course, denominated. There are no Bank of England notes in circulation that say: "This is worth *something*." And the denominations are universally applicable; they can be used to mark the value—in monetary terms, of course—of a wrench (£2.50) and a Mercedes-Benz (£43,000). And this ability to denominate makes everything commensurable. At least in theory. So if you have 17,200 wrenches, it's just like having a Mercedes-Benz. You can see why it's just the same *in theory*; but it's an "in theory" point that matters in terms of how money helps structure regimes of value.

On the face of it, these features of money—its impersonality and its universality—seem like a recipe for disaster, at least when it comes to the survival of any given culture. And indeed, many of the struggles over money are precisely of this kind—the Basotho kind, we might say—in which this particular medium of exchange and unit of

---

* When I was a teenager, one of the current urban myths was that 50 percent of the $20 bills in circulation (or some large percentage, I can't really remember; it doesn't matter) had been used to snort cocaine. Bad, bad. Now at least one prominent economist (Rogoff [2016]) wants to get rid of cash altogether because most of it is held by undesirables. In 2016 the Indian government went some way toward this by declaring, overnight, the largest rupee notes null and void. This led to huge chaos as people scrambled to change the notes within a set window of time.

value threatens to erase what is distinctive about a particular way of life by making out everything in its terms.

While most of the anthropological work on money considers it in specific contexts, there are also important pieces on its symbolic value and cultural associations. Keith Hart has written several of these. In one of his classic essays, for instance, he turns to the common coin as an object lesson all its own.[11] If you look at the coin in your pocket, he says, you'll see it has a head and a tail. We all know this. On the head is, well, usually someone's head—in the UK and much of the Commonwealth, it is that of the monarch; in the United States, it is a president (or, for $1 coins, Susan B. Anthony or Sacagawea). This is a symbol of its value and marks the provenance of its authority: it is the mark of the state that has issued it and thus the social arena in which it has original "currency." On the tail side of the coin is its denominated worth: five pence, ten pence; five cents, ten cents, and so on. Hart's argument is that, in the contemporary world, the head of the coin is coming to matter less and less. It is easy to forget about the social relations side of things, about the fact that this medium of exchange is, in some important respect, connected to personalities and communities.

It's actually amazing how much power the tail side of the coin has, at least in terms of what occupies our attention. Who cares if the monarch is on it? What you want to know is whether it says 5, 10, 20, or 50. With Bank of England banknotes, the symbolically represented persons matter even less. All the notes have the monarch—everyone knows that.* But they also feature other people:

---

*Although this has only been the case since the mid-twentieth century. With coins, however, the practice is quite old; indeed, it was a practice found in ancient Greece and Rome too.

Adam Smith and Charles Darwin, for example. But they go largely unnoticed. What one looks at is the big number: 5, 10, 20. Symbolically, though, these personalities stand not only for the greatness of the nation but for the fact—and it is a fact—that notes and coins are only valuable because we all trust that the Bank of England would, in theory, promise to pay the bearer on demand. As Hart and many other anthropologists like to point out, money is an index of human relationships of trust.

We have already seen something of how other forms of modern commodity trading try to remove the *person*; in the case of Chicago and London futures exchanges, it was quite literally by taking exchanges "out of the pits," as Zaloom puts it, and onto the computer. The relationship is supposed to shift from person-to-person to person-to-thing (computer) to, eventually, as we now know from the world of finance, a series of algorithms. Indeed, some investors now use "algorithmic trading" to make their decisions; some small-time investors are writing their own computer code at home, and the computer makes all the decisions about when to buy, when to sell, and so forth. Such moves are a logical extension of the old line that "business isn't personal"—that to succeed in business, you have to have the kind of cold heart and cool disposition that Mauss described.

Hart has explored this point even more playfully by turning to the ways in which this cliché fuels so much of the drama in movies. Drawing on both Hollywood and Bollywood gangster flicks, Hart points to what he calls "the hit man's dilemma."[12] We all know the scene. The hit man confronts his victim, gun in hand. Before he shoots, he says, *Don't take this personal, it's just business!* Bang! Bang! Bang!

Why does he say it? Well, because he has a human conscience and he's about to end someone's life. He says it because the culture in which he lives dictates that there has to be a separation between the personal and the impersonal: "So, at one level, the issue is the relative priority to be accorded to life and ideas. Because the encounter is live and therefore already personal, the hit man has to warn his victim (and perhaps himself) not to take it so. It would seem that the personal and the impersonal are hard to separate in practice. Our language and our culture contain the ongoing history of this attempt to separate social life into two distinct spheres."[13] Money forces the question of such a separation. This is true for those who have it as much as those who don't. And here we come to another key area of study.

## DEBT

When I was doing my fieldwork in Zimbabwe, young men and their parents often worried about the cost of bride wealth (often called *lobola*). Philip, my friend in Chiweshe, was still unmarried by his mid-twenties and that wasn't considered a good thing (it would have been almost unheard of even a generation earlier). But his family simply did not have the resources to meet the costs of bride wealth.

It is probably true that such worries have always existed, but they became increasingly exacerbated over the course of the 1990s because of families' changing expectations of bride-wealth levels. There were occasional stories in the newspaper about the depths to which some parents would sink in the extent of their demands: cattle would no longer do; people expected cash, mobile phones, sometimes even cars.

This could lead to a lot of fretting and tsk-ing, even as most people insisted that "tradition" was far from dead—and that the stories were surely exaggerated. Some Zimbabweans were, in any case, nonplussed by this ratcheting up of the marriage market. As one good friend explained to me, *lobola* is never supposed to be paid in full anyway; a family might set a price, but they don't expect it—indeed, don't *want* it—to be fully met. If the price is met, it is taken as a sign of hostility or disdain. Why would you cut the ties that bind? That's cutting off the social relation. This is a common aspect of such practices throughout sub-Saharan Africa: debts can have a positive social valence.

What we now see in many parts of southern Africa, though, is a challenge to the various Bovine Mystiques in place. The particular value of cattle is being eclipsed by the rise of a commodity culture and monetization of life. Christine Jeske, an anthropologist who studies the Zulu, explains that cars are beginning to gain mystiques of their own; the young men and women she got to know saw a car—rather than a kraal full of cattle—as the sign of success.[14] It is, moreover, a different kind of success, based not on the mutual ties that cattle create but rather an individualized, atomized success, which is more resistant to the claims of family and neighbors. As one young man told her, "Oh man! Oh! Car is everything! It's everything, everything, everything, everything!"[15]

This recent assessment is a far cry from what Ferguson found in 1983, not all that far from where Jeske works. In line with what many Zimbabweans told me, however, Jeske also reports the resilience of cattle in some domains;

she tells us that cars do not figure prominently in the major life-stage events, such as marriage. Even the most car-crazy people would not, it seems, consider such commodities appropriate for bride wealth: "Cars are a commodity linked to cash, not to social processes participated in and recognized by community and family."[16] And yet, what one also sees in KwaZulu-Natal (the South African province where Jeske works) is a significant drop in the marriage rates: they're down 20 percent since 1970.[17] This is in no small part because of the extent to which the market economy has reconfigured the shape of traditional customs (even when already thoroughly modern).

The fall of the apartheid regime was supposed to usher in new economic opportunities for South Africans. The rise of a black middle class, for instance, was a hallmark aspiration. The reality has been sobering, though, as no such significant class has emerged. And those who have climbed the ladder of success have done so at a cost, often racking up significant debts with banks and microlenders. Bride wealth figures in these dynamics too.

Taking a much broader view of the current economic and social climate in South Africa, Deborah James has written about the major shifts that have taken place as black South Africans aspire to succeed.[18] In terms of bride wealth—and marriage more generally—the harsh economic conditions, as well as the decline of a gift economy and patron-client ties, have left some middle-class professionals and aspirants ambivalent about "progressing" up the social ladder. Families often still insist on bride wealth (including cattle) being paid as part of a marriage arrangement, which can result in young men having to take out loans in order to purchase them. This practice serves to further muddy the water between commodity culture and custom, making it even harder to sustain the idea that such "traditional customs" have a place in the modernizing, globalizing world. The "good" debts of cattle, we might say, are being replaced by the "bad" debts of money. And it is not only the young men who worry; James features one young woman in her research who shied away from marriage because she didn't want to enter into family life with a husband indebted to the bank and her parents from day one: "The picture of modern [bride wealth] that emerges, then, is one of considerable financial constraint alongside whatever longer term moral ties it is intended to confirm."[19]

This concept of good debt and bad debt is an important one in anthropological research on value. There are dozens of studies like those of James and Jeske that trace the ways in which different regimes of value—those of the economy and those of culture, we might say—come into conflict and get reconfigured. These processes are happening all over the world, from South Africa to Mongolia. They are a current-day index of the same issues that Malinowski and Mauss sought to address.

For David Graeber, one of anthropology's foremost thinkers on value, debt has been particularly helpful in illustrating the connection between our economic affairs and moral lives. In the tradition of Mauss, for whom, as we've seen, all markets are moral—and, in a sense, all morals marketized—Graeber has devoted much of his career to an exploration of this point. As a fieldworker, he first studied politics and authority at the local level in Madagascar, exploring the lives of people in one highland village, some of whom descended from nobility and others from slaves.[20] What was most notable about this case study is how, over many decades (prior to Graeber's arrival), the former slaves managed to usurp rights to most of the land, as well as claim access to sources of supernatural power. Although not explicitly framed in terms of debt, this early ethnographic work presages many of Graeber's subsequent concerns with debt, value, morality, and authority.

These concerns really come together in his 2011 book, *Debt: The First 5000 Years*, which is the closest thing anthropology has had to a general best seller in several decades. *Debt* is not an ethnography, but it uses the ethnographic record, alongside a mix of history, economics, and personal reflections—ranging from chatter at summer parties in Westminster to the elaborate process of buying a sweater in a Malagasy bazaar—to explore and challenge some of the persistent myths about the nature of exchange and economic relations.[21] One of Graeber's main points underscores something of what we've explored in this chapter: to think of every exchange in terms of reciprocity is to leave ourselves with an impoverished view of human social relations.

This is certainly the case if the reciprocation is full and final. As we have already discussed, one of the benefits of buying a loaf of bread with money today is that we don't need to check on the cashier's happiness and health tomorrow. But in many cases, such a full and final exchange is neither warranted nor desired; there are all sorts of exchange, in other words, in which what we desire is debt— that is to say, we desire the creation or furtherance of a social relation and social connection. In a sense, as Graeber argues, this means that "exchange" is the wrong word for what's going on, since we tend to think of exchange as "all about equivalence"—canceling things out.[22] And this explains why bride-wealth "debts" are never fully redeemed, as well as why they are often transacted in terms of cattle, not cash; cash is too unambiguous in its manner of settling accounts. It is too precise and impersonal. This is also the reason exchange in the Kula Ring took place in the way it did—with the objects always circulating, with their individual value never openly questioned; with the timing of their exchange staggered, even if only symbolically to a matter of minutes. And this is why we continue to sing, "Can't buy me love!"

## CHAPTER 5

# BLOOD

Of all the concepts we're considering there's something different about blood. It's the only one you actually have. Compared to "blood," where is culture, or authority, or reason? Where, really, for goodness sake, is *hau*?

The realness of blood is both helpful and unhelpful to the anthropological project. On the one hand it gives us a set of common denominators, perhaps even universals, forever reminding us of the human constitution. On the other hand, these very commonalities can lull us into complacency when it comes to appreciating the cultural aspects of our makeup and relatedness. The realness of blood often leads us to be much surer than we should be when it comes to defining our connections to one another.

In 1871, Lewis Henry Morgan published *Systems of Consanguinity and Affinity of the Human Family*. This is the foundational text of kinship studies and is still appreciated for its achievements. It is true that Morgan couched his findings in a social-evolutionary approach, the scientific and moral limits of which we have already discussed. But his extensive work on kinship terminologies, especially among Native Americans, also provided a template with which to understand kinship as a system of ideas. It is also the case that Morgan's data had incredible depth and scope: he really did set the foundations for future work in this area.

Another way of summarizing Morgan's focus would be "systems of blood and marriage." This is basically what consanguinity and affinity mean. Blood took pride of place in his approach to kinship, and the book is laced through with an attention to blood at both the literal and figurative levels. One of the most well-known of these is his reference to the family as "a community of blood."[1]

It was precisely this emphasis that piqued the interest, and ire, of one of Morgan's most vocal critics. In the 1960s, David Schneider published a slim little book called *American Kinship: A Cultural Account*, in which he aimed to debunk Morgan's thesis.[2] Although half a century old, in many ways what Schneider highlighted is just as relevant today—not only in the United States but wherever we find ideas about kinship built up from those of biology and nature within the broader framework of "modernity." As Schneider reported, Americans consider "blood relations" fundamental and enduring: grandparents, aunts and uncles, cousins.* Americans also emphasize the link between blood and genes; when explaining certain behaviors or personality traits, they say things like

*There are terms that, in a professional register, would be taken as signs of complete and utter incompetence: they are loaded, culturally specific, and supremely vague formulations all at the same time. The study of kinship has something very near a technical vocabulary, with "ego" at its center, around which are constellated "mother," "father," "sister," and "brother" but not "uncle" or "aunt" or even "grandmother" because these must be designated as "mother's brother" (an uncle) or "mother's mother" or "mother's mother's mother" and so on. All of these terms, of course, are based on an understanding of minimal units that can be combined into a range of possibilities. They are like prime numbers, divisible only by themselves. In addition, kinship studies often come with charts, symbols, and signs detailing the various relations and relationships. Not all anthropologists like this. Bronislaw Malinowski complained: "I must frankly confess that there is not a single account of kinship in which I do not find myself puzzled by this spuriously scientific and stilted mathematization of kinship facts" (1930, 20).

"it's in my blood." While this is a metaphorical statement, it often carries the force of literal meaning. It has
certainly lost any sense of being a great figurative leap.

Kinship relations in this account of America are not
limited to blood relations; as in most other places, they
also get formed through marriage. But the bonds of marriage are subjective and dissoluble. Blood relations are
not and they define the terms of reference more generally.
When we speak of a "stepbrother," then, what we are saying is that the sibling connection is not a blood connection. When we speak of a "half sister," we are saying that
the siblings share one parent, that they are "half-blood"
siblings. Blood is the ultimate form of identity and all
other relations get categorized in terms of it. Schneider
even says at one point that blood relations take on an
"almost mystical" aspect in American culture.[3]

In Schneider's analysis, the most notable aspect of this
cultural system is the hierarchy of biological and social
relations. Biology—blood—is always the really real, the
ground upon which other relations—of step-siblings
and in-laws, to say nothing of godparents or, say, blood
brothers—are built.[*] In this American system and, as I
have suggested, what we might call the modern view more
generally, kinship and biology converge to a single point.
Kinship is really about biology and the facts of procreation. Biology always sets the terms of the kinship system.
And this is where, for Schneider, Morgan's anthropology
and American folkways come together.

Today there are footnotes to this story of nature's
reign—even new chapters being written. After all, part

---

[*] The term "in-law" is also significant here; it tells us that we need the force
of a legal system to approximate the kind of relationship that obtains "naturally" in blood.

of being modern means enjoying the advances of science, like those in new reproductive technologies (NRTs). In vitro fertilization (when an egg is inseminated not in the womb but in a test tube) and gestational surrogacy (when one woman carries the fertilized egg of another woman) are just two of the many ways in which science is challenging the limits of biology. Could anything be more *cultural* than a "test-tube baby"? Same-sex marriage is also forcing a rethink of this hierarchical nesting. Both are good examples of how distinctions between nature and culture are always changing. The institution of kinship is a good bellwether for appreciating this fact.

Although he doesn't address it himself, the logic of kinship that Schneider explores is also relevant to the logic of race. I want to turn to this in a moment but first make a point about the absence of race in Schneider's own treatments. The fact that he didn't really address race in *American Kinship* is relevant to how we understand his use of the label "American." Despite the many merits of Schneider's analysis, it also points up the difficulty of giving a "cultural account" (his term) that is abstracted from social situations and the relationships and lives of individuals. The main sources of Schneider's data were interviews conducted with "middle-class whites."[4] He goes on to note that other of his sources include materials on African Americans, Japanese Americans, and a few other minority groups, as well as people from all class backgrounds and all regions of the country. He is also clear that his approach is focused on symbols and meanings at a very general level. But even just below this level, we need to be aware of differences and qualifications.

One good example of this is Carol Stack's classic study, *All Our Kin* (1976), which is about an African American community, "The Flats," in a small, midwestern city. (The research was carried out in the same period as Schneider's, in the 1960s.) Stack's research shows that the blood connections that Schneider puts forward as fundamental are not taken as such in the Flats: she writes about how "personal kindreds," based on actual social relations of care and support, trump those of blood at the end of the day.[5] All the same, as she also notes, families in the Flats know that their "folk" system of relations is not recognized by the state, which does support Schneider's model. In part, this helps clarify that Schneider's model is presenting the normative version of American kinship: the way it is, in many contexts, perhaps, but more importantly *the way it should be* (according to the state, scientific experts, moral authorities, and so forth).

## ONE DROP

In the next chapter, I'll consider in a bit more depth one of anthropology's fundamental contributions to our understanding of humanity: what one colleague in biological anthropology calls "the myth of race."[6] Race, as it is often understood in everyday terms, is a scientific nonsense. There is no "white race," no "African race," no "Chinese race," or what have you. Inasmuch as we recognize such distinctions, they are cultural. We can't rest easy with that fact, though, or rely on the evidence of genetics to clear up matters once and for all. And there is a lot to learn by tracing the ways in which such racial distinctions have, within particular times and particular places, been naturalized.

Blood and race, for instance, are often closely linked in cultural schemes. Throughout American history, blood quantum laws and the "one-drop rule" have been used to define (i.e., construct) people's racial identity. The one-drop rule is better known and more infamous: what it suggests is that if you have "one drop" (i.e., one single ancestor) of African "blood," then you are "black." Some American states used this rule as the basis of laws meant to uphold a certain idea of racial purity. Here is how the state registrar puts it, in his preamble to Virginia's Racial Purity Act of 1924:

> It is estimated that there are in the State from 10,000 to 20,000, possibly more, near white people, who are known to possess an inter-mixture of colored blood, in some cases to a slight extent, it is true, but still enough to prevent them from being white…. These persons, however, are not white in reality, nor by the new definition of this law…. [And] their children are likely to revert to the distinctly negro type even when all apparent evidence of mixture has disappeared.[7]

The Racial Purity Act was declared unconstitutional by the United States Supreme Court in 1967. But that doesn't mean this kind of thinking has disappeared, in the United States or elsewhere. In much weaker versions, it has even been given the effect of light entertainment value. On the BBC's hit show *Who Do You Think You Are?* ex–London mayor and sometime foreign secretary Boris Johnson traced his genealogy back to Ali Kemal Bey, a Turkish politician and journalist, as well as to various royal families in Europe. "It is interesting to look at how British I feel," he says, "and yet, actually, what a completely mongrel composition I really am. What it really teaches me is that our genes pulse down our lives."[8] The intent here is certainly different from what the Virginia registrar is arguing, yet the general logic is the same. It is based on the commonly held assumption that the "blood relationship ... is formulated in concrete, biogenetic terms."[9]

Virginia's Racial Purity Act may be consigned to history, but other blood quantum laws are still on the books. Initially established by colonial settlers, and then as an instrument of the U.S. government, these have been used to determine whether Native American nations can claim special status, which in some cases comes with federal support and recognition of sovereignty. Since the mid-twentieth century many Native American nations have incorporated blood quantum laws into their own tribal constitutions (often because the U.S. government requires such laws for federal recognition of tribal sovereignty). The quanta differ but are always a lot more than "one drop": one-eighth or one-quarter in some cases but sometimes as much as a half.

The Washoe Tribe of Nevada and California is one such nation. The Washoe today are a relatively small group, under 1,500, who live in and around the Lake Tahoe area. They have a few residential colonies and some tracts of mountain land. In 1937 the Washoe were granted federal recognition by the Bureau of Indian Affairs, after agreeing to the criterion that membership is contingent on having at least one-quarter "Washoe blood." Today, you can download the application form for tribal membership from the official website; applicants are asked to list their own "degree of Washoe blood" and "other Indian blood" they may have, as well as that for their parents and grandparents.[10]

As one study of the Washoe shows, such laws are double-edged swords.[11] On the one hand, they help guarantee access to federal resources and recognition; on the other, this particular model for understanding relatedness is completely foreign to Washoe traditions (and many other Native American traditions), in which blood matters less than certain social relationships and roles.

The mathematical precision of identity in this example is telling. As Schneider might have it, it turns blood (and identity, which we'll come to in the next chapter) into a thing—a thing just like a number (1.0, 0.5, 0.25)—that provides clear-cut answers. Because the way the combination is achieved doesn't matter—it can be a "full-blood" grandmother on one side or four full-blooded great-grandparents, or maybe half-blood parents—any mathematical permutation will do. But it is a prerequisite for official recognition.

This is pretty absurd, if you stop to think about it. Let's say your great-grandparents were "full-blood" Washoe. Then let's say they moved to Los Angeles—a common destination in Washoe migration—where they had children, but these children married "out" (maybe to a third-generation Irish American man here, a Latina there, maybe even someone whose family hailed originally from Guangdong). Then these various descendants of yours keep at it, going here and there (Seattle, Piscataway), marrying all sorts of mixed-up Americans—"mongrels," as the Rt. Hon. Boris Johnson might put it—and training as car mechanics, lawyers, jazz singers, or who knows what. Maybe none of these people could pick out a Washoe

colony on the map—or even Lake Tahoe, for that matter. Then we get to you, a trainee chimney sweep in Piscataway, New Jersey, who has fallen in love with a nice
Jewish boy, adding further to your family's perfect story
of melting-pot America. And yet, according to the blood
quantum criterion, you are Washoe. Back in Tahoe,
though, your fourth cousin twice removed, who is a recognized authority on the aesthetic styles of Maggie Mayo
James, the great early twentieth-century Washoe basket-
weaver, and speaks the language fluently, is not Washoe
because her particular family tree involves one too many
blood-quantumed Paiutes, Miwoks, and a wayward
Mormon from Utah at just the wrong consanguineous
junctures.

Until about 1860, when this blood-based regime started
to develop, it would have been nonsensical to think in
such terms at all. There is even an argument to be made
that a Washoe "tribe" or "nation" didn't really exist before the mid-nineteenth century, at least not in terms of a
stable, bounded group that the U.S. government sought.
In these bygone days, if someone learned the Washoe
language, they would be recognized as Washoe. And if a
Washoe speaker married a Miwok or a Maidu, the latter
would be recognized as Washoe as long as she adopted
local practices and ways of life. In short, blood had very
little to do with relatedness or identity.

The same is true with respect to family or kin, and here
some of the older patterns of relatedness still matter. Traditionally, the nuclear family was not necessarily strong;
Washoe lived in "bunches" and often considered aunts
and uncles to be as important as parents; an aunt's or
uncle's children—any given Washoe's "first cousins" if
you will—were likewise close and, in this case, designated

by the same term as one's own brothers and sisters. As in many Native American traditions, adoption was also common, further downplaying the importance of blood per se.[12]

What we're seeing here is how blood is put to work in different cultural understandings of both kinship and race. And how they blur—dare I say *bleed*?—together. I want to move away from the category of race for the time being, but we will come back to it in the next chapter. Clearly, though, the implementation of blood quantum laws by the U.S. government was bound up with the nineteenth-century ideas of culture, race, and civilization we have already touched upon. The officials responsible for establishing blood quantum laws were perfectly Victorian in this sense.

We can see with the case of the Washoe, as much as Virginia's Racial Purity Act, and even Boris Johnson, how much cultural ideology plays a role in such fixing of identities. In fact, though, well beyond any particular cultural elaboration, what we know from work in biological anthropology is that even at this really real level, race is indeed a myth, a category mistake. Again, while I want to explore this more with respect to our next topic—identity—it's crucial to acknowledge the role that idioms of blood have played in such myth-making.

But let's get back to kith and kin. The anthropological record is full of examples in which the biological facts of relatedness play a secondary or even lesser role. Another good example comes from Iñupiaq Native Alaskans.[13] The bonds between Iñupiaq parents and children and siblings are not necessarily strong and create little in the way of a sense of necessary obligation or connection. Autonomy is such a key cultural value that even young children can make significant decisions. In one case, we hear of a seven-year-old boy who decided to move to his grandparents' house, seventy miles away, picking up his school papers en route, so his new school could have them. His mother approached this decision in a matter-of-fact way.[14] The Iñupiaq even speak of childbirth in such terms; rather than the mother "giving birth," the child "takes life." Children are said to choose to be born. Adoption is also very common among the Iñupiaq, with children moving between natal families either because they want to (much like the seven-year-old who went to his grandparents) or because one family has lots of girls and no boys—so they swap. None of this is to say that different forms of group solidarity don't matter; in fact, they do, in terms not only of family but also, say, of whaling parties. But this is a culture in which it is perfectly possible to say, "He used to be my cousin."[15]

Blood is not irrelevant outside the orbit of Euro-American modernity. And "biology" is not absent. It is not only through the channels of colonialism and global-ization, or march of science, that we find the interest in blood, even if that interest does not always look the same as we would find in the Sex Ed unit in a 7th grade class in Nashville. The Iñupiaq, for instance, may refer to their "biological" siblings as such and they recognize the me-chanics of procreation. It's just that, as we've seen, they do not consider biology to be a determining or necessary factor of relatedness. In what I've just described about the Iñupiaq I used the word "family" in a few instances. But this has to be seen as cross-cultural shorthand, be-cause there is no direct equivalent for that word in the Iñupiaq language.

So in an important sense what the Washoe and Iñupiaq do is *make* their kin, not only through marriage but at the level of even more basic family constitution. Family relations are performed and if they are not performed they disappear. At one level, of course, all family relations are "performed." Kin can be estranged, ignored, neglected, even lost and found. Ian McEwan, the famous novelist, only found out in 2002, in his fifties, that he has brother, David, whom his parents had given up for adoption. Asked in an interview if he felt a "fraternal connection" to David, McEwan replied: "I do, but it's a bit abstract when you haven't grown up together. I spoke to him yesterday and we had a long chat on the phone." Then, we are told, he pauses to think before finishing: "Well, I wouldn't be doing this with another bricklayer from Wallingford."[16] McEwan's pause was forced by the cultural role that blood plays in British understandings of kinship.

Even so, blood is not the only bodily substance that matters. The body itself as both a literal and metaphorical template is never far from our cultural elaborations. This is why I have stressed that culture is not just an idea, that it is material, it is dependent and even bound up with crickets—as we saw earlier—but even more with blood and the rest of what makes up and comes out of our bodies: the liver, the heart, hair, fingernails, semen, and, perhaps above all else, breast milk. Indeed, milk is a special candidate and deserves further attention here.

## MILK KINSHIP

Not so long ago, Egyptian anthropologist Fadwa El Guindi was in her office at Qatar University, working out a kinship chart with her colleague Laila, native to Qatar. Another locally born colleague, Abdal Karim, popped into the office and saw what they were doing, at which point he declared he could not marry Laila because he was her "paternal uncle, her maternal cousin and her brother at the same time."[17] Even El Guindi, an expert in this field, was forced to step back and think about this one.

Blood can do a lot of work in helping to decode this array of relations. But in order to crack it completely we need milk. To cut a long story short, and to spare you the kinship chart that would normally accompany an anthropological explanation, it comes down to this: Abdal Karim was breastfed by the woman who married his half brother. This same woman, whose sister married Abdal Karim's father, is the mother of Laila (and breastfed her too).

Within the traditions of Islam, milk kinship is a longstanding practice and creates a legally recognized connection between people. The most general of these is mutual affection, care, and support. But according to Islamic law, it also introduces a marriage prohibition: a man and woman who were breastfed as infants by the same woman cannot marry one another, even if they "share no blood."

Such traditions were widespread throughout the Islamic world until fairly recently. Indeed—bracketing for a moment the particular example of sharia—we can note that suckling practices have been widespread throughout human history.[18] In the days before baby formula and in the absence of wet nurses (who surely worked at Downton Abbey), what else would we expect? Exactly how suckling practices get coded can vary a great deal across cultures. It doesn't always lead to a marriage prohibition, or even a sense of being related as kin. In an Islamic frame, though, it does. All good Muslims know that they cannot marry a suckling relation. To do so would be to transgress one of the three relations of "closeness" (*qarā-bah*): blood, marriage, and milk.[19]

As with other traditions we've looked at, the decline of suckling can be put down to a number of factors, many of which are due to modernization and globalization. In Lebanon, for instance, suckling is less common because residential patterns have shifted to look more like nuclear families. Wet nurses, too, are few and far between because mothers will use formula and because, in a market-based economy, they are expensive. "Milk banks," which are increasingly common in many parts of the world, have posed particular anxieties in Muslim contexts because people worry about the long-term potential of their children inadvertently marrying someone who was fed on the same source of milk. This has led some ultraconservative Islamic scholars to demand that lists of all milk donors be kept so that any given client can know the provenance of the milk.

As we saw with cattle and bride wealth in the last chapter, however, the changing place and value of milk kinship in Lebanon has not led to its disappearance. In fact, milk kinship has received a new lease on life with the rise of NRTs, technologies that have thrown up a number of challenges to Islamic understandings of maternity.

Islamic scholars are generally in support of medical advances that aid in reproduction. Practices such as IVF are broadly accepted and can be in high demand; as in much of the world, there is a strong pressure for marriages to result in children. Some NRTs do pose specific challenges, however. In gestational surrogacy, for instance, there is debate among legal authorities, especially in Shi'ite traditions, as to whether the surrogate mother can make any claim to maternity, as well as reflection on what should happen if she did. One line of argument is that she cannot claim any such rights or connections. Other scholars, however, reason that gestation is in effect a kind of super-concentrated breastfeeding: that the principle behind milk kinship (relation through nurturing) extends to this new possibility of surrogacy.

Milk kinship continues on, then, in this and in other ways. In this book, milk kinship provides the template to understand the new kinds of relations made possible by advances in science and technology.

Still, one of the points to note, and which anthropologists must reckon with, is that, while undoubtedly important, the kinds of bonds created by suckling often *do* come second to those of blood. This is certainly the case in Islamic traditions, as evidenced by the fact that milk kin do not figure in inheritance patterns; these are determined by blood, in the diffuse sense that Schneider might put it with respect to Americans.

So we can turn away from blood, in biological and cultural terms alike. And we can certainly recognize the varied and many ways in which it figures in human understandings of relatedness. All the same, anthropological studies show time and time again that blood is something special.

## BLOOD WILL OUT

Schneider's work in deconstructing American kinship precipitated a change when it came to the study of kinship more generally. It showed how a focus on flesh-and-blood kin—and even the bonds of marriage—can limit the ways in which we understand how people, especially at the level of "family," think of themselves as related. We have already observed the pliability of kin in the example of the Iñupiaq; there are innumerable other examples to be found. And we have seen how such institutions as milk kinship also create forms of solidarity, connection, and identification.

For all this, though, blood serves as a remarkably durable symbolic resource and template, something through which human communities across space and time may express core values and interests. Among the most general of these are matters of life and death, which are in turn often tied to notions of purity and impurity. Exactly how such concerns are articulated can differ enormously; in many cultures, for instance, blood is also gendered as a female substance and this further shapes the social and cultural dynamics in question.

So we come back again to this link between the biological and the corporeal, on the one hand, and the social and cultural on the other. One of the key figures in highlighting this link has been Janet Carsten, a professor of social and cultural anthropology at the University of Edinburgh. Most of her work has been focused on Malaysia, both rural and urban, and all of it on some aspects of what she once called "cultures of relatedness."[20] Blood has been a big part of this. While Carsten has often been recognized as a leading figure in the anthropology of kinship, her interest in blood has taken her into the realms of medicine, politics, and even ghosts. Carsten has been heavily influenced by Schneider's approach to anthropological analysis; she also draws on the pioneering work of Marilyn Strathern, whose own studies of relatedness, in Papua New Guinea and the UK, have defined whole areas of research on kinship and gender.[21] But Carsten has recently articulated an approach that aims to resituate the scope of a cultural account. Because for her what we must consider is that *blood will out*.[22]

Carsten's use of this phrase is tinged with irony; as an English proverb, it means that a person's "true makeup" (blood) will always reveal itself in the end. This is more of the "it's in my blood" line of thought we were talking about earlier. On the contrary, this is *not* what Carsten means. She still stands with such figures as Schneider and Strathern, both of whom question the givenness of kin. For her, though, the phrase allows for a subtle play on the fact that not all symbols are arbitrary, that any given symbol's material properties can matter in terms of what it means. We have a lot to learn from the makeup of the physical body.

Here we might take a brief detour into semiotics, or the science of signs. This is an important area of anthropological research, both linguistic and cultural, and it is relevant across a range of interests and areas. But introducing it through our discussions of blood has a few things going for it, as we'll see.

For anthropologists, the science of signs is always linked to the work of Swiss linguist Ferdinand de Saussure. His book *Course in General Linguistics* was published in 1916 and has been of interest ever since. (The book is actually a collection of lecture notes assembled by his students— how is that for a professor's dream of fame!) As the title indicates, Saussure was focused on language, and in particular language as a system of signs (rather than their use in discrete situations). There are in fact many kinds of signs—or, in more technical terms, semiotic forms—but let's begin with language. Saussure defined the linguistic sign as "the combination of a concept and a sound pattern."[23] "Tree," for instance, is a sound pattern that calls to mind a big billowy thing comprised of wood and bearing leaves.

Ever since Saussure's work, the dominant anthropological position has been for the arbitrariness of the sign. That is to say, the words we use (cat, tree, house, love) to refer to concepts of things in the world (cats, trees, houses, *amour*) are the products of convention. If we stop referring to cats as cats and agree to call them "filipules," that would be just fine. In some ways, this is neither remarkable nor all that surprising. Of course such signs are conventional. We don't even have to start making words up; we can just point to the facts of linguistic diversity: cat (that's English) is *chat* (French), is *Katze* (German), is мышык (Kyrgyz), is *popoki* (Hawaiian), and so on. Obviously such words are often etymologically related and index specific historical relationships.* But in any case we are happy to acknowledge the principle of convention.

We've seen that things get a bit more tricky when we consider such terms as "family." For the Iñupiaq there is no such point-for-point term. "Religion" is also one of those fragile concepts. Or recall our discussion of the Ese Ejja (in chapter 2), for whom the generic "human" doesn't make sense either. These tricky cases—and there are a lot of them—can force more existential and even theological questions about the order of things. They remind us that, at the level of signs, it is not simply a matter of finding all the right signifiers in any given language (words, like "family" and "cat" and "love") to correspond to all the right things they signify ("actual" families, cats, or instances of

---

* In technical terms these are referred to as "cognates," from the Latin *cognatus*, for "blood relation." The metaphors run deep.

love). Languages are not all different versions of a puzzle that, while cut up into slightly different pieces, add up to the same picture in the end. Indeed, this is one area in which the argument about the arbitrariness of the sign actually had massive implications. Put very simply, it was part of the more general dismantling of the authority of Judeo-Christian thought. The *Course in General Linguistics* was, like *On the Origin of Species* before it, a waypoint on the road to secular social science.

In the act of creation, as described in Genesis, God names the heaven and the earth, the day and the night, and so on; then, in the Garden of Eden, God brings all the animals to Adam, who names them. Then comes the Fall, of course, which cuts off Adam and Eve from the Edenic state. Later in Genesis, all the people of the world build a huge tower in a great city that almost reaches heaven, which God takes as a sign of disrespect (the Tower of Babel). As punishment, he scatters the people and "confound[s] their language, that they may not understand one another's speech."[24] In these early examples of Judeo-Christian creation and history, what we see is an approach to language and sign-making that is fundamentally different from the anthropological approach just outlined. It is one in which everything has its proper name, place, and meaning.

A few years ago, when there was a debate in Britain over the legalization of same-sex marriage, the Catholic Bishops' Conference of England and Wales (CBCEW) issued a letter, signed by the president and vice president of the CBCEW, arguing that marriage is a sacrament and you cannot change what it means.[25] Now, they weren't talking about the English word "marriage," of course; they were talking about the institution. But the logic behind it was the same as what I've described above, which is that the meanings of things (words, institutions, and so on) are not arbitrary—are not, ultimately, artifacts of human decisions. What marriage means is "not a matter of public opinion," they write, and they call on all Catholics to "ensure that the true meaning of marriage is not lost for future generations."*

So there are different ways to approach the workings of signs. And in general, as I have said, the anthropological one holds to the principles of convention and arbitrariness. Most anthropologists would never say that marriage has a "true meaning." There is obviously an affinity here with the emphasis on culture as a construction.

But if we move away from language per se, to consider "material" things, that principle comes with a caveat. Here it is American philosopher Charles Sanders Peirce, whose work has been particularly influential. This is partly because—unlike Saussure—Peirce was interested in more than language, and certainly more than language in an abstract, formal sense. Peirce took a great interest in the material properties and qualities of semiotic forms. This is because images and objects don't work or exist in the same way as sound patterns and concepts. Does it matter, for instance, that the Ten Commandments were written on stone tablets? Of course. What the stone signifies is durability and fixity. The stone says, "These really matter." Imagine if they had been written in the dirt. Not the same thing. It is not that material properties determine the meaning of some sign, but they can shape or direct—

* We often find the same kind of sentiment and approach in contemporary human rights campaigns, even though the metaphysics might be very different or absent altogether. But such campaigns often work on the premise of absolutes and fixity; torture is torture is torture.

index, as Peirce would have put it—certain meanings and associations.

Here we can return to blood—or *Blut* (German), *dugo* (Filipino), *ropa* (Shona), and so forth. Because the actual substance is precisely such a kind of thing. Its material properties, including color (red), form (liquid), and provenance (the body), shape and direct certain meanings and associations. So, too, does that fact that it is necessary for life. As Carsten notes, for instance, its liquidity can be used to help explain why it plays such a central role across a range of domains—not only kinship, as we have discussed at length, but also gender, religion, politics, and economics.[26] Let me take each of these in turn, to give a sense of what I'm talking about.

*Gender.* Blood is not always gendered, but if it is, it is usually gendered female because of its association with childbirth and menstruation. In New Guinea, bloodletting rituals and practices have been common among the Iatmul, Sambia, Gururumba, and others. These are often group rituals held for adolescent boys and are thought to purge them of femininity; in some cases, private bloodletting is also practiced by men when their wives are menstruating.[27] Practices of seclusion for menstruating women, as well as prohibitions on cooking and sexual intercourse, are very common around the globe. Even in contexts where these practices are changing, the principle is often upheld. Among the Vathima Brahmins, women used to be sequestered to the back of the house for three days when menstruating, neither cooking nor bathing nor going out. This was central to the maintenance of household purity. These days, however, many younger Vathima women, especially those who live in cities or abroad in the United States, refuse such stringent measures. Anthropologist Haripriya Narasimhan has found that many of these women restrict their seclusion to a few hours in the morning or reduce the zone of exclusion to the kitchen.[28] This gives us yet another example of "the modernity of tradition," like bride wealth in southern Africa; the more things change, the more they stay the same. But again, blood is not always gendered in these ways. And in many cultures, there are fine-grained designations of blood. You can't just speak of blood in general. Among the Ndembu of Zambia, for instance, there are five categories of blood: of parturition (childbirth) and women (in general)—these are gendered female—but also of killing/murder, of animals, and of witchcraft.[29]

*Religion.* Having just been discussing Christianity, we might well start with the blood of Christ. We need look no further: blood is central to religion. Within Christianity, of course, we also have its symbolic and in some cases transubstantiated consumption. Both cases—the crucifixion and communion—are acts of purification and redemption. The blood cleanses rather than defiles. We need not look further, but if we do, what we see is just how common it is around the world for the most significant forms of sacrifice to be premised on the shedding of blood. Not human blood, in most cases, although there are instances in which this is seen as what one study (that of the Chukchi in Siberia) refers to as "the ultimate sacrifice." More commonly, it is the blood of a valued animal: a cow, or a goat, or a reindeer. In the Chukchi case, while the ultimate sacrifice might be taking one's own life—voluntary euthanasia in old age—in fact this very rarely happens. What is much more common is the sacrifice of a reindeer from the herd.* If this is not possible, they will sacrifice (destroy) a reindeer sausage. If this is not possible, a stick that looks like a reindeer sausage will be struck with a knife. This chain of metonymic and metaphorical associations is held together by blood.[30]

*Politics.* Another kind of ultimate sacrifice, of course, is the death of a soldier for the nation. Here, kinship, religion, and politics really blur together. There are countless examples of politicians and rhetoricians praising those who have "shed blood" for their country. And there are countless examples of antiwar slogans and forms of protest that try to turn the same imagery around. "No blood for oil" was the dominant refrain during the Gulf War in 1991. Turning once again to India, there is a genre of painting in which nationalist heroes are depicted in the act of spilling their blood. There is also a genre of portraiture in which blood, not paint, is the literal medium of expression, drawn from blood donors who see it as a patriotic sacrifice.[31] More generally, it is not unusual for some states to run more or less mandatory blood drives among soldiers, the police, and hospital staff. And in the highlands of Papua New Guinea, another reason why the Sambia practiced bloodletting rituals (up until the 1960s) was to turn young men into warriors.[32]

*Economics.* If you run a bank or a business, you want liquidity. This is a metaphor drawn from blood—because money (or credit) is the lifeblood of the economic system. Sometimes, businesses need cash infusions. We can speak

---

*The sacrifice itself is seen as an offering to the Chukchi ancestors, who wield considerable power over the mundane world. Sacrifice is often propitiatory, although in some worldviews this is denied or devalued. But it ought to come as no surprise that Marcel Mauss wrote at length about the logic of sacrifice, since in many forms it serves a similar function as gift exchange.

of the heart of the economy. The link between blood and money is not always a good one: "blood money" is part of an illicit exchange (money for life). The Nuer, who live in what is now South Sudan, have a very dim view of money, expressed through the idiom of blood. "Money has no blood," they say. What this means is that money cannot sustain or even help grow social relations; it lacks vitality, the kind of vitality that Nuer find in people and in cattle. Like other groups we have considered, for the Nuer cattle occupy a special place in the regime of value. Part of that value is linked to their blood; it is a source of vitality and has a generative capacity. The Nuer don't see money as a good investment; living, as they have, in a country that has been racked by conflict almost continually since the mid-1950s, money has never really been linked with a potential for producing "interest." All it ever seems to do is lose value through inflation.[33] After the global financial crisis of 2008, protestors in Thailand earned the moniker of "Red Shirts" because they soaked their clothes in their own blood to signal their sacrifice for the good of the nation and sense of betrayal by the government's handling of new economic pressures; the Red Shirts also spattered their blood on government buildings.[34]

All of these examples of blood's material and metaphorical relevance are a perfect encapsulation of a few key anthropological lessons. First, that—once again—it is not so easy to distinguish what we call "nature" from what we call "culture." This lesson can also be extended to the boundaries between kinship and gender, politics, economics, and religion. All of these labels and designations are inadequate and *none* marks out a discrete space. The material and symbolic bindings of blood into all of these areas make that clear.

Second, that symbols themselves often combine seemingly polar or antithetical associations. Blood is life. Blood is death. Blood purifies. Blood defiles. This particular point about symbolism has been especially well captured by Victor Turner in his treatment of symbols in Ndembu ritual.[35] In the case of blood, vitality might be the overarching theme that connects what he calls the "disparate significata." This point about symbolism is not fodder for the skeptic who finds in all such talk vagaries and woolliness, preferring rather the hard facts. The power of symbols, and the logic of their associations, may be the hardest fact of all.

And finally, then, that the body itself and the stuff of its makeup are core resources of the figurative imagination. Wherever we look, we find humans using their bodies as metaphorical and metonymical templates to consolidate, expand, and explore what they know about themselves, their relations to each other, the world around them, and the skies above. We see this with blood above all—or most diffusely—but also with milk, the heart, the liver, the skin, the head, the hands (right and left often being distinct), the eyes, and more. Our cultures are our flesh and blood.

## CHAPTER 6

# IDENTITY

We cannot begin this chapter by invoking the ancestors. The Victorians didn't really write about identity. It is not a perennial term in the pages of anthropology journals, and it is certainly one of those words—like "family"— that requires work to draw cross-cultural parallels.

You might not guess this given the importance and prevalence of the term today. A lot of anthropology now is concerned with identity. It's been this way since the 1980s. One important reason for this shift is that people all over the world have come to think in terms of "identity" and to deploy the term quite consciously. Identity is a major tool of self-definition, of political mobilization and action, of governance, and of course, as the moody teenager knows, philosophical reflection. Who am I?

"Identity" is not a new word, however, and some of its main contemporary uses are in fact quite longstanding. The first definition of "identity" in the *OED* is "the quality or condition of being the same in substance." This can refer to anything—numbers, tomatoes, stars—but in the past fifty or sixty years it has taken pride of place in our vocabularies of self and group definition. The *OED* also goes on to emphasize that this condition or quality of being the same has to be continuous over time. This second aspect of identity is just as important.

Work by psychologist Erik H. Erikson is often presented as the initiator of this change. He coined the phrase "identity crisis" in a book first published in 1968, *Identity: Youth and Crisis*.[1] Erikson's interest in youth was set against the backdrop of the era, which saw the rise of the civil rights movement, the Black Power movement, feminism, and, perhaps most broadly, the antiwar and anti-establishment protests of 1968 that sprang up from Mexico to Czechoslovakia. In all of these, the politics of identity became a powerful tool of criticism and self-definition. Take Malcolm X as an example. He took this name to signify that his given name, Malcolm Little, was not his own or his family's but rather a legacy of the slave trade into which his ancestors had been sold and through which their true names had been erased. This emphasis on name is a common way of approaching identity: it speaks to something that we often think is deep and abiding within us, even if circumstances or the forces of history try to keep it down or erase it. We can also see concerns with identity in the work of Frantz Fanon and other anticolonial intellectuals. Identity politics became central to anticolonial movements and also the struggles of indigenous groups in the context of their relationships with nation-states, from Brazil and Botswana to Guatemala and the United States.

Erikson's career can be used to appreciate how shifts in characterization take place over time, even relatively short periods of time. While his ideas on identity and youth lent themselves to an analysis of the 1960s zeitgeist, they were actually grounded in more classically anthropological concerns. In the 1930s, near the start of his professional life, Erikson worked for a spell with anthropologist H. S. Mekeel on a study of education and childhood psychology on the Oglala Sioux Reservation. Erikson's work on the Sioux is interesting in several respects, not least the critical stance he takes toward the effects of the "civilizing mission" on the psychological well-being of Oglala children. He discusses some of this work in what many consider his most influential book, *Childhood and Society*, first published in 1950. That book has a handful of references to identity, including Erikson's concern over the extent to which the Sioux had been "denied the bases for a collective identity formation."[2] In a 1937 article, though, fresh from the research with Mekeel, none of his analyses makes explicit reference to "identity" at all. But then, by 1968, identity became the headline topic.[3]

So what changed in that thirty-year period? If we use Erikson's work as a bellwether, what does it indicate? One thing is the extent to which we began to think of ourselves as rights-bearing individuals. It was an important thirty-year stretch in that respect.

We can trace the modern language of rights to seventeenth-century England and of course the American and French revolutions. Yet its fullest flowering is still the Universal Declaration of Human Rights (UDHR), one of the single most important documents of the twentieth century—and, as it happens, a very helpful index of what we might call the "modern subject." Ratified by the United Nations in 1948, the UDHR puts forward a very specific vision of humanity, one in which the individual person is the fundamental unit. Nearly all of the articles in the UDHR begin with the word "everyone." Everyone has a right to life, to free expression, to freedom of belief, to development of his or her personality, to freedom of movement, to own property, to peaceful assembly, to work, and even to paid holidays (Article 24). The state and even culture feature in the UDHR, it's true, but only inasmuch as they can help realize or possibly prevent the recognition of everyone's individual rights. The family also makes a brief appearance (as "the natural and fundamental group unit of society"), and there is a mention of duties near the end (which are very different from rights, since they require action on the part of the person). But it is the individual that matters above all else.

In the UDHR, the individual in mind is the individual *person*.* However, in my own emphasis on the individual, I don't only mean the discrete person of flesh and blood. I also mean the idea of a bounded group or culture. We're used to talking about "individuals" when we mean individual persons: John, or Selena, or Tomoko. The fact that we often treat "individual" and "person" as synonymous is proof of how important the person-centered associations have become. But we shouldn't forget that "individual" is often an adjective, not a noun. We can speak of individual Tic Tacs, individual shoes, and, yes, even individual groups. This is important because by the 1970s, it had become clear that group rights—sometimes also called cultural rights—were as pressing a concern as human (individual) rights. The inability to address this is a major shortcoming of the UDHR. It was written in a way that suggests people can exist outside of a cultural context. Some of the earliest opponents of the UDHR were Boasians for whom this made no sense whatsoever. It also struck them as absurd to frame the rights as if everyone was a factory worker in Manchester or Detroit. (Paid holidays are all well and good—don't get me wrong. But if you're a peasant farmer in Oaxaca, this is nonsense.)

This gets us to another important mid-twentieth-century shift, which is the extent to which self and group under-

---

* The first meaning of "individual" in the *OED* is "one in substance or essence," which is nearly synonymous with "identity."

standing became increasingly framed in relation to what we now call globalization. In anthropology, globalization has been defined as the process of creating "an intensely interconnected world—one where the rapid flows of capital, people, goods, images, and ideologies draw more and more of the globe into webs of interconnection, compressing our sense of time and space, and making the world feel smaller and distances shorter."[4] There is plenty to unpack here. For now, though, the point I want to make is that one effect of the intensity of interconnectedness is to force the question of identity. Are we all becoming identical? Is globalization forcing difference to give way to sameness?

In the face of such questions, one response has been to assert a strong cultural identity. Take an example from Belize.[5] In the late 1980s and early 1990s, more and more people in Belize started having access to satellite television. In a relatively short period of time, the connections that Belize had to Britain, its former colonial master, were loosened. Local people were no longer as dependent upon a diet of television provided by the postcolonial state broadcasting system, much of which recycled old and outdated shows from the BBC and American networks. In important ways, local people started to feel connected to the broader world—part of the same time, if you will, as everyone else. Satellite television was *live*; it was not mediated and it was not delayed in ways that marked Belizeans as "backward"—a lingering colonial image. All of a sudden, they had access to the cable news channels and baseball games in the United States (very popular). Satellite television served as a marker of entry into the global arena, and in key ways this was empowering. Yet for some it also sparked concerns about Belizean identity. We see this in part through another shift that took place during this time: an upsurge in the popularity of Belizean music traditions, including the "punta rock" style (kind of like calypso). Whereas under the older colonial model of relations such local music was something of a quaint throwback, now it became a source of real interest and pride. It was distinctive, a showcase for local talents and a contribution to that ever-expanding genre, "world music," that didn't get broadcast on MTV.*

One beginning of a lesson here is that globalization does not necessarily lead to the erasure of cultural difference. Anthropologists regularly find that the threat of cultural homogenization, real or imagined, is the best way to ensure new cultural flourishings. Sometimes they're revitalized traditions, as in the case of music in Belize. Sometimes they're invented traditions. Oftentimes it's some combination of both. Think of it this way: a violin is also a fiddle. You might expect that it is meant to produce a concerto if you are from Vienna. But in the hands of a virtuoso from County Cork, or Elkins, West Virginia, that's not what you get. The spread of string instruments hasn't been a major focus of debates on globalization, but the point I'm making holds for a lot of other stuff from television, to mobile phones, to Coca-Cola, to, for that matter, pamphlet versions of the UDHR handed out by UN agencies and human rights NGOs.

I've presented the example of Belize at a high level of remove. From such a distance it's easy to acknowledge that a national identity can change. All identities change

---

* "World music" is of course a catchall category for music that's produced outside the West. Michael Jackson isn't "world music"; Thomas Mapfumo, a popular singer in Zimbabwe, is. This is strange, though, when you think about it, because it's Michael Jackson's music that enjoys worldwide popularity. This is in no way a slight on Thomas Mapfumo's excellent work. But what it tells us is who gets to call the shots and identify the labels.

over time, partly in relation to historical and social factors. Even something as seemingly simple as a new television platform can, when set against the background of British colonial rule and foreground of globalization, contribute to that change.

Events always matter to the equation of identity. So do circumstance, perspective, and location. Every social scientist who has ever written about identity seems to make this point. Identity is relative. It is calibrated to the other. When I'm in Ghana, I say I'm from the United States (but that I live in London). When I'm on the East Coast of the United States, I say I'm from New York, but if I'm in California, I might just say I'm from the East Coast. When I'm in New York, I say I'm from the Capital District. When I'm in the Capital District (that's the Albany area), I say I'm from Schenectady (pronounced \skə-ˈnek-tə-dē\ in case you didn't know; derived from a Mohawk term for "beyond the pines"). When I'm in Schenectady, I say I'm from near the park or that I went to Linton High School and so on. If I'm talking to a fellow anthropologist in any one of these places and we get to Schenectady, I might also note that Lewis Henry Morgan went to college there. These are all "identities"—or at least an effort at identification—and they are all me.

Then there is the growth in online social media. This makes my situated identifications vis-à-vis Schenectady and Lewis Henry Morgan look like child's play. Studies of online social life and virtual worlds by anthropologists show how we give full rein in cyberspace and other media to the construction of new identities. Take Second Life, one of the longest-running virtual worlds, which now has over one million members. On the Second Life website, people are invited to join and create their "avatar"—

their online presence, as it were. "Create, customize, and completely change your virtual identity whenever you like," we are told.[6] One anthropologist who did field-work on (and in) Second Life, Tom Boellstorff, tells us of men who appear as chipmunks, elves, and voluptuous women, as well as an adult who identifies as a child and even gets "virtually" adopted.[7] What's been made clear in anthropological studies of the virtual, though, is that this doesn't mean it isn't real or that it's all play and so doesn't matter. "The avatar represents who I really feel inside," says one woman in a Second Life promotional video.[8] Virtual identities, as Boellstorff and others note, are be-coming actual. They represent what is in fact a more gen-eral trend toward thinking of ourselves as self-fashioning creatures. So that stereotypical teenager's question—*Who am I?*—is now increasingly complemented by a more open-ended, postmodern question: *Who do I want to be?*

## RACE, AGAIN

And yet, despite the widespread recognition that identi-ties can change and that identities are situational, there is a persistent tendency—even in a globalizing world full of rights-bearing individuals, expressing themselves freely—to think of identities as fixed, enduring, and abiding. Re-member, blood will out! Not in Janet Carsten's subtle sense but in the gross sense we find in the logic of racism and the one-drop rule.

I want to come back to race here because it has posed one of the most significant challenges for anthropologists when it comes to such questions of identity. On the one hand, anthropological research can be used to show that, biologically speaking, race is a myth. On the other hand, it is a myth—like all myths—that carries a great deal of cultural significance. Race may be a myth, but "race" is a powerful category nonetheless.

One of the hallmark studies in this area is Ashley Montagu's 1942 book, *Man's Most Dangerous Myth: The Fallacy of Race*. A student of Franz Boas and Ruth Benedict (although introduced to anthropology in Bronislaw Malinowski's London seminar), Montagu covered an incredible range of materials, from studies in biological sciences to the history of ideas—a history that shows quite clearly that the modern conception of race is rooted in European colonialism. In terms of the science, of course, the evidence base in 1942 was not as extensive as it is today. By the 1990s, physical anthropologists and geneticists had clearly shown that, in biological terms, there is only one human race; there are no human "subspecies," to put it in more specialized language. Genetic diversity is very slight among human populations, especially when compared to other large mammalian species. Moreover, hypotheses about distinct evolutionary lineages (African, Eurasian)—much more common in Montagu's day—have been questioned by advances in tracing evolutionary history through molecular genetics. As one of the leading researchers in this area puts it, "All of humanity [is] a single lineage, sharing a common long-term evolutionary fate."[9]

In chapter 1, I referred to an argument by Ruth Benedict that she made in support of this same point. Benedict, of course, did not have the data on genetics and evolutionary biology that are available today; she made her arguments more along the lines of culture and custom. It was an important set of arguments to make, however, and they were aimed against the likes of the state registrar in Virginia, whose position against so-called miscegenation was grounded in the racist assertion that, eventually, the "negro type" would emerge from anyone who carried just one drop of "colored blood." To counter such arguments that race and cultural behavior were linked, one of the examples that Benedict used was a hypothetical "interracial" adoption. She writes: "An Oriental child adopted by an Occidental family learns English, shows towards its foster parents the attitudes current among the children he plays with, and grows up to the same professions that they elect. He learns the entire set of cultural traits of the adopted society, and the set of his real parents' group plays no part."[10] All of this is in service of her antiracial and antiracist point: "Culture is not a biologically transmitted complex."[11] Blood will not out. There is no true black, white, Occidental, Oriental, or other such racial identity.

Yet Benedict's turn toward culture in the effort to get rid of the biology of race is misleading. In America, or Britain, or any number of other modern places in which the legacies of Orient and Occident obtain, you can be very sure that the "cultural traits" of a child's "real parents" will play a *major* part in the determination of identity. This isn't because blood will out, it's true. But many of the Occidental people around this child will think it does play a part—whether they say it or not—and the child will be made to think in relation to a racial identity, even if that also means being left betwixt and between.

In that earlier discussion of race and culture I also referred to the contemporary work of Lee D. Baker. A professor at Duke University, much of his writing is on the history of anthropology, in particular the involvement of Boas and his students in the debates about race and culture. What I want to focus on for the moment, however, is something in Baker's own biography, because he uses it in one of his books to make an important point about identity.[12] Baker is African American, but he was adopted by a white (Swedish Lutheran) family and grew up in an almost wholly white community in Oregon. From a very early age, though, he started to think in terms of race, of being black. It began with the garbage men—the only other "hegros" he had met, as his three-year-old, 1969 self put it. This identification came not from within but from what was around him—what was said and unsaid, lovingly and with the best intentions by his parents, sometimes cruelly by children at school. Over the course of his childhood and into college, he tells us, he "worked hard at being black." "The idea that one has to learn to perform whiteness or model blackness was always at the forefront of my socialization," he writes.[13]

Baker could not be Benedict's hypothetical adoptee. While in Benedict's big picture anthropologists can cheer the status of race as a cultural construction, the danger is that we assume our knowledge of this fact has a definitive bearing on the world at large. As Baker puts it, "Race in the United States is at once an utter illusion and a material reality."[14] Biological fiction; cultural fact. Geneticists and biological anthropologists recognize this too. In a recent article in *Science*, one team of researchers acknowledged exactly the paradox to which Baker refers. We cannot ignore the extent to which racial identities have cultural significance, they argue, but "the US National Academies of Sciences, Engineering, and Medicine should convene a panel of experts from biological sciences, social sciences, and humanities to recommend ways for research into human biological diversity to move past the use of race as a tool for classification in both laboratory and clinical research."[15]

## IDENTITY IN MASHPEE

There are few better cases that attest to the modern messiness of identity than that of the Mashpee Indians.[16] Mashpee is a town on Cape Cod, Massachusetts. In 1976, the Mashpee Wampanoag Tribal Council, Inc., representing approximately three hundred members, went to the federal district court seeking the rights to roughly three-quarters of the township land. Their move was part of a broader one at the time within the United States of Native American claims to land and sovereignty, especially in the Northeast. This was in fact the start of a wave that has seen indigenous groups around the world make claims to land rights and sovereignty—from Brazil to India to Australia. By the early 1980s cultural rights had emerged alongside human rights as a major issue with a powerful moral force. And the strength of the claims has often depended on the strength of the identity politics marshaled.

Many of these efforts have been successful. There were major land rights acts passed in Australia in 1976 and 1981. In Brazil, indigenous rights were formally recognized in the 1988 constitution (not that it led to immediate shifts). In Guatemala, Rigoberta Menchú Tum became arguably the first "global native," following the publication of her autobiography (*I, Rigoberta Menchú*) in 1983 and the attention it brought to the plight of the Mayan groups. In the case of the Mashpee, however, there was a preliminary question: Could they be rightfully recognized as an indigenous group to begin with? Did they have a cultural identity?

Mashpee had been recognized as an "Indian town" since its incorporation in 1869, and the area was associated with a group, once called the South Sea Indians, since Puritan times. The recognition was informal, but it was reinforced by the fact that until the 1960s, town politics was dominated by Indian families, allowing them to enjoy a certain kind of sovereignty and self-determination. In the 1960s, however, as Cape Cod became an increasingly popular tourist and retirement destination, the population balance of the town shifted and the Indians lost political control, as well as their numerical majority. Until the 1960s, the ratio of Indians to whites was 3:1. By the end of that decade, it was more like 1:4—a complete reversal. While the Indians had initially welcomed the new sources of tax and commercial revenue that tourism brought, this gave way to complaints of overdevelopment, especially the loss of lands they had used for hunting and fishing. The Tribal Council was incorporated in 1972 and petitioned the Bureau of Indian Affairs for recognition in 1974.

It was the political control of Mashpee that had long provided a sense of group identity. Most people in the area recognized and accepted it as a matter of course. Beyond this, however, there were not many distinguishing aspects of a Mashpee Wampanoag culture. While there had been periods of cultural revivalism, these were occasional. And while some cultural traditions survived, or colored the course of life, they were few and far between.

The political structures themselves were not "tribal" per se; the Indians governed largely in accord with small-town conventions and state law. The indigenous language, Wôpanâak or Massachusett, had died out in the nineteenth century, so that wasn't a bond. There was no strong tradition of indigenous religion either: most of the Indians were Baptists.

The federal court case took forty-one days, over the course of which the plaintiffs aimed to paint a picture of tribal identity that was not lost but submerged and sensitive to the broader social and political dynamics of New England. Pointing back to the Puritan era, the Tribal Council argued that conversion to Christianity had been necessary just in order to survive. Integrating themselves into the local and regional economy, playing a part in Massachusetts, was likewise vital. How could they exist otherwise? To strengthen their case, the Indians could point to those periods in which revivals took place, including the 1860s and 1920s. For the plaintiffs, in other words, their Indian identity had been continuous, and authentically held, but not marked by many outward signs because of the power imbalance often faced by colonized peoples.

Lawyers for the defense took a very different tack, arguing that what the Tribal Council plaintiffs had painted as an effort to keep a core identity intact in the face of external pressures was, in fact, just another version of the American story. The Indians in Mashpee had become Americans. They had assimilated into the system and could not rightly claim otherwise. Where was their culture?

Several anthropologists were called as expert witnesses by the plaintiffs. The defense lawyers (to say nothing of the judge) made minced meat of them because the anthropologists refused to respond in the yes/no terms that the court system demanded. Culture, as I have been at pains to explain throughout this book, is not an easy thing to limn or define; cultural identity cannot be reduced to tick-box questions. In short, what the defense argued was that there was no such identity there. In terms set by the popular imagination in America, the Mashpee didn't look like Indians, didn't sound like Indians, didn't act like Indians. Simply put, the Mashpee weren't cultural enough. This argument won the day. The Mashpee lost the case.

The Mashpee case sits in the gray area of indigenous identity politics. More black-and-white cases, which have managed to fulfill the definition of identity we find in the *Oxford English Dictionary*—the same in substance, and continuously so over time—have been more successful. When the courts, political elite, or any members of the mainstream public are asked to consider claims such as those of the Mashpee, often what they expect to see is a colorful display of difference.

If you want to be indigenous, you need to be different. You need to be traditional and wear your culture—quite literally—on your sleeve. The same logic holds in global tourism. If you've ever been to a safari lodge in Kenya or resort in Bali, chances are you've been greeted off the bus by a troupe of "natives" dancing to some traditional music, welcoming you with open arms. What you'd probably acknowledge, if you stopped to think about it, though, is that in between your busload and the next, those natives are checking Facebook on their smartphones.

Identity is, like race, both an utter illusion and a material reality. And identity is, like race, something we treat as both nature and artifice. We assume it is to be found deep within and yet we would also recognize it as performed—sometimes quite literally—by, for example, those dancing Masai at the safari lodge in Kenya, or maybe the chipmunk man on Second Life—and sometimes as more in terms of navigating the everyday and society's expectations, as Baker explains of his own American coming-of-age.

## LANGUAGE IDEOLOGY

If Massachusett had still been spoken by the Mashpee in the 1970s—even if by just a few of the older folks, who kept it alive in the community—their case would have been undeniably stronger. Language and culture are often treated as two sides of the same coin. Like blood, language is often understood to capture the essence of character and being as constitutive to identity as the nose on your face. Mother tongue; mother's milk; blood: the figurative chain is clear.

In the four-field approach of anthropology, sociocultural and linguistic anthropology have often had the strongest links. This makes practical sense, certainly from the perspective of social and cultural anthropologists. You can do most fieldwork projects in London or Lagos without needing much recourse to paleopathology records or carbon-dated pot shards. But you can't do it without attention to language.

Not all of linguistic anthropology involves fieldwork, or close attention to language in use. What you learn from studying grammar, syntax, or, say, the comparative structuring of Bantu noun classes in the abstract—that is, from textual sources and records—is valuable, but it also tells you something distinct to the study of language use in day-to-day life. This is sometimes glossed as the difference between a focus on *langue* (language) and *parole* (speech), labels that come from the work of Saussure (who focused on *langue*). Much of the work in linguistic anthropology, however, does focus on language use—*parole*—sometimes also called sociolinguistics or, more technically, pragmatics. One of the research interests in this tradition is on how the speakers of a language understand its cultural value.

Over the past forty years, one of the richest areas of research on language use has concerned what the specialists call "language ideology" (or sometimes "linguistic ideology").[17] I want to spend some time explaining this here because it can be very helpful for appreciating cultural approaches to identity. Indeed, more generally, if you understand something of language ideology, you get a fantastic insight into the workings of culture.

We all have a language ideology. We may not know it, or think about it, but we do. Basically, what this means is that we all make certain assumptions, or hold certain beliefs, about the structure, meaning, and use of language. Our language ideologies tell us something about how we understand such concerns as the order of things and the nature of authority, what values are important, and even what we take reality to be.

One popular example of language ideology in action is what I've done at several points in this book: quote the definitions of words from the *Oxford English Dictionary*.[18] What does this tell us? That I think—or maybe think *you* think—that dictionary definitions give us the real meanings of words. This in turn tells us that I—or you, or maybe we—assume that truth or the real is authorized by textual sources produced by experts. I could never have written, "As my mom once told me, identity means *the quality or condition of being the same in substance*"—not if I expected you to treat the definition as, well, *definitive*. We trust books over people and experts over ordinary people—even mothers—when it comes to such matters (especially experts at Oxford University Press?).

Another popular example is related to this and is also something I've done in this book: trace terms etymologically. *In its oldest uses, taken from the Latin, "savage" means ...* I wrote something very close to this back in chapter 2. So what does this tell us? That I think, or maybe think you think, that something of a word's real meaning is also linked to its original use. And often, that in my use of a word, something of that buried original form makes itself felt. For example, religion: from the Latin, *religare*, "to bind," and *religio*, "sacred/reverence." Ah, yes! Religion is about community—and the links between humans and the divine!—and also, yes, that *sacred* stuff. That pretty much sums it up. In the West, of course, Latin and Greek have a special cachet (which in turn tells us something about the premium value of antiquity). It also suggests that the metaphysics of meaning lingers in our collective consciousness. The strident atheists among us should not kid themselves that only Catholic bishops can think that marriage has a "true meaning."

There are a host of other examples. One of my favorites involves an atheist, in fact—the comedian and composer-musician Tim Minchin. He is the type of atheist for whom unbelief is a cause; he's not just a live-and-let-live atheist. Once, to prove his point that there is nothing supernatural or mystical out there, he said to a fan-filled audience at a literary festival, "I hope my daughter dies tomorrow in a car crash."[19] There were audible gasps. In saying it, he was highlighting some characteristics of Anglo language ideologies. First, that our speech should be sincere; we tend to think of language as a medium for truth. "Say what you mean, and mean what you say." This isn't the point he was trying to make, but he made it anyway. The point he was trying to make concerned a second aspect of our language ideology, which is that our speech can have a material effect not only on others but also on the course of events. "If you can't say anything nice, don't say anything at all." This is also why we say "touch wood" or actually touch wood when we say something, and then worry about it not happening. "He'll get the job! Touch wood." Not many people know why they say "touch wood," but that's not relevant in this case: what's relevant is the incantation-like expression, the "magical" effect. And that's precisely what an ardent atheist wants to challenge. Minchin was trying to shock his audience out of its superstition-filled, linguistically ideologized stupor. He was trying to convince them that (a) there is no supernatural force out there listening in, just waiting for you to say something reckless; and (b) such utterances, in any case, have no effect whatsoever on the future course of events. (This is also why ardent atheists think prayer is so irrational.)

Over the past twenty years, many linguistic anthropologists have contributed to mapping the macrolevel terrain of language ideologies in modern Western societies.[20] Simply put, they argue, what we find in the contemporary West are two major types: the ideology of authenticity and the ideology of anonymity. While in some respects these are distinct, they share a common grounding in what Kathryn A. Woolard calls sociolinguistic naturalism in a major recent study of language ideology and identity politics in Catalonia.[21] I'll want to come back to the details of this study in the next section, but for now let's consider the general arguments.

The ideology of authenticity is related to much of what we've already covered in this chapter. It is based on essentialism and suggests that our language expresses something integral to who we are, both individually and corporately: "The primary significance of the authentic voice is what it signals about *who* one is, rather than *what* one has to say."[22] There are some choice stereotypes of this in popular culture: the dashing Frenchman whose dashingness is tied to his mellifluous sweet nothings. The profound Russian poet whose profundity, and ability to capture in words what the winter sunlight reveals, is tied to her verse. But the impetus to emphasize authenticity often comes from being in a minority position. It has been central, for instance, to the nationalist projects in Quebec and Brittany. It is also commonly found within minority communities, especially in poor, urban areas. Class can be a major determinant, as well, as expressed in accent and pronunciation. In all such cases, the register of language indexes a local communal identity, grounded firmly in a place and often expressing a particular character or sensibility. We see it in the Cockney accent in London, the particularities of New York or West Coast rap, and the distinctiveness of Soweto slang. As we might expect, such authenticity cannot be learned. You either have it or you don't. This doesn't stop some people from trying to "get real" or "get down" with the people. Mainstream politicians often seriously embarrass themselves in this respect. Throughout his political career, Tony Blair was mocked for his habit of slipping from his Oxford, Westminster-bubble primness into a more salt-of-the-earth, real-people, working-class "Estuary English." In these moments, he was trying to sound like a boy from Basildon, although every time he did it, he only seemed to annoy people more.

The ideology of anonymity is what stands behind the legitimacy of dominant languages. English has the widest currency as such a language. In many contexts, it is not expected to index place but instead to transcend place—to be the language of everywhere and nowhere. Because English is a global lingua franca, native speakers—especially in England—have had to give up some of the strongest claims to authenticity on account of its globally recognized value. True, a lot of people, maybe especially Americans, love a good English accent. But those same Anglophile Americans would never feel that English was any less theirs than for Hugh Grant or even Queen Elizabeth II. This ideology is crucial for the proper functioning of a public sphere. Here, then, it's not only about global languages like English or Spanish but how any dominant language works within a political arena that includes different groups or communities. Indonesian is another good example, because it was constructed in an effort to create a common medium across a nation of islands in which over three hundred languages are spoken.

As we can appreciate, ideologies of authenticity and anonymity often apply to the same language; the distinctions are relevant depending on the level of remove or context. If you're from Basildon in Essex, it's perfectly possible to: (a) be annoyed when Tony Blair tries to speak as if he grew up next door to you; and (b), at the same time, support the use of English as a lingua franca at the

United Nations because you'd acknowledge that it belongs to everyone equally. Indeed, for the secretary-general of the UN to make a public address in Portuguese, Korean, or Akan, especially to an international or global audience, could be seen as divisive or exclusionary.

What underpins both of these ideologies is what Woolard calls sociolinguistic naturalism. This means that the ideology in question is taken to be natural. Given. Just the way it is. In other words, the authority of authenticity or anonymity is not seen to be a result of human decision, political engineering, or economic circumstance.

## FROM PEOPLE TO PERFORMANCE

If in the period between the 1930s and 1960s we saw a rise in recourse to identity, in the time since then other shifts have occurred. In terms of research, it's still the case that anthropologists often find an expectation or assumption that cultural identity is what it is—that it can't really be changed. There is still a high premium on exotic difference; Masai can still get sidework in safari camps, dancing for British tourists.

But in the early twenty-first century, the more performative approach to identity has gained traction and credence. This is evident not only in the virtual worlds of Second Life avatars but also where we might least expect to find it: in nationalist movements in Europe.

Nationalism in Europe doesn't always have a good name. With some exceptions, most are on the right and, often, far right wing of the political spectrum: Jobbik in Hungary, the Front National in France, the British National Party (BNP), for example. These types of parties trade on xenophobia, either openly or with dog-whistle tactics. They have very twentieth-century, blood-will-out understandings of identity, and their understanding and use of language are premised on an ideology of authenticity and sociolinguistic naturalism. The BNP even supplements this by using imperial language in reverse: on one of their website postings, they say Tower Hamlets in London has been "colonized" by Third World migrants and the "indigenous population" displaced.[23]

Catalonia is a different case. In 1978, after the fall of Francisco Franco's dictatorship, a new Spanish constitution was adopted. Catalonia became one of seventeen "autonomous communities" wielding considerable power in its own right and enjoying a strong degree of self-governance. Catalonia is one of the largest of these communities within Spain, in terms of population. It is also one of the wealthiest. The regional language, Catalan, is distinct from Spanish (or Castilian, as it is generally known in Spain); it is not, as people sometimes assume, a dialect of Spanish. Well into the 1980s, Catalan's authority was based on just the kind of ideology of authenticity described above. Catalonians were considered born, not made. Over time, however, this has changed, and the premium on local rootedness and "the mother tongue" has given way to a much more flexible sense of belonging and identity, one in which authenticity can be made, not only given.

Woolard began studying Catalonian identity politics in 1979, right at the start of the post-Franco chapter. It was a brilliant choice of field sites for a linguistic anthropologist. As a language, Catalan has a large and stable base of native speakers; it has also played a central role in the political work of partisans to assert Catalonia's distinctiveness. What is more, because the economy of Catalonia is quite strong relative to other areas of Spain, the language and identity carry a certain prestige value. But native Catalan speakers are not only a minority vis-à-vis the larger context of Spain; within the autonomous community itself, roughly three-quarters of the population have migrated there since 1900. Even today, less than a third of the population speaks Catalan as a first language; 55 percent are native speakers of Castilian.[24]

From the early days of autonomy, Catalonia's new government put in place a number of language policies in order to shore up a clear sense of national identity. Much of this was done through the education system. Schools were increasingly required over the 1980s to offer lessons in Catalan, first as an elective but eventually as the main medium of instruction. By the 2000s most of the curriculum was being delivered in Catalan.

Given the importance of educational policy to what Woolard calls Catalonia's "project identity," it is not surprising that she spent a good deal of her fieldwork in schools. In 1987 Woolard studied a class of teenagers in a high school that was generally perceived to be pro-Catalan in outlook. The school drew in a range of children, so there was a good mix of those who came from Catalan- and Castilian-speaking households. In the latter case, they tended to be the children or grandchildren of working-class migrants. What Woolard found generally confirms what we see in other contexts where the politics of identity is staked out in essentialist terms. The Catalan and Castilian speakers were generally marked as distinct, with the latter coming from working-class families not considered local (even if they had been there for a couple of generations). In her discussions with the teenagers, Woolard heard that Castilian was coarser, rougher, and more unrefined than Catalan. "The people who speak Castilian are people who don't have much culture, let's say," one young man said.[25] While this prompted a spirited debate, it was nevertheless confirmed by the extent to which Castilian speakers expressed a sense of institutional (and peer-group) marginalization. As some of the Castilian speakers also said, when they spoke in Catalan they felt a sense of embarrassment and shame, as if they were faking it and as if they didn't really have the right to do so.

In 2007 Woolard was able to track down several of the people she had first met as students in the 1980s. Among most of those whose first language was Castilian, many of whom had once expressed a sense of being excluded from the nationalists' "project identity," she found some distinctly different attitudes. Now in their mid-thirties, these men and women had almost all come to identify themselves as Catalans and to speak the language with increasing confidence, even a sense of ownership. The hurt of those teenage years had not gone away: the exclusions they had felt were meaningful and real. By and large, however, they put this down to the toss and turn of teenage existence. For them, moreover, the uptake of a Catalan identity was not necessarily tied to larger political projects or statements; indeed, most emphasized that it was personal, and derided strong nationalistic expressions. Their approach to identity had become "a both-and rather than either-or model of being."[26]

When Woolard returned in 2007, she not only tracked down many of her original informants; she also did a repeat study in the same school. She found a very different situation, one in which the rough-and-tumble of coming into your own wasn't gone but wasn't about which language you spoke in your family. The second time around, teenagers did not think of language as constitutive of identity in the same way that they had in 1987; Catalan and Castilian had lost that iconic role. When Woolard asked how they identified each other, none of the young people turned to language as a marker. It was all about style: clothes, music, and other staples of pubescent concern. As a language, in other words, Catalan had become more anonymous, in the terms described earlier—something that anyone could take up. As an identity, it had been opened up to anyone who chose to adopt it, the primary criterion being a commitment to the distinctiveness of the identity itself. "We don't have a problem here," Woolard heard, again and again.[27]

Woolard is mindful of what such heartwarming statements mask; the situation in Catalonia is more complicated than this, and we also hear from local Castilian speakers who feel anything but at ease and accepted, who still feel a sense of marginality. This is to say nothing of more recent waves of arrivals in Catalonia from Africa and beyond. But at both an interpersonal, microlevel and the level of national politics, the shifts are notable. The president of Catalonia from 2006 to 2010 came from a working-class family with roots in Andalusia; his command of Catalan was poor and he was often mocked because of it. Yet he did become president. From 2010, Catalans began protesting for independence from the rest of Spain. In September 2012 over 1.5 million people marched in the streets of Barcelona for the "right to decide" their own future. "Catalunya, nou estat d'Europa," read the banners—in Catalan of course (meaning "Catalonia, new state in Europe"). But at that march, and in much subsequent campaigning, it was not only children of the soil, in classic nationalist fashion, in the front ranks. Native Castilian speakers were right there with them.

## MASHPEE TODAY

The 1976 court case had not been the end of the road for the Mashpee Tribal Council. They persevered and in 2007 were granted federal recognition as a tribe in a ruling by the Bureau of Indian Affairs (BIA). In its Final Decision (FD), the BIA made lengthy reference to the 1970s legal case, arguing that, contrary to the opinion at the time, cultural distinctiveness was not a necessary criterion for recognition as a distinct community. In this respect, the FD offered a blunt assessment of the expert evidence provided in support of the defense: it was both immaterial and unrealistic. It was immaterial because BIA regulations "do not require a petitioner to maintain 'cultural distinctiveness' to be an Indian tribe or community." It was unrealistic because the expectation of what culture is demanded no change whatsoever. On this score the FD is particularly incredulous, noting that one historian's expert view (echoed by the judge and reinforced by the opinion of the jury) "required unchanged culture, including maintenance of traditional religion and essentially total social autonomy from non-Indian society."[28]

In 2001, a prominent legal anthropologist published a paper on culture and rights in which she noted a puzzling situation.[29] On the one hand, it was settled science within academic circles that culture is always changing and fluid. It had also long been recognized by academics, as well as the United Nations, that our understanding of rights is subject to change, modification, and expansion. Since the UDHR in 1948, with its emphasis on the individual person, the international community has gone on to ratify a host of declarations and conventions based on more specific, categorical identities, including children, women, and indigenous communities. On the other hand, despite these various recognitions, within the arenas of rights-based activism and policymaking, culture and rights were often seen as antithetical and as fixed as ever.

I don't know if the authors of the BIA's Final Decision on the Mashpee have read much anthropological culture theory, but any teacher of anthropology would be ecstatic to see such a rebuke of the idea that Indians must have an "unchanged culture" in order to be recognized as a distinct community with group-based rights.

Culture, though, is far from incidental to the Mashpee's sense of community and identity. Since its founding in the 1970s, the Tribal Council has put culture front and center in efforts to gain sovereignty and recognition. In 1993 a language reclamation project was launched. Its founder says: "reclaiming our language is one way of repairing the broken circle of cultural loss and pain. To be able to understand and speak the language means to see the world as our families did for centuries. This is but one path that keeps us connected to our people, the earth, and the philosophies and truths given to us by the creator."[30] In 2009 the Tribal Council established a Language Department to "recognize the role of language as central to the protection of the customs, culture, and spiritual well-being of the people."[31] We might see in all this a language ideology of authenticity. If so, it is combined now with a recognition that that authenticity has to be actively cultivated. It doesn't come from nothing.

CHAPTER 7

# AUTHORITY

When Annette Weiner first arrived in the Trobriand Islands in 1971, following in the footsteps of the late, great Bronislaw Malinowski, she was struck by gaps in his presentation and analysis. All such figures have their critics, and all anthropological accounts are partial—even if, as with Malinowski, the supreme confidence of the voice suggests otherwise. But if we take Malinowski's account as comprehensive—and authoritative—we would be mistaken. As Weiner makes clear, it cuts out important aspects and domains of Trobriand life, including many of those pertaining to women.[1] Reading Malinowski you might think that Trobriand women have nothing to do with the realm of production and exchange, for instance. Emphasis is placed upon the Kula Ring and secondary-level exchanges that take place around it. All of these exchanges are carried out by men.

Indeed, you might think that the Trobriand case simply confirms a common stereotype of sex and gender roles: that men produce and women reproduce; that men are public and women private; that men do "culture" (things like politics and work) and women do "nature" (things like childbearing and cooking). But you would be wrong. With respect to the Trobriand case, Weiner points out several problems with this line of thinking. One is that it doesn't describe the empirical situation. Women do produce: they make cloth from banana leaves and fibers. They also control its circulation. This cloth is extremely valuable because it is crucial to the maintenance of a strong matriline and its political stability. (Trobriand culture is matrilineal.) At the death of a matrilineal relative, women distribute cloth wealth to settle the deceased's social debts, accrued throughout the course of life. Ideally this cloth is new and unused (in contrast to Kula objects, remember, which gain value with age and circulation) because that newness symbolizes the purity of the matriline. While not a form of direct political or economic authority, then, cloth does provide women with important forms of agency and autonomy. In other words, the hierarchy of gender relations is not as cut and dried as it might otherwise be made to seem.

Another point Weiner makes is that Malinowski reproduces the biases of his own upbringing. In a word, his account is androcentric. "For me," Weiner writes, "my first question in the Trobriands was, would Malinowski have ignored Trobriand women's banana leaf wealth if men had produced and exchanged it?"[2] In terms of ethnographic authority, it is vital to pay attention to the fact that "natives" might have more than one point of view. Throughout this book I have referenced Malinowski's famous summation of the anthropological mission: to present "the native's point of view." We can surely appreciate by now that, while not as catchy and crisp, a better summation is *the natives' points of view*. Not just "*his* vision of *his* world," as Malinowski went on to elaborate, with his 1922-style pronouns, but—for a start—hers too.

I have begun this chapter with something of a return to the mechanics of anthropology rather than its findings— something of the manner of its presentation. This is important to do because when it comes to a focus on "authority," anthropology has always been at its best when it considers its own, in addition to how it should be located and understood within the general dynamics of social and cultural life.

Malinowski gives us a wonderful object lesson in this respect. His rhetorical flourishes and confident prose leave little room for doubt as to the authority of his accounts. But oh, the irony. For what we see here is how one form of authority—ethnographic authority—runs the risk of reinforcing a more generally held set of assumptions about authority per se.

## "PROBLEMS WITH WOMEN"

Cloth production in the Trobriands is only the beginning of the story. As Weiner notes, what we find throughout the ethnographic record is that cloth often serves as a key symbol of political authority and power, from the cloaks and mats of tribal chiefs to the robes of royalty, clerical vestments, and sacred shrouds of the dead. And it is women, by and large, who produce it all. The Trobriand case is in fact relatively minor in this respect; in many parts of Polynesia and the wider Pacific, cloth is a dominant symbol of power, prestige, or authority. Weiner even argues that to understand Mauss's argument about the gift—that every gift demands a gift in return because of its "spirit" (or *hau*, in the famous Maori example)—we need to appreciate the political importance of Maori cloaks, which, like Kula valuables, have something of a personality and agency in themselves.[3]

Correcting for partial views aside, though, many of the ethnographic examples we've considered thus far do beg the question of patriarchy's predominance. Yes, Malinowski gave women short shrift in his analysis. But even Weiner notes that the authority and agency women enjoy through the production of cloth are limited compared to those of men. Or consider the complexes of honor and shame; this is often clearly gendered in the sense that men win honor while women lose it. Then there are the Basotho, with their Bovine Mystique; women don't do so well out of that. The mystique around cattle is used by Basotho men to assert their authority within the household and within the community. One might even want to raise the very idea of bride wealth, upon which a good part of the Bovine Mystique rests. Many critics, from Victorian missionaries to contemporary feminist activists, have likened this to treating women as goods to be bought and sold. But what about matrilineal kinship systems? This is undoubtedly a form of authority defined by women. At the same time, if you read accounts of political relations in matrilineal societies, you could be forgiven for thinking that all it really seems to amount to is the recognition of different men being in charge: not women's husbands, that is to say, but rather their brothers. And what about "blood" more generally? We have discussed how blood is a powerful symbol of vitality and life but also how it is associated with female pollution, danger, and death. "Modern" Vathima Brahmin women have reconfigured the extent and scope of menstrual seclusion and taboos, but the practice of seclusion still remains. What is more, many of the women themselves insist upon it.

So, is it the case that cultures are always, in the end, patriarchal systems? Are women the second sex?

The short answer is no. The slightly longer answer is: these are the wrong questions. Neither answer is meant to deny or downplay the many ways in which women's social roles and standing—to say nothing of women themselves—have been overshadowed by those of men. And it is not to gloss over the ugliness of power that often obtains. But inasmuch as the answer is "no," it is to make clear that we cannot naturalize gender relations; we cannot say, in good anthropological conscience, and on the basis of the ethnographic evidence, that the Kula Ring, or the Bovine Mystique, or even the customs and laws of inheritance that shape the drama of *Downton Abbey* are indicative of the fact that men are always already—and in the end—on top.

Inasmuch as the answer is "these are the wrong questions," consider two points. One is the simple matter of perspective, of how the politics of value shape our assessments of authority, prestige, and power. What if we do put cloth production at the center of our accounts? Or child-rearing? Or, for that matter, the role of primary school teachers—most of whom, in most places, are women? If there is a "patriarchal system" out there, or in us, it reflects something similar to what we observed in an earlier chapter, in the encounter between European missionaries and Africans: a colonization of consciousness.

The second point is less straightforward but may be even more important. Because in some instances it is not even a matter of perspective but whether there is, in fact, any fixed thing to perceive. For some anthropologists the mistake comes in assuming that "men" and "women" are the figures on the board and that they are playing the same game—or are locked in the same struggle—as we are.

This argument has been made by a number of anthropologists but finds a seminal expression in the work of Marilyn Strathern. Her book *The Gender of the Gift:*

*Problems with Women and Problems with Society in Melanesia*, published in 1988, crystallized it. The "problems" to which Strathern refers in her subtitle have to do with the assumptions Western analysts—anthropologists, feminists, and feminist anthropologists chief among them—make about gender relations in Melanesia. For Strathern, many Western critiques of gender relations and male domination of women don't go nearly far enough in considering the native's point of view—his *or* hers. In fact it is more as if Strathern wants us to get away from this standpoint metaphor altogether, because it assumes that all of the differences we can catalogue nevertheless rest upon the same ground.

In most of what follows, I want to stick with matters of perspective, although in two of the examples (a study of fatwas in Egypt and of the Chewong hunter-gatherers) we find approaches that resonate with Strathern's. Let's pick up the point on perspective, then, by returning to the practice of bride wealth. For it certainly prompts the matter of authority vis-à-vis a certain "problem with women."

## GENDER AND GENERATION

Bride wealth is the practice of one party (usually a man's parents or kin) giving certain things (usually not just commodities, in the everyday sense, or money but also special things) to another party (usually a woman's parents or kin) on the occasion of a marriage. As I have noted, the term "bride wealth" might strike some contemporary readers as a politically correct euphemism for what is, in fact, the practice of treating women like commodities. Indeed, in an earlier era, it was sometimes referred to as "bride price," which might seem a more honest label. As long ago as 1931, however, the renowned anthropologist E. E. Evans-Pritchard suggested scotching the term "bride price" altogether because it was so misleading.* His suggestion came within the context of a debate carried out over two years in the pages of a major journal, in which several possible terms were suggested—some of them quite odd. Evans-Pritchard argued that "bride wealth" was the best of them, and was glad in any case that "bride price" seemed to have few champions:

> On one point at least there seems to be fairly complete accord among specialists, namely about the undesirability of retaining the expression "bride price." There are very good reasons for cutting the term out of ethnological literature since at best it emphasizes only one of the functions of this wealth, an economic one, to the exclusion of other important social functions; and since, at worst, it encourages the layman to think that "price" used in this context is synonymous with "purchase" in common English parlance. Hence we find people believing that wives are bought and sold in Africa in much the same manner as commodities are bought and sold in European markets. It is difficult to exaggerate the harm done to Africans by this ignorance.[4]

Evans-Pritchard was right. As much later work would go on to underscore, we cannot assume Western understandings of exchange, gender relations, and social personhood are universal. And a very specific understanding of each of these is necessary in order to see bride wealth as an

---

* He actually wasn't renowned at the time; his star rose later. We'll come to some of that stellar work in the next chapter.

unambiguous sign of women's subordination, secondary status, or commodification.

But there is more to say on this topic. Because when it comes to questions of authority, what bride wealth primarily indexes is not a gendered divide but a generational one. A focus on the bride is misleading in several respects, not least the fact that in most cases the bride wealth does not pass to the bride but rather to her parents. Indeed, a good argument could be made that if we want to find a root inequality in human societies, then we ought to be thinking about age, not sex or gender. Elders almost always call the shots. What is more, there are cases in which bride wealth has served as a source of empowerment for women.

Let's consider this by turning to an example of bride wealth in China. For over thirty years, Yunxiang Yan has been studying transformations of social and cultural life in a village in northeastern China. In the broadest terms, these can be characterized by what he calls "the individualization of Chinese society."[5] Many of these changes have taken place since the 1980s, when China started to realign its economy along more market-based lines. That realignment has been increasingly informed by the dynamics of globalization, including the flow of ideas and rhetoric on individualism. As Yan also stresses, since 1949 the Chinese Communist Party (CCP) has implemented policies that contribute to these shifts, often ironically, since the policies were based on socialist principles of communitarianism and mutuality.*

---

* China's longstanding (though now withdrawn) one-child policy can also be seen as part of this picture, although it was a policy that did not affect family dynamics in the kind of rural village Yan studied nearly as much as it did in urban areas. Finnish anthropologist Anni Kajanus (2015) has also re-

One of these policies concerned the abolition of bride wealth. The party banned marriage payments in the 1950s. For the Communists bride wealth was a backward, traditional practice that stood in the way of socialist modernization. The CCP wanted to reorient social bonds away from the extended family and toward a nuclear ideal, in which the state could have a more prominent role. Another factor here has been the strong tradition of "filial piety." Especially important in areas of China where Confucianism is dominant, the ideal of filial piety demands obedience to one's parents. This means not only respecting their wishes and caring for them in old age but making decisions in life (such as whom to marry) that reflect their interests (which is to say, the lineage's interests) and desires. Under a strongly directive state, this value is obviously one that might divide loyalties. For the CCP, indeed, the aim has been to replace (or at least complement) filial piety with what one anthropologist has called "filial nationalism."[6] As we have already noted, it is often the case that political leaders encourage thinking of the nation in terms of kinship.

Bride wealth has not died out in China. When it was outlawed in the 1950s, local people simply came up with new categories of marriage transactions to get around the formal prohibitions. But the CCP's campaigns did have an effect and during the Cultural Revolution forced a crucial shift in the structure of the practice. To relieve the political pressure and scrutiny, in the 1970s families started transferring bride wealth to the bride herself. This shift away from the bride's family and toward the bride

ported how the one-child policy helped fuel significant investment in the education of girls among urban families.

as an individual was reinforced in later decades by the increasing influences of marketization and globalization. By the 1990s, young women in the village Yan studied had a new vocabulary with which to stake their positions, one drawn from the rhetoric of freedom, choice, and rights. They also had four decades' worth of CCP efforts to challenge the legitimacy of the traditional family and once unquestionable logic of filial piety.

Through an odd combination of communist and capitalist principles—equal parts Chairman Mao and Milton Friedman, it seems—bride wealth became a vehicle through which young women could assert and wield real authority. For one thing, young people in general have gained a much greater say in selecting a spouse. The statistics are striking. In the 1950s, 73 percent of marriages in the village Yan studied were arranged; by the 1990s, none were.[7] But even more notable, according to Yan, is this new figure in the equation of the bride. At various points in the 1990s and into the 2000s, Yan observed brides-to-be driving extremely hard bargains with their future in-laws, negotiating and renegotiating the terms of bride wealth—not to mention the directional flow of domestic support. Filial piety has not disappeared, but it is offset by the idea of the "parental heart"—mothers, fathers, and in-laws ceding to the desires and in some cases demands of their children.

The example of one twenty-two-year-old woman sticks out for Yan. She was such a ruthless negotiator with her in-laws that some people in the village thought she was being selfish. She did not care. "Look what has happened since then," she told Yan. "I have a lovely son, two dairy cows, all the modern appliances in my house, and a good husband who listens to me! My parents-in-law respect me and often help me with household chores. I would not be able to have had all this had I not had individuality [*you gexing*]. Girls in our village all admire me."[8]

Is this "selfish"? Well, that is a matter of perspective. For one thing, while we don't hear much from this particular well-behaved husband, the groom is often fully supportive of his bride's hardball tactics, since he benefits as well. These new forms of marriage transfers, then, are in support of couples, not individuals. A different kind of corporate unit—the nuclear family—has moved alongside an older one, that of the patrilineal clan. Moreover, in producing a son, a couple like this is living up to some very "traditional" expectations, chief of which for the husband and father (and his parents) is continuation of the patriline.

Yan himself expresses a sense of loss, and something like regret, at the emergence of this new youth. But in another reading, we hear the case for thinking of such shifts in authority as sincere efforts to live ethically in the face of significant economic and political shifts.[9] It is nevertheless the case that here, once again, efforts to be modern often rely upon the trappings of tradition in seemingly counterintuitive ways.

## FROM THE LIVING TO THE DEAD

It is not only in the realm of marriage customs that we find the lure of the modern approached through the refashioning of personhood. In fact, it is not only in the realm of the living. Even the dead play their part.

Bride wealth was only one of many "backward" customs the CCP worked to stamp out. More broadly, many forms of ritual became targets, partly because they divided loyalties (ritual and religion suggest other, higher forms of authority than the Communist Party) and partly because their emotional charge—variously marked by loud music, dancing, possession, or wailing—frustrated the ideal of the rational, socialist peasant.

Like bride wealth, then, ritual laments came under significant pressure in the first several decades of CCP rule. Throughout many parts of China, as indeed elsewhere, ritual laments are performed during funerals and in periods of mourning. To the outsider, these laments might easily come across as uncontrolled and over-the-top crying and wailing by groups of women (it is often women who perform this particular ritual work). In actual fact, they are carefully calibrated and well-established forms of poetic expression. Lamentations are an excellent means of processing grief, not only for those performing them but for other mourners too. Outside observers sometimes question the sincerity of the tears. Are those women *really* that upset? Not all of them might be, it is true, but this is because the lamenting is only partly about its therapeutic value. Laments are also a means of expressing collective misgivings about the wider social or political situation. They allow people to voice concerns and critiques via the event of a death (which is another reason the CCP has not always been very keen on them). Even more than such this-worldly concerns, though, laments are part of a larger ritual complex showing respect to the ancestors and acknowledging the cosmic order of things. In all these ways, they make a death "good."

The desire to make deaths good is very commonly found and is hardly unique to peasants who embarrass Communist Party officials. This is why the U.S. government, for example, has spent so much money to recover the remains of military personnel killed in action in Vietnam; the state, as much as the families, want the remains because within the American cultural system (as indeed in most cultural systems) proper handling of remains is considered essential for coming to terms with the loss and laying the person to rest. (In the case of the government, it also indexes state power and authority.) Similarly in tragic cases of the disappeared in Chile or the abduction and murder of a child in a suburb of London, or Bath, or, for that matter, Bangkok, what the families always want, above all, are the remains of their dead: without them, the process of making that death good is always incomplete, always haunted by ghosts.

Coming back to ritual laments in China, what we see is that, traditionally, they were about much more than the person who had died. Indeed, in key respects, the individuality of that person was minimized in the process of lamentation itself. This is certainly what Erik Mueggler found during fieldwork in the early 1990s in a rural mountain valley in Yunnan Province.* As throughout the country, by the 1990s people in Yunnan were able to openly revisit and revive certain aspects of traditional culture. Many of the locals were bringing back the long-derided traditions of lamentation at funerals, and they were intent on maintaining the old ways of doing so as closely as possible. Authenticity and faithfulness were what mattered, and this meant that the laments greatly downplayed

---

*Yunnan is a long way from where Yan studied the changes in bridewealth practices; in fact Mueggler works not with Han Chinese but an ethnic minority group called the Yi, who speak a Tibeto-Burman language. Even the designation "Yi" is open to question because it is a label that the Chinese state applied to a broad range of peoples, not all of whom identify with one another.

the person as an individual. In his analysis of the laments, what Mueggler found was a rich array of metaphors and imageries that emphasized social and familial roles.[10] The formality of this oral poetry does not sit well with bespoke recollections. What matters are "conventional assemblages of social relations."[11]

When Mueggler returned to Yunnan in 2011 he found a very different situation. Laments were still popular and valued, but their purpose and focus had been radically altered. Similar to what Yan found at the opposite end of the country, in the southwest Mueggler speaks of the ways in which desires to be modern, shaped by state-level economic reforms and the dynamics of globalization, pushed individuality to the fore. Now, laments are very much about the person, about Yi efforts to index their modernity by focusing on the character of the deceased, on specific memories and life-shaping events. The art of lamentation has changed too. The most powerful performances are not judged in terms of technical skill but, rather, heartfelt emotion. In the twenty-first century, it is sincerity, not formal competence, that makes these rituals efficacious.

## RITUAL AND AUTHORITY/AUTHORITY IN RITUAL

This is a good place to stop and consider some of the basics of ritual. Anthropologists love studying ritual because they tend to think it contains a map of whatever larger territory they're exploring. Crack the ritual and you crack the culture. Not all anthropologists think this way, it is true, but many do. I want to bracket this aspect of ritual studies, though, and focus more on what they can tell us about the workings of authority.[12]

Ritual often entails spectacle or performance. Some rituals are more colorful, more fragrant, and noisier than others, but they are all marked in some way that sets them apart from the ordinary course of life. This theatrical quality is something that many anthropologists have commented upon, in no small part because it raises the question of authority. In ritual, who—or what—calls the shots? And toward what end?

There is no consensus on how to answer these questions. Broadly speaking, anthropologists fall somewhere along a spectrum. At one end is the argument that ritual is all about authority: a tool of tradition, a device used by the powers that be to keep the people in line. At the other end of the spectrum is the argument that ritual enables agency—that it is a vehicle of human creativity and critique, the means by which real change can be affected, real opinions voiced.

What most anthropologists do agree on is the character of ritual itself: its set-apartness. You tend to know a ritual when you see one. The people are doing un-ordinary things, like dancing or wailing. Or doing ordinary things in un-ordinary ways, like speaking in a singsong voice or moving about on their elbows and knees. Ritual is also often marked by what people are wearing (or not wearing at all): special outfits, heavy makeup and paint, expensive and often impractical headgear, masks, or jewelry.

In terms of cultural communication, what these aspects of the ritual character convey is a metalevel message: "what's going on here *tells* us something important about the Order of Things." In other words, if you want to understand "the meaning" of a ritual, don't limit yourself to what people say or do; think also of how they say and do it.

It's not difficult to appreciate the argument that ritual is all about authority, about putting people in their place. When you participate in a ritual, you can often feel the weight of tradition bearing down upon you, the facts of your individual existence—thoughts, feelings, and opinions—muffled by the collective demands of it all. Of course for many people it is precisely this feeling that is valuable, a feeling of being part of something larger, perhaps even larger-than-life. But if you have ever (1) been at an Anglican church service, or (2) found yourself singing the national anthem at a sporting event, and you're (1) not a Christian, or (2) not a nationalist or patriot, you might well have been saying to yourself: *hold on*, (1) this isn't me, and yet here I am, singing praise to God and "Amen, Lord have mercy upon us," or *wait*, (2) I'm not sure about this "God save the Queen" refrain or this line about "the land of the free and home of the brave."

One way ritual exerts such authority, then—one way in which it *disciplines* its participants—is precisely by using a set script: formal prayers, a liturgy, a national anthem, and so forth. Maurice Bloch, one of the most prominent ritual theorists in this tradition, puts this in a memorable way: "You cannot argue with a song."[13]

The set script, though, as well as set routines of action—kneeling before an altar, making the gesture of Namaskara or Namaste (a Hindu greeting offered to one's superordinate), throwing rice at the bride and groom as they come out of the church—serves another important function. It places the authority of the action itself beyond the person performing it. In a ritual, you're not supposed to be making things up as you go along. When anthropologists ask ritual participants *why* they are doing something—Why do you cross yourself three times? Why

is the shaman's face painted white? Why are the boys
secluded for three days?—the answer is often something
along the lines of "Because that is how it is done." Or,
more flatly, "I don't know." Or, "Oh, you have to ask the
shaman." It is the kind of question that anthropologists
seem compelled to ask, even though the answer is almost useless—except inasmuch as it confirms that what's
taking place is a ritual, whose "authors" have been lost
in the mists of authority. Bloch refers to this as ritual
"deference."[14]

Consider the Anglican Church service. Take a look at
the liturgy. It doesn't include a byline. Who wrote it? Who
is the authority? It's not the priest. The priest standing in
front of the congregation is just a person. A well-trained
person, yes—ordained and maybe even pious. But you
don't look at him or her and take what he or she is saying
as *his or her* words. If it were a matter of the priest saying, "Well, in my opinion, the Lord is the God Almighty,"
the congregation would empty out. The authority of the
words is put beyond any individual person, giving it a
timeless or transcendent quality. The more a ritual can
rely on being timeless, or expressing something beyond
the here and now, the more authoritative it becomes.

Repetition can also serve this function. It is not so
much that the more you say something, the more likely it
is to come true (although we do often hold that view). It
is that repetition creates a gap between what is said and
who says it. In an important sense, it makes the words
"object-like" and thus free of individual human intentions
and opinions. The same point can hold for ritual actions.
Rituals often involve series of repetitive acts. In some
cases the success of the ritual is seen as dependent on the
proper execution of these acts—not necessarily whether

one performs them sincerely or even with belief. One effect of such repetition is to deemphasize the agency of the person or persons performing them and suggest, or even aim to reproduce, a larger cosmic order or hierarchy.

There is a strong link between authority and stability. The point of many rituals is to maintain the status quo—again, often by reproducing that status quo through a series of ordered, repetitive sequences pregnant with symbolism. This is often the point of funerals and mortuary rites, for instance. A death is a disruption to the community, a tear in its fabric. The funeral is part of the act of mending that tear, not only in terms of its therapeutic value but also as a symbolic means of showing how life conquers death. The imagery in funerals is often about the regeneration of life: signs of rebirth, regrowth, and regeneration.[15] Food, alcohol, and reproduction are staples in this imagery. Moreover, because funerals and mortuary rites often follow a common format, their individual enactments serve the added function of suggesting stability to the social order. The same thing, performed again and again, conveys continuity.

A funeral is also a specific kind of ritual that has been of great interest to anthropologists: the rite of passage. Circumcision rituals, weddings, and funerals are all rites of passage. They bring about a transformation in the status of persons: child into adult; unmarried into married; living into dead. So rituals are not only used to maintain the status quo or assert the continuity of a social order, they are also crucial to the act of changing the social position or even makeup of individuals or groups of people.

Within some types of ritual (including many rites of passage), authority is also on display through a particular use of language. In ritual, words can have the power to do what they say. Think about some of the commonly known examples: "I now pronounce you husband and wife." "I hereby sentence you to life in prison." In a more diffuse (and debated) sense, we could also include the repetitive utterance of mantras by Buddhists aiming for enlightenment. These are examples of speech acts that have what the philosopher John Austin called "illocutionary force."[16] Austin's idea has been popular within anthropology, in no small part because it helps account for the seemingly "magical" ability of words to do things, of speech to be a kind of action.*

This magic is often central to the workings of modern state power. Politics relies upon ritual as much as the most spectacular, exotic religious tradition we might be able to dream up. And we can see this best when those ritual workings go wrong. Take the first presidential inauguration of Barack Obama. The stakes of illocutionary force were brought to the fore during his swearing-in ceremony in January 2009. To go from being president-elect to president, Obama had to swear an oath, administered by the Chief Justice of the Supreme Court. During this ritual act, the Chief Justice read out the words of the oath in a slightly wrong order; this caused Obama to stumble in his repetition of them. Some of Obama's advisors worried that this meant he wasn't really president; they were certainly concerned that his political opponents might suggest as much. And so, for the avoidance of doubt, and what the White House Counsel called "an

---

* Illocutionary force is not unique to ritual language; it is also found in a number of more everyday interactions and exchanges. It is especially common in rituals, though, because they are often performed in order to "do" something (marry people, bury people, cleanse sins, restore divine power to images of Shiva, cure a young woman's stomach pains, and so on).

abundance of caution, because there was one word out of sequence," the oath was administered a second time, the day after the inauguration. Fidelity to the script really matters; everything in its right place.[17]

Did Obama *really* have to take the oath again? There is no "really" here, other than in its perception. Austin called this "the securing of uptake."[18] In other words, the authority of an illocutionary speech act depends on the extent to which it is socially recognized.

As a particular kind of context and event, ritual helps legitimize that authority. The second time the Chief Justice administered the oath it was without all the pomp and circumstance of the formal inauguration—all the things that say "this is an important event." No hundreds of thousands of spectators, no past presidents and dignitaries onstage, no Aretha Franklin singing, and no Yo-Yo Ma on his cello. The second time the Chief Justice simply slipped into the White House, shortly after 7 p.m., summoned at short notice, for a quick in-and-out retake. No pomp, no circumstance. Obama didn't even put his hand on the Bible. Only one thing was extraordinary. The Chief Justice *did* put on his robes. He still felt the need to communicate, via those black gowns, that he had the power and authority to perform and that this was a set-apart moment demanding special focus and having special force.

The black robes of American judges are also instructive here. For they, too, require a kind of "uptake." Why do they matter? Because we assume they do. "Because that's what judges wear," we say. Again, this is what Bloch would call ritual deference: timeless traditions, and all of that. In fact, there is no requirement in the U.S. court systems to wear such robes. Where did they come from? No one seems to know for sure, but one story is that

Thomas Jefferson suggested simple black robes in order to distinguish them from the rather more elaborate robes of the judiciary in England.[19] This in itself can be taken as a comment on different understandings of and attitudes toward authority. In imperial England, we find an exaggeration of difference and rank; this underpins the logic of hierarchy that has long been central to English (and British) society and politics. In the new United States, we find recognition of the value of difference, but it is minimized according to the principle of equality. Only simple black robes and the same look for all judges.

## ARGUING WITH A SONG

So yes, it is true that rituals can have a number of disciplining effects, that they shape our actions, reactions, and understanding in and of the larger course of life. But all the same, we also know that such formalized, prescribed, and marked behavior—ritual—is often a source of creativity too. Of things made new.

We have already considered an example of this. Try as it might, the Chinese Communist Party's decades-long suppression of traditional funerals in Yunnan Province could not extinguish the people's desire for a particular kind of good death. Like most communities, the Yi understood such rituals as central to the proper functioning of their social life. The traditions were suppressed, but not forgotten, and when a space opened up to perform them again, it was taken. And to start with, that meant fidelity to the form—doing it just the way it should be.

We might take this fidelity as evidence of the power that ritual has over us—that, in other words, it robs us of agency, choice, and deliberation. And yet we also know that twenty years later "the same" rituals were anything but. In the 1990s, laments reflected the general order of things: relations between children and parents were set out in well-established yet generic semantic couplets; the forms of suffering that each bore for the other reflected an endless cycle of generations. The Yi did not lament a particular mother, they lamented with respect to motherhood itself. While they relied on many of the same formal structures and patterns, by 2011 these laments had been slowly transformed through the incorporation of new imageries to better reflect local revaluations of individuality, biography, and the sincerity of personal grief. In 2011, Mueggler heard not of daughters and mothers in the abstract but of the pain that had wracked particular mothers on their deathbeds ("my feet hurt up to my head"), the grief of particular daughters ("I speak my suffering to the mountains / the wind in the mountain pines replies"), and even political commentary on the day ("now government policies have improved / not in time to give mother good food / not in time to give mother clothing").[20]

Paradoxically, it is sometimes in the moments of seemingly greatest constraint that we find people exercising the faculties of critique and levers of innovation. You *can* argue with a song. Or, at least, *through* one.


## AUTHORIZING AUTHORITY

A focus on the formality and structuring of ritual can tell us a lot about the mechanics of authority in general, even if the provenance of that authority seems to shift between different planes. In some cases the authority of a ritual is like something transcendent—it comes down to the just-because character of the words and actions, the seemingly timeless and comforting-yet-controlling feel of it all. In other cases, it is quite mundane—like the lamentations of a particular woman in the Júzò valley, a daughter unusually close to her mother and angry enough with the government to throw caution to the wind and criticize the slow pace of economic development. But even this example of something mundane is only made possible by other factors: the impacts of globalization and cultivation of desires within a community to mourn sincerely in "modern" terms.

There is no set formula or surefire way of knowing why some rituals—or institutions, or religious traditions, or political leaders, or peasant women—get taken up. It is not down to the mechanics alone. And it is not simply a question of "power," be that from behind the barrel of a gun, with the threat of jail, or even, say, the power of control over pension payments. These are all forms of authority that strong states possess. But we know that such power is not always effective. Not even the Chinese Communist Party has been able to have everything its own way, and it heads a very powerful state indeed. Authority is never only a question of force or power, baldly conceived. The persistence and even flourishing of bride wealth and funeral lamentations in China are evidence of that.

To understand authority, then, we also need to understand the nature of its legitimacy. We need to understand why people accept certain forms of authority and not others. How is authority *authorized*?

To consider this question, let's turn to an anthropological study in Egypt by Hussein Ali Agrama, which explores people's very different attitudes toward two important institutions: personal status courts and the Fatwa Council.[21] Personal status courts address family issues, including those pertaining to marriage, divorce, maintenance (alimony), and inheritance. The Fatwa Council addresses similar issues, although it can be consulted on a range of other matters as well.

In addition to the issues they address, the courts and council are similar in that both are state bodies. And, perhaps most important, both are governed by Islamic sharia. In the media, this is often referred to as "sharia law," but it would be a mistake to limit the idea of sharia to law in the Western sense. While it does pertain to certain rules and normative expectations, at root it concerns the ethical question about what kind of person to be. Sharia is the "path" upon which the pious Muslim must embark.

The courts and the council do differ, though. Take their legal standing. Sharia is not reducible to the concept of "law," but the personal status courts are governed by sharia via the law. Their judgments and rulings are legally recognized. Those of the Fatwa Council are not. In other words, the courts are part of the formal legal system, judgments in which are binding, while the Fatwa Council is merely advisory. Fatwas are not legally binding and indeed are not generally put forward as such by the sheikhs who offer them.

There is a lot of misunderstanding about fatwas in the West. Since 1989, when the Ayatollah Khomeini issued a fatwa calling for the death of Salman Rushdie, the term has evoked the image of an angry cleric making very public pronouncements in favor of an illiberal, "political Islam" (as many would now put it). This image has only grown more vivid since 9/11.

Most fatwas are nothing like this. Simply put, they are the opinion or advice of a learned figure (sheikh), often but not always a trained Islamic scholar (mufti). Most fatwas are sought by individuals when they feel they need advice on how to live as a good Muslim and in accordance with sharia. In other words, fatwas are most often very private and very particular to the life and situation of the person in question. The mandate of the Fatwa Council in Egypt is in fact to assist ordinary people with their everyday affairs (not to denounce novelists).

Agrama spent two years in Cairo studying personal status courts and the Fatwa Council in the early 2000s. During this time he noted a seemingly curious pattern. While both institutions allowed people to address a range of family matters, the council was much more popular, and positively viewed, than the courts. What is more, while the opinions and advice offered in fatwas are not binding, people tended to follow that advice much more than they did the formal, legally enforceable rulings of the courts. This was the case even when the fatwas went against the interests or desires of those seeking them. Generally speaking, if someone doesn't like the advice contained in a fatwa provided by the sheikh, there is nothing to prevent them from consulting another sheikh. But in Agrama's experience this rarely happened. In one case a family followed the fatwa of a sheikh even though it cost them dearly in a bitter dispute with extended relatives over the inheritance of some land.

One of the more notable aspects of Agrama's findings is just how flexible the sheikhs are in their application of sharia. Sheikhs listen, but they also ask questions. They try to get as much of a sense of the broader situation as possible. They also try to take the measure of a person. Is *this* fatwa-seeker level-headed? Is *that* fatwa-seeker genuinely remorseful? As a result, it may well be that two people with the same issue are given totally different advice. In one case, a couple that seeks to reconcile after a divorce may be told they cannot; in another, they might be told that they can. It depends on the situation and on the demeanor of the couple (or the man, or the woman). The same sheikh might himself take different attitudes and approaches; in some cases he might be stern, in others joking, in others scolding. It all depends.

Flexibility is also evident in some of the advice given. When it comes to the messiness of morals and life, sometimes sheikhs would take a lesser-of-two-evils approach. In one case that Agrama observed, a young man who had committed adultery with the same woman twice was told that when he was tempted to do so in the future, he should "do the secret thing" (i.e., masturbate) instead. The young man was surprised, since masturbation is *makruh* (reprehensible); yes, said the sheikh, but adultery is *haram* (forbidden) and that is worse.[22] This kind of advice is all the more notable because it is widely understood that sheikhs bear some of the responsibility for the suggestions they make. The fatwa initiates a kind of relationship, one that ties the sheikh and the fatwa-seeker together in some way.

Agrama's anthropology of the fatwa speaks to much more general issues and dynamics within the anthropological record that are relevant well beyond concerns with religious piety. Whenever we consider matters of authority, we are also very likely considering matters of ethical concern. Fatwas are obviously about ethics. They help Muslims address the question of how to live. And the Fatwa Council in Egypt gets its authority because of the extent to which it facilitates a "journey of ethical cultivation."[23] The personal status courts do not serve that function.

Thinking of authority with respect to ethics can help us understand why people act the way they do, why they align themselves with particular institutions and not others, and why certain values come to be seen as cardinal or paramount. I want to come back to ethics as a topic in its own right in chapter 9; it has become a major area of anthropological interest in recent years. In the final section of this chapter, though, I'd like to explore the points just discussed by turning to one of the near mythical cases in the anthropological record when it comes to the question of authority, the test-limit case of egalitarian societies, in which the only authority is often none at all.

## STATE AND STATELESS

Lewis Henry Morgan wasn't drawn to a study of Iroquois kinship only out of his interest in consanguinity and affinity; he was also fascinated by how political authority worked in a matrilineal system. Who is in charge, and on what grounds? For the social evolutionists these were crucial questions in the calculation of a culture's stage of development. Long after social evolutionism lost its hold, these questions have continued to interest anthropologists. Whatever else they may be—the anthropology of kinship, the anthropology of religion—the studies we've considered on China and Egypt are also contributions to the anthropology of politics, and even more specifically the anthropology of the state.

The state has always played a central role in how anthropologists approach understandings of political organization and authority. For a long time—up until the 1970s, really—the state was in fact a central point of reference. Until that time, when it came to political organization, anthropologists often broke societies down into one of two varieties: "state" or "stateless." There could be different categories along that scale. Reading through the literature, you will come across references to "primitive states," "modern states," "complex states," and so on. Statelessness has its own diversity. In one of the classic studies, which focused on African political systems, the editors distinguished between (1) societies in which political authority is based on kinship relations, in particular lineages, and (2) those in which "political relations are coterminous with kinship relations and the kinship structure and political organization are completely fused."[24] The idea of fusion would be avoided by most anthropologists these days, since it suggests there is a thing called "politics" and a thing called "kinship" that can be welded together. We know from our discussions of blood that kinship and politics are not such "things."

Fused together or not, the second condition of being "stateless" is the more thought-provoking when it comes to questions of authority and the workings of power; it is in such cultures that we find the closest thing to egalitarianism within the human family. There are some small-scale, hunting and gathering societies in which authority and discrimination are not easy to locate.

The Chewong are a small aboriginal group on the Malay Peninsula, one of several such groups known in Malaysia as Orang Asli, or "Original People." Over two periods of fieldwork in the late 1970s and early 1980s, Norwegian anthropologist Signe Howell spent twenty months living among them as they pursued their livelihoods in the tropical rain forests.[25]

The Chewong are—or at least were, until the mid-1980s—the kind of society that sparks a tinge of wonder in even the most postmodern, not-Victorian anthropologist.* Until Howell's fieldwork, no outsider had ever lived among them and as a people they had had little contact with the wider world, with the exception of a British park warden stationed in the area in the 1930s. Almost nothing in the anthropological tool kit proved of use for Howell—a situation that is not unheard of when the focus is on such a remote people.

Does Howell's account give us a glimpse into our own past? No. Is it a glimpse into human nature, unadorned and unadulterated? No. But it does help us appreciate the possibility for what anthropologists sometimes call "radical alterity." The Chewong way of life is like a different way of being, one in which hierarchy, status, and authority are all but absent. Social relations are egalitarian and autonomy highly valued.[26] Like the Ese Ejja, with their reluctance to win at football, the Chewong actively avoid competition and if someone is better at a particular task—due to physical strength, dexterity, or what have you—this is never commented upon or highlighted. Children do not play competitive games. When it comes to sex and gender roles, there are some acknowledged differences, but these do not get hierarchically ordered. Moreover, Chewong mythology and cosmology stress equality between the sexes; in their creation myth, both sexes are created at the same time and in the same manner, both the man and woman participate in childrearing, and the father is taught by the mother how to breastfeed the child. In everyday life, this sense of equality and equal

---

* The Chewong were settled in villages by the Malaysian government in the mid-1980s. Such state-backed programs have been common in many countries, including Botswana and Namibia, where San peoples (Naro, Jul'hoan, and others) live. These settlements and relocations have often been forced upon them and resisted fiercely.

participation in nurturing the child is borne out as a two-stage process. In effect, men and women take turns. The man nurtures the child during pregnancy by having sexual intercourse with his wife right up until the birth. Each act of intercourse provides the fetus with semen, which is lexically equivalent to milk, and which is believed to be essential for the development of the baby. Then, after birth, the woman takes over, providing her milk from the breast. During a pregnancy men and women observe the same food taboos.[27]

For the Chewong, as indeed for some other hunting and gathering societies, hierarchy and authority are not so much anathema as imponderable.[*] Their traditional way of life can help us appreciate the kind of argument put forward by Marilyn Strathern, outlined earlier: that there are limits to what our own categories—and ethical projects—can provide for in our understanding of others. Questions of authority don't really come up among the Chewong. Nor, it seems, do the "problems with women," as Strathern might put it. If Strathern tried to balance Western feminist critiques of women's subordination with the "distinctive nature" of what Melanesians understood themselves to be up to, in Howell's study such a balancing act would seem unnecessary altogether.

---

[*] Sometimes it is anathema and not imponderable. For the Hadza, in Tanzania, another hunting and gathering society, minor forms of authority do exist—in the form of nominal group "leaders," for instance. Yet the authority of such leaders is checked by a number of factors, including the fluidity of group membership and lack of property rights. No one is bound to belong, and no one can accumulate prestige or power. The Hadza and a handful of other African examples of egalitarian societies are the subject of a seminal essay by James Woodburn (1982).

## CHAPTER 8

# REASON

We've heard a lot about the native's point of view. This is definitely the most common summary of what anthropology is after. But there's another one too, and it also has a long tradition: how natives think. Not the eyes, then, but the mind. Not how people see, but how they reason.

It isn't either/or. In fact, all of the founding figures in anthropology were concerned with reason in one way or another. For Bronislaw Malinowski the emphasis on thought and the mind was probably the most important thing, at the end of the day. To have a point of view in his reckoning is to have an opinion; it is to have a thought, to "see" something in a particular way. The same goes for Franz Boas with his *Kulturbrille*, or cultural glasses. Yes, perception mattered for his understanding of culture, but the mind and mental capacities were complementary concerns. His book *The Mind of Primitive Man*, published in 1911, makes this clear in no uncertain terms; of all his works, moreover, this is one of the most accessible, emphasizing what he felt was important for the general public to know. This commitment to thought also underpins what comes closest to an anthropological doctrine: the psychic unity of humankind. Anthropologists have never seen much point in separating out culture and the senses from the mind. We are in the world and the world is in us.

It's time we tackled the matters of thought and cognition, and I want to do so by braiding together some different strands of anthropological work, all of which address the matter of "how natives think" and all of which raise some of the more philosophical and head-scratching questions anthropologists have posed. When it comes to reason, what we often find is anthropological dalliances with an even more daunting r-word: reality. Let's introduce reality by considering first how it is bound up with language and thought.

Picture two petrol drums: one is marked "empty," the other is not. Which is more dangerous?

Back in the 1930s, a fire safety inspector in Connecticut found that people who worked around petrol drums in factories and depots would often assume the full drums were more dangerous and would accordingly be extra careful around them. They'd stop smoking, handle them gently, and so on. In reality, though, an empty drum is much more dangerous because, while empty of petrol itself, it is likely to retain vapors that are highly flammable and explosive. Smoke around an "empty" drum, and you're likely to go out with a bang. The problem, the inspector concluded, was with the labeling of the drums. By marking them as "empty," he argued, workers simply extended their sense of what this word often means to judge the risk level at hand. "Empty" in this context means "nothing; nil," just as we would think an empty gun and an empty threat pose no danger. But here language fails us because language gets it wrong; it provides a false sense of security. As the inspector writes, "We always assume that the linguistic analysis made by our group reflects reality better than it does."[1]

The inspector in question was named Benjamin Lee Whorf, and in addition to being very good at his job for the Hartford Fire Insurance Company, he was also an accomplished linguist and amateur anthropologist. In his work in anthropological linguistics, Whorf—probably more than any other figure in the discipline—has driven home the point that language, thought, and reality are closely interwoven. Language is not a clear window onto the world and thought is not a process that takes place independent of that world. And isn't this kind of like saying *we are in the world and the world is in us?*

## REASON AND LANGUAGE

When he wasn't traveling throughout Connecticut in the service of fire safety, Whorf was poring over texts on the grammar and lexicon of Hopi, Mayan hieroglyphics, and ancient Aztec. He was a brilliant and largely self-taught linguist, although he did come under the wing of Boas's student Edward Sapir, who was a pioneer in his own right. Whorf lectured for a year at Yale University, where Sapir held a professorship.

In his most famous essay, "The Relation of Habitual Thought and Behavior to Language," published in 1939, Whorf argued that the structure of the language we speak shapes the ways in which we perceive and act within the world. He makes this point simply with a set of examples like the one above, drawn from his work in the insurance industry. But Whorf's conclusions were much more far-reaching than what we get in individual examples of human error brought about by the mismatch between linguistic signs ("empty drum") and objective states (empty drum = drum full of highly flammable fumes). Taken by itself this might just tell us something about the language ideology of Americans; they place (too much?) trust in the written word. What Whorf meant to suggest is that language shapes our very experience of reality, our understandings of space and time.

To make his case, Whorf compared articulations of space and time in Hopi with those in what he called Standard Average European (SAE) languages. His point here was that in order to understand how language shapes behavior and experiences of reality, we need to juxtapose languages from distinct families (in this case Uto-Aztecan and Indo-European, respectively). It won't do to dwell on some of the interesting but nevertheless minor differences between English and German. When we compare languages at this level of remove, we can see just how significant spatial and physical metaphors are within SAE. And we can see this so clearly because they are almost entirely absent in Hopi.

SAE objectifies nearly everything. In English, we treat chairs and days in the same way. You can have ten of each. "I have ten chairs." "I have ten days to paint the house." But "ten days" is clearly quite different from "ten chairs" because a day is a length of time that is measured as such—as a thing. But it is not a thing like a chair. The Hopi seem to recognize this better than SAE speakers. In Hopi, there is no equivalent when it comes to days. You cannot say "ten days" in Hopi but have to express numeration in terms of a relation. You express "ten" in ordinal form, which puts it into such a relation. So whereas in English you would say, "They stayed ten days," in Hopi you would say, "They left after the tenth day."

Another example Whorf gives of this patterning is about the phases of temporal cycles. Take summer, which in SAE is a season marked by a start date and an end date according to the astronomical calendar (in 2016, this was June 20 to September 22 in the Northern Hemisphere). In Hopi, "summer" is the *experience* of heat; only warm days are summer, so if the warmest days happen to be May 23 and September 29—according to the Gregorian calendar—they are summer, which means what Whorf glosses as "when heat occurs." Moreover, in Hopi you would not use a determiner to mark summer, you would use an adverb. So you don't say "this summer"; you say "summer now."

SAE, then, is a language structure that predisposes its speakers to objectify subjective experiences, such as those of time. In Hopi, there is no such predisposition. The connection between time, events, and persons is more relational and subjective.

None of this is to say the revolution of the earth on its axis, indexed by the rising and setting of the sun, is irrelevant to what we understand a day to be. Nor is this to say the Hopi don't realize each day brings a new dawn.* But in each language structure there is a way of apprehending reality that affects behavior and the patterns of thought.

One minor example that Whorf gives in his book concerns the use of gesture. Speakers of SAE often use hand gestures and their bodies, especially when they are

---

* This is a very important point. We know that within any given culture, people can operate with more than one comprehension of time or experience of temporality (Munn 1992). Moreover, the basic sense of temporal linearity and causality is a general feature of cognition (Bloch 2012). Anthropologists have yet to discover a culture in which people eat boiled eggs and *then* boil them.

speaking about more abstract topics, such as justice or love. This is because of the heavy emphasis on objectification, as if the gestures help concretize the ideas. The Hopi use very few gestures.

In a more recent study, we see how categorizations of space can shape awareness of the immediate environment.[2] Among the Kuuk Thaayorre, an aboriginal community in Australia, space is defined in cardinal terms; relative terms are not used. For the native English speaker, relative terms are very common. A person is likely to distinguish two trees from one another by saying something like "the tree on the left" or "the tree on the right." This assumes a certain subject position, of course—but then again, native English speakers often assume that their own subject position is the one that matters! So in technical terms, this is a relative spatial distinction (which smuggles in an ideology of the absolute individual). It is perfectly possible for the same English speaker to say "the eastern tree" and "the western tree" in accordance with cardinal terms. But you're only likely to get such precision by technical experts of one kind or another: tree surgeons, perhaps, or an army scout giving directions through the forest. Among the Kuuk Thaayorre, however, linguistic distinctions are always cardinal, even when it comes to the most trivial and specific matters. So you wouldn't say, "you smeared some paint on your left cheek"; you'd say, "you smeared some paint on your west cheek." In terms of sensibility and behavior, what this means is that the Kuuk Thaayorre are much more attentive to where they are at all times; they are excellent navigators and orienteers.

In Whorf's original work, an even more significant and potentially far-reaching example concerns what he refers to as the Hopi penchant for "preparatory behavior." This is partly the result of their attitudes to time, as reflected in language. The Hopi, he tells us, make elaborate preparations before undertaking significant activities, such as sowing crops. This can involve a range of things, from private prayers and meditation, reflecting on the activity itself, to public announcements (delivered by a special figure called "the crier chief") and various forms of practice, which might include symbolically sympathetic actions such as running and other forms of intensive exercise (to make the crops "strong" and "robust"). Such actions are, moreover, thought to influence the event. Being well prepared for a major journey or the sowing of crops is thought to increase the likelihood of their success. For the Hopi, thought is a kind of force in the world and "leaves everywhere traces of effect."[3]

Although there was no direct link between their projects, it's not difficult to see that what Whorf is describing in Hopi language and culture can be related to Marcel Mauss's understanding of exchange in what he calls "archaic societies." Recall how, in cultures of the Kula Ring, or among the Maori, many objects are thought to have agency and personality—in essence, "to leave everywhere traces of effect," as Whorf might have put it. Gifts are reciprocated because they contain something of the spirit of the giver (Maori: *hau*), which demands a return. These are understandings of the world in which the boundaries between the animate and inanimate, the personal and impersonal, and spiritual and material are much more porous than in a modern, Western framework. Indeed, one could argue that the structure of SAE languages plays an important role in the Western ideology of exchange. It is part of what makes everything thing-like in the first place, as opposed to person-like. It is another aspect of the Western penchant for objectification.

Does this help explain why capitalism developed in the West? Is there something about the structuring of SAE that helped support the development of an economic system in which the value of things could increasingly easily be objectified and quantified—everything from the labor of our hands to the sands of time? Even love? Whorf does not reach such sweeping conclusions. Nor does he suggest that language is the *only* factor in shaping patterns of thought and behavior.[4] This is something that his critics often seem to misunderstand. But language *is* a factor, and Whorf does feel confident enough to offer a thought-provoking reflection on developments in Western culture since the Middle Ages, developments in which language, economics, and science have to be seen as mutually constitutive. "The need for measurement in industry and trade," he writes, "[the] standardizing of measure and weight units, invention of clocks and measure of 'time', keeping of records, accounts, chronicles, histories, growth of mathematics and the partnership of mathematics and science, all cooperated to bring our thought and language world into its present form."[5]

If we want to understand how people reason, it can be useful—very useful—to consider the principle of linguistic relativity. As we already know, any time the word "relativity" enters the mix, its detractors cry foul over the lack of baselines or concerns that it means anything goes. Just as I've argued with respect to moral and ethical issues, however, when it comes to language it's important to recognize that the principle here does not mean we can have no baselines. The starting point for Whorf is reality. This is not even "reality" with scare quotes—he's perfectly happy with the really real. Whorf knew all about reality; after all, he was an insurance man. If a petrol drum has fumes in it, it might well blow up. It doesn't matter if that petrol drum is in a pueblo or on the shop floor of a New England factory. Clearly, though, how we encode such things as danger and risk in language can have significant consequences.

## "WE ARE PARROTS"

Another aspect of the interest in language, thought, and reality has to do with questions of meaning and comprehension. This gets us to a perennial anthropological interest: the seemingly odd and outlandish things people sometimes say. Anthropologists have always been interested in sound bite–worthy claims, some of the classics being "we are parrots" (the Bororo of Brazil) and "twins are birds" (the Nuer of the Nile Valley); in some contexts, the Nuer will also speak of a cucumber as an ox. These classic cases have their contemporary equivalents; among the Makonde in Mozambique, for instance, there is talk of lion-persons, while among the Araweté of Amazonia, jaguars are people too (so are many other animal species, although not all). Nearly all of these cases raise controversial questions and sometimes even heated and politically charged exchanges: one of the most well-known, in 1779, was whether or not the Hawaiians, when they killed Captain James Cook, thought he was an incarnation of their god, Lono. More generally still, there is much anthropological interest in certain idioms of reasoning and ways of speaking—not necessarily attention-catching statements such as "we are parrots" but, rather, more diffuse registers linked to the supernatural, the mystical, or the occult. I have been in more than one anthropological seminar where I've heard about cosmic spiders, the activities of witchcraft familiars, fat stealers, vampires, and the like. I have been informed of an underground army (i.e., a secret army stationed under the ground) in the Solomon Islands, young men in Abidjan, Ivory Coast, who think Tommy Hilfiger shirts have mystical potency, and New Age seekers in Arizona who, in between firespinning sessions, derive energy and insight from the ley lines in and around Sedona.

Before we go any further, it's important to know that anthropologists *never* ask each other whether they "believe" in cosmic spiders, vampires, or ley lines—whether they think any of this is really real. In that seminar on cosmic spiders (in southwest China, in this case), for example, during the Q&A, no one in the room stopped to say, "Excuse me, but *what* are you talking about?" When less diplomatic people do pose such queries, or even more polite ones, the most common reply is based on an appeal to the "social fact." That is to say, whether it's real or not, it informs the ways in which the people in question understand the world and act within it. I spent eighteen months in Zimbabwe studying a church in which exorcisms were held on a weekly basis. I observed dozens of them. I did not see it as my job to play the part of theologian, philosopher, or ghost-buster. I was there to understand how the people who performed them, underwent them, and witnessed them fit possession into their broader takes on personhood, moral and physical wellbeing, the legacies of colonial rule, and Christian ethics. None of that required knowing whether the spirits were spirits.

And yet this is not the whole story; nor does it allow us to address some of the more important questions about what anthropology can teach us about reason and reality. Having listed a whole range of what are sometimes glossed as "apparently irrational beliefs," I want to back up and begin again at the beginning, with the people whose words have been pored over more than any other, the Bororo.[6]

The Bororo people live in areas of the Amazon basin extending between Brazil and Bolivia. They have been the subject of anthropological interest ever since Karl von den Steinen, a German ethnologist and physician, undertook two research expeditions to central Brazil in the 1880s. One of the things von den Steinen reported is that the Bororo say "we are parrots." This statement has been remarked upon by what sometimes seems like every other major figure in the discipline, certainly through the 1950s: James Frazer, Émile Durkheim, Mauss, Malinowski, E. E. Evans-Pritchard, Claude Lévi-Strauss, Clifford Geertz; they've all had something to say about the Bororo being parrots. The interest in them has been more sporadic since, but it's still there.

As you might well guess, it's not as straightforward as recognizing the Bororo as poetically inclined. We might easily understand a phrase such as "we are parrots" as a figure of speech. But that is not how the earliest anthropologists understood it. Their belief was that when people like the Bororo said such things—people, that is, who are "primitive"—they meant it literally.

In the Victorian world and fin-de-siècle France, the ability to use figurative thought and language was considered another marker of evolutionary development. Just as Edward Burnett Tylor and his contemporaries looked at kinship systems, political organization, and so on, they also turned to matters of the mind and mental skill when coming up with their evaluations. In *Researches into the Early History of Mankind and the Development of Civilization*, Tylor approached this largely through what he saw as the inability of savages to grasp "subjective connexions," by which he meant the symbolic connections between a sign and its referent.[7] He uses the example of a man's portrait. Among primitive peoples, he argued, the difference between a portrait and the man depicted in it will not be recognized; the two will be seen as parts of the same whole such that, for instance, harm done to the portrait will result in harm to the man. Primitive peoples were likewise said to populate their worlds with "fetishes": inanimate objects mistaken for animate forces. (For Tylor, in fact, such confusions extended well beyond the stages of savagery; even Roman Catholics fell into this trap, what with all their relics and icons.)

Von den Steinen, as it happens, took a slightly more qualified view. Nevertheless, his remarks on literal intention are what piqued others' interest, and none more so than the French philosopher Lucien Lévy-Bruhl, who addressed it in his monumental study, *How Natives Think*, published in 1910.* Like Tylor, Lévy-Bruhl argued that primitive peoples could not grasp figurative thought and language. Unlike Tylor, Lévy-Bruhl made this argument in terms of their being. In other words, he denied what nearly every anthropologist accepted, then and now: the

---

*Actually, the original French title is *Les fonctions mentales dans les sociétés inférieures*. The English translation wasn't published until 1926, and its English title reflects more of the Anglo penchant for the term "native," though it doesn't detract from the French interest in the mind and mentality. In fact, if anything, French anthropology has been more committed to the mind, as we'll discuss when we get to Claude Lévi-Strauss.

principle of psychic unity. For Lévy-Bruhl the Bororo were not simply lower down the ladder of social evolution; they were Different beings altogether, capital D.

*How Natives Think* considers a wide range of ethnographic data, but that on the Bororo (gathered by von den Steinen) takes pride of place. Again and again, Lévy-Bruhl comes back to the claim, "we are parrots," and von den Steinen's reflections on it. "It is not a name they give themselves," Lévy-Bruhl writes, "nor a relationship they claim. What they desire to express by it is actual identity."[8] He explained this identification through what he called the "law of participation." This refers to a "primitive mentality [in which] objects, beings, [and] phenomena can be, though in a way incomprehensible to us, both themselves and something other than themselves."[9]

Lévy-Bruhl is going further here than his slightly younger compatriot, Marcel Mauss. We have already considered the ways in which Mauss argued that certain objects can be "themselves and something other than themselves." We can even recognize this line of thinking in Western societies, with respect to family heirlooms and national treasures. With the law of participation, though, Lévy-Bruhl was making a more significant claim about the workings of the mind and insisting on a kind of difference that not even the social evolutionists had distinguished.

Lévy-Bruhl was consistently criticized for his disavowal of psychic unity, even by those who otherwise found his work insightful. Many anthropologists also charged him with overplaying the differences between people like the Bororo and people like the British, with the former less exotic and the latter less dull when it came to how, as natives, they think. There is certainly a lot to be said for this argument against overplaying difference. For every respect in which a Bororo man might claim to be a parrot, there are likely to be nine times the number of perfectly "reasonable" and often downright unremarkable claims and convictions voiced.

## WITCHCRAFT AND COMMON SENSE

One of Lévy-Bruhl's most important critics was Evans-Pritchard, whose classic work, *Witchcraft, Oracles and Magic among the Azande*, has been recognized as a book-length rejoinder to Lévy-Bruhl's most infamous positions. It's recognized for a lot more than that; this book is one of the all-time classics in anthropology, something that every generation of anthropology students must read and that still generates debate and interest well beyond the confines of African studies.

Evans-Pritchard, or E-P, as he is often known, took his PhD at the London School of Economics, where he was a research student in the 1920s. After spells in Cairo and Cambridge, he moved to Oxford where he remained for the rest of his academic career. Much of his fieldwork took place in what is today Sudan and South Sudan. In addition to studies of the Azande, he is also well-known for his work among the Nuer (about whom we've already heard a little, with respect to their attitudes toward money and blood).

*Witchcraft, Oracles and Magic* sets out to explain the role of these things within Azande society (E-P was there in the late 1920s). E-P tells us that anyone spending a few weeks or more among the Azande will realize how important these things are, for they form a central part of

None of this is to say that the Azande cannot recognize the workings of physical, chemical, and biological sciences—the workings, that is to say, of the laws of nature or, more plainly still, the real world. What it means, E-P explains, is that the Azande make a strong distinction between *how* something happens and *why* it happens; witchcraft is what links how and why together. One of his famous examples concerns the collapse of a granary. The Azande store their grains in slightly elevated granaries in order to protect them from vermin and the worst effects of humidity. The underneath of these granaries provides a nice source of shade, which the Azande often exploit. On rare occasions, however, granaries collapse—the humidity still affects them, and termites are also a risk—and thus the occasional Zande gets buried in a heap of grain. The Azande understand perfectly well that granaries collapse because of humidity and termites; the question they pose is why, in such-and-such an instance, did such-and-such a granary collapse on such-and-such a person? The answer is witchcraft. That person is being made to suffer on account of something done to upset or offend a witch. His or her actions and well-being bear the load of moral relations.

Again and again throughout his work, E-P reminds his readers that of course witchcraft does not exist; it is not really real. At the same time, he consistently works to make the Azande less exotic and his Western readership less unexotic than we might otherwise conclude. Yes, of course it's strange, he says, and it defies a certain common sense. But he also argues, in a subtle and polite way, that the common sense is indeed of a certain kind and that, taken on its own terms, the Azande belief in witch-

people's everyday concerns and interests. Mishaps
misfortune are thought to be the results of witchc
while oracles and magic each, in their own way, l
guard against or mitigate witchcraft's effects. While
three are important, and interlocking, I'll concentra
here on what E-P has to say about witchcraft, in part be
cause studies of witchcraft remain central in the disciplin
to this day. Indeed, witchcraft is yet another of the seemingly "traditional" customs found in the ethnographic
record that is perfectly at home under the conditions of
modernity.

It will come as no surprise that witchcraft is practiced
by witches. And yet one of the first and most notable aspects of witchcraft among the Azande is how little they
care about witches per se. They have elaborate and sophisticated understandings of who—in the abstract—witches
are, as well as what a witch is. Both men and women can
be witches; it is an inherited "trait" passed from father
to son and mother to daughter (but not crosswise); it
resides, as a physical substance, in the small intestine.
Azande don't care about witches, E-P tells us, because
people do not necessarily know they are witches, at least
when they are performing witchcraft. Part of the reason
is also because there is much less emphasis on the idea of
individual and bounded personhood to begin with.

Witchcraft, then, exists in discourse and in its effects.
People talk about it—they "think" with it, we might say—
and observe its influences. In this way, E-P approaches
witchcraft as an idiom, a way of speaking and of reasoning about events in the world, above all about unfortu-
nate occurrences: illness and death, family strife, poor
crop yields, a journey frustrated, and so on. All of these
would be understood as being the result of witchcraft.

craft is perfectly reasonable. At core, he says, it functions to regulate people's relationships—to reinforce their cultural values. It is also an admirable system of natural philosophy; don't we all ask "why" about the wonders and puzzles of life? "Belief in witchcraft is quite consistent with human responsibility and a rational appreciation of nature."[10]

At one point E-P even suggests that the Azande idiom of witchcraft sounds a lot like the Western idiom of luck. This effort to put the more haughty Western reader in his or her place is part of what marks E-P as such a nuanced analyst. He has a point. If we were sitting under a granary and it collapsed, we'd probably say it was bad luck. We might even ask, like the Azande, why us? What did we do to deserve this? In fact, given the obvious nature of such questions, I think the point about luck can be taken even further than E-P intends. He draws a line when it comes to illness, for example, resting easy with the facts of medical science. We know that cancer is not the result of wronging a neighbor; we even know that while contracting HIV may be the result of using the infected syringe of another heroin addict, there is no causal relation, at the moral level, between drug use and testing positive. And yet the stigmatization of HIV-positive patients persists; the moral loading of AIDS is a social fact. It has effects regardless of its basis in reality. The same is still true of cancer; it often invites stigma and it frequently prompts people to ask that question: What did I do to deserve this?

So, returning to an old-school register, "we" are not as civilized and "they" are not as primitive. We are not as modern, they are not as traditional. We are not as scientific, they are not as mystical. We are not as rational, they are not as irrational. "The attribution of misfortune to witchcraft does not exclude what we call its real causes but is superimposed on them and gives to social events their moral value."[11] Swap "witchcraft" for "luck" or "bad behavior" or, for that matter, "sin" and you are not so far from Cleveland or Colorado Springs.

Evans-Pritchard's efforts to de-exoticize the Azande are part of a long and distinguished tradition of anthropologists pulling down the Enlightenment's very own idols. And while E-P did not hesitate to talk up common sense and talk down superstition, he also gives the occasional hint in his writing of being open to the world of enchantment. In his work on the Azande this comes early on in his discussion of witchcraft, which, at the moment of its occurrence, the Azande say appears like a fire or light. "I have only once seen witchcraft on its path," E-P writes, without skipping a beat or departing one degree from his clear and sober Oxbridge prose. E-P saw such a light during one of his regular nighttime strolls and could not trace its source. The next morning, he learned, a neighbor died. Maybe, he says, the light was "possibly a handful of grass lit by someone on his way to defecate, but the coincidence of the direction along which the light moved and the subsequent death accorded well with Zande ideas."[12]

Many anthropologists would be open to such possibilities themselves. They would at least not openly scoff. Nevertheless, most would never commit it to print, and most work hard—not without justification—to suggest the ways in which apparently irrational beliefs, forms of mystical participation, witchcraft, and so on make sense on their own terms, and often even in ours.

## BACK TO THE BORORO

The disciplinary discussion over what the Bororo mean by referring to themselves as parrots certainly went in this direction. After Lévy-Bruhl, interest in what the Bororo said turned squarely to explaining it in terms of the figurative; they were not denied the play of tropes for long. Lévi-Strauss, for instance, had little time for Lévy-Bruhl's conclusions, arguing that the assertion was metaphorical and spoke to the importance of totems in such cultures. Then, in the 1970s, when an anthropologist named J. Christopher Crocker finally did the kind of in-depth, field-based study of Bororo that was needed, he filled in a number of important details.*

First of all, Crocker informs us, only men say they are parrots, and they only do so in certain situations. Second, parrots (or more specifically, red macaws) are associated with spirits, both because spirits and parrots are brightly colored and because they can be found in remote cliff-face aeries and in the tops of certain trees. Part of what this means is that the parrots (all parrots, not just red macaws), and more specifically their feathers, are important accoutrements in ritual performances, in many of which men take the lead. For this reason, parrot feathers are highly valued; men and women alike keep personal collections in safety containers constructed out of palm-tree trunks. Many of these feathers are taken from wild birds, but parrots are also kept by the Bororo as pets— the only such animal. The Bororo do have dogs, and

* Until that time, the debate was based on von den Steinen's early remarks, a few studies by some Catholic priests, and a handful of writings by Lévi-Strauss, who only spent a few weeks with the Bororo in the 1930s.

chickens and pigs have been introduced by the Brazilians, but none of these animals are regarded with affection. Parrots are loved, named, and even given funerals (unlike other animals). Although they do suffer some indignities: before a major ritual in a village, these beloved pets will have all their feathers plucked out, making them, at least temporarily, "pathetic denuded bundles of flesh and bone."[13]

Clearly, then, the parrots are important. They are a symbolic link that ties together men, spirits, and corporate groups (clans) via a complex ritual system. But here is the key: all pet parrots are owned by women. And so, in a way, are men. Bororo society is matrilineal, but it is also uxorilocal (which means that men live with the families of their wives). So a man is pulled in two directions and has two sets of obligations and attachments. He is responsible for looking after his sisters and their children, back in his natal home, but he is also a husband to his wife. Crocker tells us that marriage is often a bond of love; nevertheless, the man is always made to feel like something of a stranger among his wife's kin. One of his escapes is through the ritual system, in which he plays a significant role through enacting the spirits. In saying that they are parrots, then, men are making a metaphorical association between themselves and the parrots, an association based on a number of key characteristics they share with the birds. Like parrots, they are a vital part of the ritual economy; but also like parrots, they are a kind of pet. Powerful, and yet not. In control, and yet not. In saying "we are parrots," what men want to do is "express the irony of their masculine condition."[14]

Crocker's conclusion has not been the final word in this debate. One leading figure in the study of Amazonia,

Terence Turner, took issue with Crocker's emphasis on metaphor and irony; he argued that what we have here is synecdoche—indeed, not only that but what he calls a "super synecdoche."[15] I will not take up space here to explain the argument or what can make synecdoche super; I will only say that it is a brilliant analysis that nevertheless begs the question: *And?* In any case, we are now onto matters that tend to excite only the most gifted and devoted of literary critics.

But this is not just academic acrobatics. Debates over the finer points of synecdoche and irony can matter in terms of how we understand a cultural logic. Paying attention to figurative expressions within any given community is a good way to learn about not only that community's values but also how its members order knowledge and make categorical distinctions. It is in figurative language that we often make clear what matters to us and what does not, which categorical distinctions have purchase and which do not, what we understand and what remains unclear or inchoate.

One of my favorite examples of this is a very simple one, but telling nonetheless. For Christian missionaries working in locales very distinct from the Mediterranean world, it was sometimes necessary, in colonial and more remote postcolonial contexts, to upend conventional metaphors and images found in the Bible. So, for the Guhu-Samane in Papua New Guinea, the "lamb of God" became "the roast pig of God."[16] Local people had no idea what lambs were, so to convey the importance of Jesus' sacrifice, the translators turned to pigs, about which the Guhu-Samane know a lot (and which are commonly sacrificed in Melanesia). This is how metaphor and other figures of speech work: the predication depends on making sense of what you don't know (the character and qualities of Jesus) in terms of what you do know (the character and qualities of pigs). What the metaphor does is highlight shared meanings and associations. Of course, in many other ways Jesus and a lamb, or pig, are different and distinct. When a Guhu-Samane person hears for the first time that Jesus is the roast pig of God, what she learns is that Jesus is like the animal in some respects—above all, the subject of an important sacrifice.

It was Crocker's intimate knowledge of Bororo cosmology, totems, gender relations, kinship system, ritual life, and practices of pet keeping that allowed him to appreciate—and communicate—the figurative aspects of what Bororo men (sometimes) say. Yet there is still a nagging issue in all of this, one that bothers some anthropologists. For is there not a danger, especially when we are trying to understand how ("exotic") natives think, in assuming that what is "literal" and what is "figurative" is consistent across cultures? We are back again to reality.

This is the kind of question that some anthropologists have always wanted to pose when it comes to the debates over reason and rationality. Taken to an extreme, the reliance on analogy (talk of witchcraft is like talk of bad luck) and the play of tropes (Bororo men are being ironic) risks reducing cultural differences to the point of inconsequence. "They are really like us" might sound respectful, but it might also give another meaning to the phrase "colonization of consciousness." Turning what other people say into elaborate figures of speech lends them a certain "cognitive respectability," as one anthropologist puts it, but we might be better served to "view literal statements about the world as such, no matter how strange their content, rather than treat them as merely another example of the differentiating structure of the mind at work."[17]

Some anthropologists do this—or try. Some even move away from the language of literal and figurative to begin with; that framing in itself relies upon certain assumptions. Evans-Pritchard is like this in some moments, for instance, above and beyond his witnessing the light of witchcraft. When he turned his attention from the Azande to the Nuer, who say that "twins are birds," he did try to render this into the shape of something figurative, but he also pointed out (and did not wholly dismiss) that, from the Nuer point of view, neither "literal" nor "figurative" really captures what they are on about. Crocker also slips in a remark about how Lévy-Bruhl's analysis of the Bororo statement, based on the idea of actual identity, is more accurate—at least at the level of the point of view— than that of Lévi-Strauss, which relies on the metaphoric safety net of universal reason.

## ANOTHER POINT OF VIEW

Over the past twenty years, one of the anthropologists most closely associated with a dismantling of the metaphoric safety net has been Eduardo Viveiros de Castro. A professor at the National Museum in Rio de Janeiro, Viveiros de Castro has done extensive fieldwork among the Araweté, an Amazonian group in the Tupi-Guarani language family.* He published an influential book on the Araweté in 1986 (the English translation was published

---

*The Araweté never called themselves this; it's a name that was given to them by the National Indian Foundation in Brazil in 1977. They had always just referred to themselves as *bïde*, which means "human beings" or "people."

in 1992), but it drew much more widely on the ethnographic record, situating them in relation to other Amerindian groups. It was in this book, and a follow-up essay on what he calls "Amerindian perspectivism," published in 1998, that his approach really came into sharp focus.[18] Simply put, what he asks us to do in this work is to resist the impulse to make Amerindians intelligible in Western terms, to slot them into a landscape of cultural differences built up on a substratum of universal reason or the really real. In this kind of anthropology, the task doesn't end with figuring out how natives think. That's only the first step. The second step is to think like the natives, at least to the extent that it dislodges our own regular manner of doing so.

Viveiros de Castro argues that among the Araweté, as with many other Amerindian groups, there are a number of fundamentally distinct premises and presumptions about the cosmos. Perhaps the most important one is that, if we consider Amerindian myths, what we see is that humans and animals shared an original condition. This condition, however, is not exactly what we would find in the Judeo-Christian framing, in which humans rule over animals and are of a distinct nature. Nor is it what we find in the science of evolution by natural selection, in which humans are animals, albeit a distinctive species of animal, unique in their acquisition of culture. In Amerindian cosmologies, "humanity" is the original condition; it is what all living creatures share. What makes humans different, then, is not their development of culture (as it is in the Western view, whether that development is divinely ordained or the result of evolution or both) but rather the development of nature. In many Amerindian myths, we find animals losing their humanity, whereas in Western myths and science, what humans do is transcend their animality. In order to understand how *these* natives think, Viveiros de Castro is arguing, we need to take this distinction seriously. And one important thing it suggests is that the human-centered approach of anthropology, based on a clear set of distinctions between human and non-human, culture and nature, subject and object, and so on, is neither exhaustive nor the only way of thinking things through.

If animals have lost their humanity, this does not mean they have been rendered blind as creatures of nature. Indeed, as Viveiros de Castro and many other anthropologists have argued, a common feature of Amerindian cosmologies is the emphasis on "perspectivism." Many animal species are thought to retain agency and self-awareness; they have "points of view" just like humans, and they occupy their own cultural worlds. Part of what this means is that Amerindians have a much more relational and interconnected view of the world. When they think about what they do, and how they do it, they do so with the understanding and expectation that other sentient creatures do so as well.

So, all of those divides between human and non-human, subject and object, are not as clear-cut for the Araweté as they are in the Western formulation. "Amerindians put a wide berth between themselves and the Great Cartesian Divide," notes Viveiros de Castro, referring to the mind-body dualism made famous by René Descartes.[19] The Amerindian view of the world is one in which everything is connected and mutually informing; boundaries and distinctions are much more porous than in Western or Westernized schemes. Amerindian perspectivism is an example of what another important anthropologist in this area calls "relational non-dualism."[20] Everything is connected.

By getting rid of the metaphorical safety net, Viveiros de Castro is not getting rid of metaphor. He remarks—without much handwringing or hypocrisy—that what the Bororo say has to be taken as a figure of speech. "Bororo men and Nuer twins do not fly," he confirms in his book on the Araweté.[21] At the same time, he approaches Amerindian perspectivism, in which animals see themselves as persons, in a very matter-of-fact way: "This 'to see as' refers literally to percepts and not analogically to concepts."[22] In other words, it's not metaphor. Or irony, or super synecdoche.

Perhaps the best way to understand this both/and approach is to return to the intention behind this kind of anthropology. This is a point-of-view approach that goes beyond what Malinowski and many others have championed—one in which how natives think alters the anthropologist's own standpoint. As far as Viveiros de Castro is concerned, every anthropological project should contain within it something alien and other, something that not only challenges and unsettles scholarly terms of analysis but redefines what they mean and the thought-work they can do. With this approach, anthropology should always be open to the possibility of wonder.[23]

In Viveiros de Castro's work, the key is to understand that when Amerindians speak of themselves as parrots or, say, jaguars, we should not think in terms of parrots and jaguars (only) as animals in the world, referenced by words that we call "nouns."* In the Amerindian perspec-

---

*Viveiros de Castro doesn't write a lot about parrots, but he often makes reference to jaguars, which are important creatures (people) in many Amerin-

tive, "jaguar" is more like a quality of action than a noun. "Jaguar" really means something more like "jaguar becoming"—an awkward term in English, to be sure, but one that better captures the fact that the focus should be on "a quality of the verb, not its predicate."[24]

Reading the work of anthropologists like Viveiros de Castro is like reading a novelist who is pushing at the conventions of the form: a James Joyce, Gertrude Stein, or David Foster Wallace. You cannot really understand what they are trying to do without fully devoting yourself—surrendering yourself, in a sense, to their worlds. This is even the case with such anthropologists who seem to write in clear prose. Take Marilyn Strathern. If you read her work, it will always begin well. Her writing is relatively straightforward and easy to digest. Any given sentence from her masterpiece, *The Gender of the Gift*, for instance, should be comprehensible. But if you go on to a full paragraph of her perfectly welcoming sentences, you'll start to lose your bearings. After a chapter in the book, you might start pulling some hair. She is not using the English language in a normal way; she has let Melanesia inflect it. She is asking her readers to think in a different way. So, to really get what she's on about, you have to give yourself over to the logic of her prose.

In one way or another, all of the approaches set out in this chapter are getting at the same thing. From the off-beat linguist Benjamin Lee Whorf to the reasonably reasonable Sir Edward Evans Evans-Pritchard to the self-described radical Eduardo Viveiros de Castro, the point being made is that we cannot take our categories and

---

dian cosmologies, including that of the Araweté. In his book, he focuses on one case, for instance, in which a chief told a German explorer in the sixteenth century, "I am a jaguar."

domains of knowledge as self-evident. The order of things is sometimes also a flow of being. For most anthropologists, what this amounts to is cataloguing other ways of living. For some, however, it also opens up other modes of life.

## LIFE EXPOSED

I want to provide a final example on this point, one that takes us a long way from the forests of the Amazon and the humid undersides of Azande granaries.[25] It is a useful one to include, however, not least for showing us how the order of things can be radically reconfigured, how common sense and reason are culturally conditioned—even when, as in this case, "culture" comes close to being both literally and figuratively annihilated.

In April 1986, in the middle of the night, one of the units in the Chernobyl nuclear reactor in Ukraine exploded, sending a radioactive plume eight kilometers into the air. The explosion was the result of a botched experiment by engineers to test how long the reactor could go without a supply of steam. In the days that followed, as the Soviet authorities tried to contain the situation, the damage was made worse both by the way in which the authorities tried to extinguish the burning graphite core (dumping tons of sand, dolomite, and other smothering substances on it, which only intensified the heat) and by silence on the part of the Kremlin; the disaster was not publicly announced for eighteen days. In that period tens of thousands of people were exposed to radioactive iodine-131 and within four years cases of thyroid cancer skyrocketed. Soviet efforts focused on 237 workers at the site, all of whom were taken to an institute in Moscow specializing in radiation treatment. All told, however, one estimate is that 600,000 people have died or suffered serious health problems because of the meltdown.

In 1992, Adriana Petryna began anthropological research on the Chernobyl disaster, focusing on the dense web of relations among scientists, medical experts, politicians, and, above all, the victims themselves, many of whom were firemen, soldiers, or workers employed to clean up afterward whose problems started well after the explosion. Petryna began her fieldwork just after the breakup of the Soviet Union, and part of what she was interested in was how, as a newly independent, post-Soviet state, Ukraine was approaching the lingering crisis. Until the collapse of the Soviet system, a hard line was maintained on limiting any acknowledgment of the effects of Chernobyl. In newly independent Ukraine, this line was all but erased, as the state significantly lowered the threshold for recognition of victimhood. Over the course of the 1990s, 5 percent of the Ukrainian population—3.5 million people—made claims for reparations and special forms of state support. In this same period, 5 percent of the annual national budget was devoted to dealing with Chernobyl and its aftereffects, environmental and human. Close to 9 percent of Ukraine's territory was deemed contaminated, and to this day there is a thirty-kilometer zone of exclusion around the site.

Evans-Pritchard tells us that it didn't take him long to start to think like the Azande: "after a while I learnt the idiom of their thought and applied notions of witchcraft as spontaneously as themselves in situations where the concept was relevant."[26] His point is a simple one, which is that we adjust ourselves to the world around us. Studies of disasters such as Chernobyl add a further observation that such shifts can also take place at the societal level. They are signal events, and they point both to the fragility and pliability of life, cultural and biological alike.*

In Ukraine, as Petryna shows, what this amounted to was a wholesale reconfiguration of what it meant to belong to a nation—to be a citizen. Claims on the state, which in "normal" cases are understood to be a matter of birthright or naturalization, came to be defined in terms of suffering. Petryna calls this "biological citizenship." Over the course of the decade, getting by in everyday life—and getting anything much from the state—was dependent upon one's ability to navigate the scientific, medical, and legal knowledge of radiation poisoning. It required a new language, a new way of thinking, and a new common sense.

The disaster at Chernobyl is a particularly dramatic, tragic, and clear example of the extent to which "how natives think" is shaped by cultural factors. Yet it is also a reminder of how such an event, even if man-made, cannot be divorced from the reality of which Whorf spoke. However "cultural" this example is, it is also profoundly natural, profoundly dependent upon the workings and laws of nature itself. It is to nature, in fact, that we now turn.

---

* Anthropologists have also shown this in their studies of the Bhopal chemical plant explosion in India in 1984 (see Das 1995) and the Indian Ocean tsunami of 2004, which devastated a wide region in Southeast Asia and in particular Aceh, Indonesia (see Samuels 2012).

## CHAPTER 9

# NATURE

Palestinian literary critic Edward W. Said, whose work focused on colonialism and empire, was a great fan and devoted student of Western classical music. It was from his study of music that he developed a trademark style in his work, the style of "contrapuntal reading."[1] In music theory, contrapuntal motion refers to the relationship and connection between melodic lines. They are separate and can be separated, but taken together they can become something more than the sum of their parts. For Said, the best literary criticism has to produce something similar, something that cannot be reduced to one line or one voice (a real danger, he argued, when reading Western fiction set in the age of empire).

Throughout this book "culture" and "nature" can be viewed as the melodic lines of anthropology, whose contrapuntal motion gives the discipline its distinct character. To be sure, much of what we've considered places the stress on culture, with nature as a kind of steady, background drone. This norm has been challenged on some occasions, from our treatment of blood to our more recent discussions of reason. In some of the examples, in other words, nature seems to rear its head—ugly or not—and assert itself. Blood is not just another substance. The laws of chemistry, biology, and physics matter; "empty" petrol drums *are* dangerous, thyroid cancer is deadly, and Bororo men cannot fly.

250 ■ Chapter 9

It might seem that, for many anthropologists, nature is a rather dark melodic line, something that they work to mute as best as possible. Figures such as Ruth Benedict, Clifford Geertz, and Marshall Sahlins are cheered on for their passionate defenses of culture, social and historical specificities, and recognition of the extent to which reality is not something to which we can ever have unmediated access. In all cases this passion has been driven by political positions, above all by what Sahlins once called "the use and abuse of biology," the most serious being what Benedict, Franz Boas, and colleagues addressed with respect to the spurious science of race.[2]

It is also worth noting that while anthropologists have a whole drawer full of definitions of culture, the same cannot be said for nature. I can't recall ever being presented with a definition of nature in my undergraduate courses, and such definitions are difficult to find in the extant literature. Where they do appear, it is often with respect to culture, and in some cases even in cultural terms (nature's construction, its discursive character, and so on).

The situation is so clear, it seems, that the largest professional association of anthropologists recently left "nature" off a list of more than a hundred keywords. For the 2011 meetings of the American Anthropological Association, presenters who registered their papers had to use this controlled vocabulary of terms to classify their interests, so apparently you weren't even allowed to address nature in your research.[3] Activism, Africa, Borders, Ceramics, Education, Evolution—that's close!—the list goes on—but no Nature.

It is tempting to say that nature's absence is a sign of anthropological disdain, but this would not be wholly accurate. We should not forget that Boas began his career in anthropology in no small part out of an interest in the environment of Baffinland and in the field of physics. Bronislaw Malinowski was even more wedded to nature via human biology: he approached all cultural life in terms of biological needs. He proposed a theory of "functionalism" in which underneath all the weird and wonderful cultural elaborations of any given people is a human body driven by needs and desires. Even so, in the main, nature has always been the drone.

One important exception to this norm is Claude Lévi-Strauss. For Lévi-Strauss, recall, the great diversity of cultures is not in itself anthropology's main concern. It is what lies behind this diversity—which he sometimes speaks of in terms of its chaos and messiness—that really matters. And that internal structuring is a matter of nature, of the mind.

## LÉVI-STRAUSS IN MIND

Claude Lévi-Strauss was born in 1908 and died just short of his 101st birthday. He spent most of his life in Paris but with formative stretches in Brazil and the United States. It was in Brazil, in the 1930s, that he became interested in anthropology, having previously studied law and philosophy at the Sorbonne. This education of sorts was completed during World War II, most of which he spent in exile in New York City, trolling through endless books on Native Americans (North and South) at the New York Public Library and soaking up the wisdom and sensibility of Franz Boas. Despite a lifelong reverence for and use of the work of Boas and his students, Lévi-Strauss did almost no fieldwork himself: just a few months of touring around the Brazilian interior that today, at least, wouldn't qualify as fieldwork at all. His time with the Bororo could be counted in weeks and he never learned their language.

While I have emphasized the importance of fieldwork as a method, and while the armchair approach of the Victorians has been largely discredited, a discussion of Lévi-Strauss gives me the opportunity to reiterate that not all anthropologists think fieldwork is the sine qua non of the discipline. There are still traditions in France, for instance, in which fieldwork is secondary, and many of the most influential texts in Anglo traditions are wholly theoretical or conceptual analyses. Mary Douglas, for instance, studied a group in Africa called the Lele, but almost no one reads her book on them; people read *Purity and Danger*, much of which is a structuralist analysis of books in the Old Testament and takes more inspiration from Marcel Mauss and Lévi-Strauss, who did little fieldwork, than Malinowski, who put fieldwork at the center of his vision of anthropology. (I can thoroughly recommend *Purity and Danger*; it is a great book.)

It was Lévi-Strauss who developed structuralism in anthropology, an approach he adapted from Ferdinand de Saussure and another major figure in linguistics, Roman Jakobson (a fellow Jewish exile in New York, whom he got to know there during the early 1940s). Lévi-Strauss had a huge admiration for linguistics, and he argued that anthropology needed to mold itself in a similar fashion. Structural linguistics got it right on several counts, Lévi-Strauss argued. First, it focuses on what he calls the "unconscious infrastructure" of language, something about which the speakers themselves may have no clue. Second, it locates meaning not in terms themselves—"cat is cat" (meow)—but in relations between terms—"cat, not dog" (meow, not woof). Third, such relations are situated within a system; it is ordered and structured. And finally, it seeks to locate general laws.[4]

If you go on to read any structural anthropology it will look very different from most other anthropological studies. It will probably not feature many colorful, full-blooded characters: Chief Chiweshe, say, or Janet, the maternity nurse in Sarasota. It will probably have a lot of encyclopedic information, such as on the folk taxonomies of marsupials in Australasia. It may well be focused on myths—myths have been a source of keen interest for structuralists because, it is argued, they encompass the workings of a lot of that "unconscious infrastructure"; if so, don't expect a good Brothers Grimm tale. Expect a surgical dissection. Lévi-Strauss himself is not a story-teller and the point isn't to enjoy a wonderful tale; it's to understand how the myth, broken down into its constituent parts, tells us something about both the system of the culture from which it is drawn and, even more, the workings of the mind. Indeed, all of these elements will be used to shore up Lévi-Strauss's case for the universal structures of thought, cognition, and classification.

It might seem a slight to the greatness of Lévi-Strauss to turn to someone else in an effort to summarize what structuralism is all about. That the summation was written over a century before Lévi-Strauss was setting out his position might further be seen as adding insult to injury. But I am not alone in doing so, because it is this quote from philosopher August Comte that Lévi-Strauss uses as the epigraph for his short book, *Totemism*: "The laws of logic which ultimately govern the world of the mind are, by their nature, essentially invariable; they are common not only to all periods and places but to all subjects of whatever kind, without any distinction even between those that we call the real and the chimerical; they are to be seen even in dreams."[5]

That pretty much sums up structuralism. "Primitive" or "civilized," Bororo or Briton, shaman or scientist: there is no difference at the level of mental structure or cognitive capability. What anthropology must do is sift through all of the very significant differences and seemingly incommensurable divides between cultures to uncover the universal elements of the human condition. In *The Savage Mind*, one of his most well-known books, Lévi-Strauss makes this case at length. "The savage mind is logical in the same sense and the same fashion as ours," he concludes, after 250-plus pages of analysis that covers everything from the classification of Artemisia in the Americas to necronyms (identifying someone in relation to a deceased relative) among the Penan of Borneo to the skills and approach of the modern engineer to the philosophy of Jean-Paul Sartre.[6]

Lévi-Strauss is one of the few figures in anthropology who can be seen as a naturalist of sorts. He never abandoned or downplayed the importance of cultural differences, but he understood them as situated within a more fundamental register of cognition and thought. Maurice Bloch has recognized Lévi-Strauss as "the first of the modern anthropologists to consider seriously the necessity of taking into account the full implications of the functioning of the mind."[7]

The first of the modern anthropologists and not the last, yet an interest in the mind, at least in the sense concerning Bloch, has been a minor pursuit within the discipline. Much of it, moreover, has been done in relation to cognitive science, a field that—somewhat surprisingly—Lévi-Strauss himself took little interest in. For Bloch, who has become a leading figure in cognitive anthropology, this lack of engagement with cognitive science has greatly weakened the discipline and makes it all the more difficult to recognize humankind's place within a natural history.

For many anthropologists, though, the sticking point is that appeals to naturalism have always come up short. Social evolutionism has produced very little of lasting value, even bracketing its moral high-handedness. Lévi-Strauss's work, as well, has not had staying power for many anthropologists, at least in an unqualified form. While he is unrivaled in terms of his erudition, there are nevertheless frequent moments in his work where leaps of faith or sleights of hand seem to take place: interpretations of myth, for example, that are very difficult to account for. Even more seriously for most anthropologists is the extent to which structuralism seems to erase the possibility for human agency to bring about genuine change in a system. This is the challenge that Sahlins and Bourdieu set themselves: to recast structuralism as something that could take account of history and human agency—as something that is indeed structured but possible to change.

I want to consider some work in cognitive anthropology later, as well as another way in which some anthropologists today are trying to reconcile the focus on nature with the focus on culture. But before turning to this, it is not a bad idea to consider further why nature gets such short shrift.

## NATURE'S LIMITS?

For most people, in most times and places, the boundaries between nature and culture are blurry at best, if they exist at all. And in many places they are not in play. This is one of Marilyn Strathern's key points in her treatment of Melanesia. Melanesian groups do not think in the same terms as Westerners. Among the people of Mount Hagen, for example, among whom Strathern conducted fieldwork, classifications are made in terms of wild or domestic rather than nature or culture. This approach leads to cuts across what we would normally understand to be the lines of nature versus culture. Pigs, for instance, are understood not in terms of their pig-ness, as it were—their "animal nature"—but rather whether they are wild or domestic. So whereas we might say, "Okay, yes, certain animals are domestic or kept as well-loved pets, but they are *still* animals, they are *still* part of the natural world," this would not occur to a Hagener. It is not possible to equate the wild (*rømi*) with nature or the domestic (*mbo*) with culture. It's a fundamentally different way of carving up the world and relations within it.

The people of Mount Hagen are far from alone. Certainly, for many societies that have historically lived so "close to nature" we should not be surprised that the concept has little traction or relevance. If you spend most of your time with pigs, or in a garden, or hunting in the forest, or fishing, or tending cattle, the conceits of belonging to a cultural order won't necessarily make sense. Even within Western traditions of thought, in fact, the insistence on a nature/culture split is of fairly recent making.

It was over the course of the eighteenth and nineteenth centuries that this split took its current form. This is an understanding of nature in which all living things are connected but within which there is nevertheless a ring drawn around humanity. What happens within that ring is made possible because of the unique faculties of humankind, of which there are several but chief of which is the brain. The human is thus distinguished by the possession of, and ability to create, culture. In many ways, of course, this involves the domestication of nature: growing certain crops, raising certain animals, making medicines and shelters, and clothing. And yet one of the chief conclusions of this period is that nature is, in the final analysis, an autonomous realm. Slowly, over time, the divine hand pulled away and left us facing It.

Nature in this sense has to be understood as both a modern term and a *term of modernity*. And with it have come a number of associations and oppositions. Under the umbrella of the nature/culture divide, we also started to think in terms of objects and subjects, given and made, non-human and human, the passive and the active, unintentional and intentional, immanent and transcendent, and so on. In some ways, it wasn't that such distinctions were new or even unique to Western thought (though they were understood to be uniquely well grasped in Western thought). More important than this, really, was the belief that moderns could keep them separate, hold them apart. Recall the arguments of men such as Edward Burnett Tylor and Lucien Lévy-Bruhl; their point about primitive thought—premodern thought—was that it confuses and blurs things because it cannot handle the separation. It is not sophisticated and evolved enough to process information along clear channels. The triumph of modernity is that of recognizing the true order of things.

Except it isn't. For it is not only that "moderns" impose their own way of thinking about the world onto everyone else—blind to the specificities of the Araweté, Hageners, Nuer, or, for that matter, Han Chinese—it is that they fail to live up to it themselves. As French anthropologist Bruno Latour puts it, "We have," in fact, "never been modern."

In a short book, published in 1991, Latour shook up the human sciences in a way that rarely happens. *We Have Never Been Modern* is almost like a sermon—an admonishment of "us"—about the failings and sometimes downright hypocrisy of the contemporary West. Ranging over everything from the history of science to the anthropology of Amazonia, from climate change (in the headlines even back in 1991) to the fall of the Berlin Wall, Latour traces the ways in which, from the seventeenth century onward, a story of our break with the past—with tradition at home and other ways abroad—came to define who we are. In that story, God dies (or is at least crossed out), science rises, and democratic politics take hold. A new world order emerges, one in which the messy, muddled ways of the past—and non-Western others—get left behind for a rational and reasonable approach to the relationship between nature and culture. It is a relationship, to be sure, but one in which propriety is maintained by each side not collapsing into the other, making it difficult to tell them apart. After all, that is where our own ancestors failed and how much of the rest of the world continues to do so.

This is the story we tell ourselves, Latour argues, but it is not true. We have never actually managed to keep

nature and culture distinct and pure; we have never completely given up the allure of magic for the assurances
of science; and so on. The presidential inauguration in
the United States is the pinnacle of modern ceremonies,
drawing on the rich traditions of liberal democracy and
Enlightenment values—except that it is dependent on the
same kind of magical power of words as we might expect
to find in a Hindu ritual. Business is business, remember;
it's nothing personal. Except that's not true: we are very
bad at separating business from our human connections.
A gift is a gift and a commodity is a commodity: they are
very different things. Actually, we know that is not so.

Let's take one more important example that brings us
back to human-animal relations: pets. We keep pets; pets
are animals. And yet you don't have to be a trained anthropologist or ethologist to know that many pet owners—
perhaps even most pet owners, and certainly good and
decent pet owners—treat their animals in very human
ways: naming them, talking to them, taking pictures of
them, buying things for them (toys, cardigans, insurance),
loving them like crazy, and, when the bell tolls, mourning
them deeply. There are some people, most of whom happen not to own pets (especially dogs; dogs are clearly the
best pets in the Western world), who see this kind of treatment for what it is: a flagrant violation of the nature/
culture divide. It is an irrational outpouring of what should
be directed toward humans (love, money, time, social life)
being channeled toward non-humans. But if these level-
headed people are properly modern in their attitude when
it comes to dogs and other creatures, chances are they
fall short of modernity's demands in other areas. (Maybe
they don't trust their doctors, or they pray to saints, or
they *hate* flying because it seems so "unnatural," or they

only eat the meat of animals they kill themselves, rather than buying it, like they should, cut up into joints or ground up and then wrapped in polyethylene.)

Sometimes it's not at the supposed back end of modernity but at its vanguard that we find the nature/culture divide most under pressure. Being not fully modern is a foregone conclusion if you're a Roman Catholic, or darn your socks, or own a family business. But it affects doctors, too, and moral philosophers, as we know from one anthropological study of organ donation.

## DEATH IN MIND

Margaret Lock is a medical anthropologist at McGill University in Montreal. She started out as a specialist on Japan researching indigenous medicine. Her interest in organ donation came later and was the result of what she found to be a very different set of debates surrounding it than what took place in Canada and the United States.[8] The difference was that in Canada and the United States, there was no real debate being had, especially around the increasingly common situation, due to advances in medical technology, of "brain-dead" patients. When a patient is brain-dead, it is possible to harvest their healthy organs, since the bodily functions that keep the organs going continue. In Japan, on the other hand, Lock noticed not only that there was a lot of opposition to organ donation but also that many people, including some medical and ethical experts, refused to recognize that the death of a person should be determined in relation to their mental capacities.

Within North America, Lock tells us, the success of organ donation and acceptance of brain death is put down to early efforts to cast it as the ultimate gift: the "gift of life."* While this language draws on Christian notions of charity and the sacrificial tradition, it is also made possible by the shift, over the course of the early modern period, from death as a religious matter to death as a medical matter.

Today, for instance, it is worth noting that, as far as the state is concerned (American, Canadian, or for that matter British), death is determined by the doctor, not the cleric. It is the doctor, or medical establishment, that has both the legal authority and duty to declare a death. The cleric or religious figure often still plays a role, of course, at the funeral. But keep in mind that nothing legal happens at a funeral. You are not required, by the state, to have a funeral, and in many Western contexts it can be conducted by anyone; it doesn't have to be an ordained religious figure. It can be done by your Uncle Jim, if you want, or for that matter Zippo the Clown. This "medicalization of death" in turn structures the ways in which we are able to see the body as a body—as a thing, or collection of things, including organs that can serve a valuable purpose in other bodies that are still living people.

Personhood is also important here, and it is not difficult, given much of what we've already discussed, to understand why the brain, as the engine of mind, should be seen as so important to the definition of personhood. In North America, individualism is a paramount value;

---

* She focuses on North America, but the argument could be extended to several contexts in Western Europe.

freedom, autonomy, and choice are what people cherish—what they "live" for. Freedom of thought and conscience are part of this and so when one cannot think, when one is not conscious or in control of one's body, as a free agent, one is not a fully-fledged person. When it comes to brain death, the metaphor that we use is telling. To be brain-dead is to be in a "persistent vegetative state." In a more everyday setting, you may have been told by a relative that they'd rather die than "be a vegetable." Maybe you feel this way yourself. It's the kind of thing we discuss with loved ones at the end of a holiday dinner, in which the talk has turned to life's big questions, or after learning of someone in the community who has suffered terrible head trauma in a car accident. For many of us, to be human is to have a mind, to be self-aware and the agent of our destiny. In North America, brain death shifts the body from something that is cultural to something that is not. Brain death reduces us to the state of nature, which is no place for a person. And in such a state, the one last thing we can do is give that "gift of life" to someone else.

Different values and traditions of thought are relevant in Japan. And perhaps inevitably, part of the understanding is also informed by longstanding concerns with the integrity and distinctiveness of Japanese culture and worldviews. Japan is a resolutely modern nation: it is a G-8 economy, its population is literate and highly educated, and it is technologically advanced—perhaps even more technologically advanced and innovative than the United States or Canada. And yet it is still Other, still understood to be modern in relation to and as a result of Western influence. It is not only culture that helps explain the difference between Japan and North America, then: it is the *politics* of culture as well, the extent to which public figures in the debates over brain death use "Japanese tradition" to shore up nationalist sentiments of Us versus Them. As Lock points out, though, and as we can appreciate from even the brief remarks above, culture and the politics of culture are at work in North America too. It's just that their mobilization has been much more successful, such that it appears (to us) as common sense or a matter of fact. But there is nothing given or natural in thinking of a brain-dead person as a "living cadaver."

Lock points to several values that orient the attitudes of many Japanese. In Japan, she tells us, death is not understood as something that happens in a split moment or that hinges on a binary state—death is a process. What is more, most Japanese do not privilege cognition as the seat of personhood; the body plays an equally significant role. Tied up with this is an understanding that individuals are not autonomous; they are part of a larger whole, which is the family. In Japan, families and even individuals within families are unwilling to accept death as something atomistic or divorced from the collective. Finally, although the medical profession is both well established and well-developed, medical science has not garnered the air of prestige and authority it has within North America. Death has not become fully medicalized, nor the body correspondingly naturalized. This makes it difficult to think of a heart or a liver or a kidney as something akin to a "thing." Lock even found that some medical professionals downplay their right to make such calls. One physician told her: "I don't think we really understand what is going on in the brain at death, and a death that can only be understood by a doctor isn't a death, as far as I'm concerned."[9]

As we saw with new reproductive technologies in Lebanon (in chapter 5), a ventilator, a bowl of ice, and an operating theater are enough to raise fundamental questions about the boundary between nature and culture, life and death. The very idea of a "living cadaver" is a perfect example of why, as Latour would put it, we have never been modern. It is to most ears an oxymoron. A dead body that is not dead. (Latour calls this a "hybrid.") No sooner do we have a clear understanding of something as natural and biologically unambiguous as "death" than the understanding shifts. Death is not what it used to be. And advances in scientific technology, as well as new arguments in ethics, will ensure its reinvention and redefinition for a long time to come. Seen through the lens of medical advances "it is doubtful whether demarcations between nature and culture can ever be settled."[10]

## SCIENCE/FICTION

Another reason anthropologists have been skeptical about the purchase of nature is the extent to which certain scholars take liberties with the scientific authority they are given. Scientists are certainly held in high esteem. A 2015 poll in the UK listed "doctor" as the most trusted profession; scientist came in fourth, with teacher and judge coming in between (hairdresser was fifth place).[11] In a similar exercise in the United States, nurses, pharmacists, and doctors came in the top three spots, followed by high school teachers.[12] Keeping in mind that doctors, nurses, and pharmacists are trained in biology, chemistry, and pharmacology, it's clear that science is a standout field of virtue and value.

dard presentation, she found, was the description of oo-
genesis (the production of egg cells) as inefficient. One
textbook even says flatly that it is "wasteful." Now, it is
true that of the roughly seven million egg germ cells produced in the ovaries, only 400 or 500 will, in the course
of a woman's lifetime, be released as fully formed eggs.
Fine. Yet this is a drop in the ocean compared to what
happens with sperm. In the course of a single day, a cau-
tious estimate is that a man produces 100 million sperm;
that's over 2 trillion in a lifetime. Yet this is never described in the textbooks as wasteful, or even odd. If anything, it is taken as a sign of male productivity. But if we
say, for the sake of argument, that the average couple has
two children, couldn't we then say that women are in
fact much less "wasteful" than men with their little bits?
For every 200 eggs the woman produces, she produces a
child: a ratio of 200 to1. For a man, on the other hand,
the ratio would be 1 trillion to 1.

Another gendered aspect of the descriptions concerns
the passivity of the egg and the activity of the sperm.
Eggs are said to pretty much just lie about; sperm are on
a "mission" to "penetrate" the egg. Martin even found
one textbook that described the egg in the following
terms: "a dormant bride awaiting her mate's magic kiss,
which instills the spirit that brings her to life."[13] As it
happens, the period in which many of these textbooks
were written, the 1980s, saw a number of changes to the
understanding of insemination. Researchers began to
understand that the egg plays a much more active role in
the process and that sperm aren't nearly as "forceful" as
previously thought. The process came to be understood
as part of a chemical reaction, dependent upon both the
egg and the sperm. As Martin reports, however, sperm

continued to be written about as the more active partner. In some cases, too, this finding simply shifted the emphasis of the gender stereotyping. Eggs started to be described as "trapping" the sperm. Poor little sperm! Eggs went from being damsels in distress to something more like vixens or sirens.

As if this wasn't dangerous enough, Martin also points out that the adoption of dramatis personae at this micro-level runs the risk of pushing the seat of personhood even further into the body. Never mind the brain and all the controversy it stirs up with respect to the definition of life. Taken to its logical extreme, the language of science textbooks would suggest that anthropology's real subject matter lies under the microscope. Trobriand Islanders be damned, this approach makes the sperm into a native too. Damsels in distress. Men on a mission. "That these stereotypes are now being written in at the level of the *cell* constitutes a powerful move to make them seem so natural as to be beyond alteration."[14]

Cells, however, have turned out to be very twentieth century. We are now much more micro than this. The entire logic of what Martin describes has more recently been mapped onto genes with barely a bump in the process.

## GENES ARE US

Genetics has become an absolutely central aspect of the anthropological project writ large. It is especially central to biological and physical anthropologists in a number of areas: debates about race, the population distribution of inherited disorders (such as sickle-cell anemia), demographic history, and even in one study in the Democratic

Republic of Congo of how war-related stress is affecting gene expression in pregnant women.[15] For some authors, however, including a number of high-profile evolutionary psychologists and their followers, genetics has become akin to a secret decoder, something that can finally make sense of the mysteries not only of human makeup but also of human behavior. If we understand genes, then we understand humans. Nature begets culture.

In 2005, anthropologist Susan McKinnon conducted an exhaustive analysis of this turn to genetics as the key-to-everything. As she shows, it ends up telling us more about the cultural and ideological positions of the authors than it does about the human genome.

McKinnon calls the approach in this work "neo-liberal genetics." That is to say, the picture of human nature that it reveals bears a remarkable resemblance to the way Milton Friedman and Margaret Thatcher viewed the world, as well as what motivates humans as economic actors. The particularly striking thing, though, is that the evolutionary psychologists who paint this picture of human behavior move freely between the present and prehistory, covering, in the same stroke of the brush, the average man in contemporary America and a hunter from two hundred thousand years ago when, during the Pleistocene period, *Homo sapiens* first appeared. In this reckoning, individuals are what matter; society and history are secondary. Freedom and choice are good; control and regulation are bad. Self-interest and the maximization of profit or one's position are virtues and they drive all our decision-making processes.

It is the last of these points—self-interest and maximization of profit—that really fuels this trend. As McKinnon points out, the common commitment in this work is to a particular understanding of the sex drive and, with it, gender roles, marriage, and the family. Kinship is all about genetics. And within that frame, men and women are both seeking to "maximize" their positions, which comes down to the production of offspring. This does mean that men and women developed (or rather, were programmed, through genetic coding) certain "preference mechanisms" in choosing mates. Men are said to look for young, shapely, and attractive females. Women are said to look for men who show signs of leadership, ambition, and success.* Men are also said to have what some of these evolutionary psychologists call a "Madonna-whore switch." Basically, men want to marry a Madonna and have sex with lots of whores on the side. This allows them to have what they need in order to continue their genetic line (i.e., a family), while at the same time meet their inborn need to sow their seed. (The availability of whores is somewhat curious, though, since women are understood to want to restrict their reproductive "investment" in one of these leaderly, ambitious men. So they cannot have whore genes, one supposes, since that is maladaptive and all the whores would surely have died out over the past two hundred thousand years.)

In addition to certain switches with labels clearly indebted to historical Christian and medieval character types, these evolutionary psychologists also proffer the existence of ultraspecific genes. At least, they sort of do. Following the basics of what we know about genetics,

---

* Shapely? Given what we know about human history and prehistory, to say nothing of many contemporary non-Western aesthetics, your average runway model is anything but the desired norm. Fat and girth have often held considerable appeal. See Popenoe 2004 for a study of fatness and beauty in the Sahel.

they acknowledge that in fact it is not possible to isolate links between genes and certain behaviors, character traits, or dispositions. But then they go on to come up with just such fictions. These include: a fidelity gene, an altruism gene, a club-forming gene, genes for helping relatives, a gene that made a child murder his newborn sister, a shame gene, a pride gene, and—my favorite—even "shady accounting genes."[16]

McKinnon provides dozens of examples from the ethnographic record to counter each and every just-so story in this field—every shady account, we might say. Some of the examples are drawn from cases we have also considered, including the Chewong, the Iñupiaq, and the Trobriand Islanders. McKinnon notes, for example, how Malinowski seems not to have located the Madonna-whore switch among the Trobrianders: men and women alike were quite open in their sexual relations and encounters; women in the Trobriands did not fall into the categories of Madonna *or* whore. Such value-laden language, which some evolutionary psychologists want to write into the genome itself, was simply irrelevant—to men and women alike. In short, though, the point is that this approach to genetics is simply the latest in the search for a simple, universal, natural history of humankind.

## OUR NATURAL AND SOCIAL HISTORIES

It is very difficult to find universals of human behavior and cognition that have much in the way of substance. There is little evidence from the anthropological record of a hard-wired human nature. Sure, we can find some kind of "kinship" or, more descriptively, "relatedness" in every known human grouping, but to gather the Che-wong, the Han Chinese, the Iroquois, and the Bavarians under the same umbrella term doesn't really tell you all that much. Anthropologists would be as happy as the next lot of academics to find such universals: If it's true it's true; why not work with that? But what anthropologists really, *really* don't like is when "science" and "nature" are yoked together without much in the way of a concern for the evidence or critical self-reflection.

Gallant sperm and Madonna-whore switches are just two of the reasons that we find such strong anthropological commitments to the importance of cultural particularities, social context, and historical dynamics. Good reasons—and yet Bloch is right when he says that the discipline ignores work in the cognitive and natural sciences at its own peril. If we cannot seem to locate a Madonna-whore switch, or any other switches for that matter, the legacy of Lévi-Strauss, as well as the more general disciplinary commitment to the psychic unity of humankind, behooves us to take naturalism seriously. In closing this chapter, I'd like to highlight two areas of research in which this is happening with productive results.

One is in the combination of traditional fieldwork methods with experiments in cognitive psychology.[17] Rita Astuti has been studying a small fishing community, the Vezo, on the coast of Madagascar for close to thirty years. In the early 2000s, after publishing a number of important works on Vezo kinship relations, livelihoods, and identity, she began a comparative project with two cognitive psychologists looking at conceptual representations in the domains of folk biology and folk sociology. The trio wanted to know about the everyday understanding and rationalization of such processes as biological inheritance: What do the Vezo think about the processes of inheritance? Who is a child said to look like, and why? How does that identification affect how a child might act, and so on? Following on from the answers, which, set against the backdrop of Astuti's long-term fieldwork, they gathered through a series of specially designed psychological tests (in which people were asked hypothetical questions about inheritance and personal identity), a more basic question was posed. Are there constraints on conceptual development? In other words, are there certain categories of knowledge, or understanding of the "facts of life," that are wired into human cognition? Does "everyone really know" that a duck begets a duck, a tiger begets a tiger, and that Mr. and Mrs. Smith beget little Johnny Smith? (Even if that duck is raised by a goose, the tiger is raised by an elephant, and little Johnny is raised by Mr. and Mrs. Jones?) Clearly, these questions on constraints to conceptual development can be raised in the context of some of the major debates in anthropology we've considered in this book, such as Benedict's and Lee D. Baker's points about adoption and nurture, Lewis Henry Morgan's analysis of kinship terminology, or, for that matter, what Bororo men mean when they say they are parrots.

The questions are especially interesting in Astuti's study because the Vezo have a strongly performative approach to identity and relatedness.[18] As for many of the other small-scale, non-Western societies we've considered, who and what you are is a matter of what you do and the social relationships you develop.* The Vezo are not Vezo because they're born that way: they're Vezo because they

* And the Catalans too, of course—at least in recent years.

act that way. To be Vezo you must do Vezo things, most of which revolve around family, fishing, and the sea. This performative, socially oriented approach to identity is so strong that the Vezo even say that if a pregnant woman makes a good friend during the course of her pregnancy, the baby will grow up to look like that friend.

Yet the cognitive experiments did not accord with this ethnographic account. It seems the Vezo understood perfectly well that certain "facts of biology" matter in terms of intergenerational inheritance. In the hypothetical examples presented in the tests, Vezo adults gave a clear indication of understanding that a child gets its "template" (as they put it) from its birth parents. In other words, they recognized that genetics and key aspects of "who you are" are not social constructions or shaped by performative acts. What the research trio also found, however, was a systematic denial of this knowledge by the Vezo when it came to thinking in terms of their own lives. Within Vezo communities, too much emphasis on biological relatedness was considered antisocial and possessive; it pushed against the core value of Vezo life, which is to have as many relations (i.e., "kin") as possible. What Astuti and her colleagues discovered is that the Vezo "do not attend to what we know they know."[19]

For Astuti and her colleagues, these findings raise the important point that anthropologists who do not engage with what we're coming to understand about cognition and conceptual development are shooting themselves in the foot. If the goal of anthropology is to understand the native's point of view, isn't that goal only aided by knowing something about constraints on conceptual development? They clearly don't take away from the significance of culture, since the Vezo "override" them. On the contrary, then, they might ultimately suggest just how significant culture and values are to our constitution. Even Benedict might be emboldened by this recent research. After all, her example of "interracial" adoption is, at core, addressing the same issue: what makes us who we are. And yet what the Vezo case suggests is not the existence of some hard-wired, strongly prescribed pattern of culture. Instead, it indicates that there might well be something wired within us to recognize the "facts of life," but this is clearly underdetermined and dependent on cultural elaborations.

Another good example that bridges the approaches of natural and social histories comes from the anthropology of ethics.[20] This has been a growing subfield in recent years, with a number of contributions that offer serious engagement with the work of Aristotle, Immanuel Kant, Michel Foucault, and others in the grand tradition of philosophy. Research in this area has focused on everything from the highly elaborated ethical projects of religious subjects—as we saw with the examples of fatwa-seekers in Cairo and Pentecostals in Papua New Guinea—to the struggles of drug addicts and the "ordinary ethics" of getting by in everyday life. Most of the work reflects the emphasis in anthropology on questions of social and cultural construction.

In his recent book, *Ethical Life: Its Natural and Social Histories*, anthropologist Webb Keane, one of the most highly respected cultural anthropologists working today, questions the sufficiency of this sociocultural approach, not least since ethics is such a major area of research in the fields of psychology and child development. Much of this other work is more naturalistic in orientation; it addresses itself to the age-old question of whether our moral values and ethical reasoning are innate.

Keane does not reject the importance of social histories and cultural context. Far from it. They are central to his account, and he spends a lot of time looking at how ethical projects have developed in such distinct contexts as revolutionary Vietnam, the Islamic piety movement in Cairo, and the consciousness-raising campaigns of Western feminists. He also attends very closely to the ethical dimension of personal interactions: how exchanges between people in everyday, ordinary settings can reveal something of their commitments and values. Inferences we make during the course of a conversation, exchanges we have on Facebook, and the frustration that we feel on being corrected by a Starbucks barista over the wrong use of coffee-ordering vocabulary (short, tall, grande, venti, wet, skinny) are all ethically charged and can be profitably studied through anthropological methods of observation and sociolinguistic analysis.

But Keane also attends to work in psychology and child development because these areas of research tell us a lot about some of the most fundamental building blocks of any ethical life. They include the importance of human play, empathy, and altruism, the point at which children start to make self/other distinctions, the point at which children begin to recognize the existence of other minds and the ability to take a third-person perspective. The evidence suggests that children do not need to learn to be empathetic, that they develop propensities to cooperate and share even when no self-interest is at stake, and that they value fairness. Parenting, schooling, and other forms of socialization are not preconditions for the expression of such intuition.

At the same time, as Keane advises, that does not make any of these actions or reactions "ethical" in themselves. Rather than think of them as intuitions or impulses, we should think of them as "affordances," a term he borrows from a psychologist to capture the way in which experiences and perceptions make certain things possible. To adapt an example Keane provides: if you are on a long hike and start to get tired, a flat, smooth rock that comes up to the same height as a chair might well serve you as a make-do chair. You can stop and rest. It is not a chair, but it "affords" itself as such, serving the same purpose. Similarly, in other circumstances, a chair might "afford" itself as a stepladder or something with which to tame a lion. None of these uses or existences is fixed or predetermined: they result from a combination of objective and contingent factors. The rock needs to be a rock, and a certain kind of rock (sturdy, level). But you need to be tired, too, and aiming to sit down.

What Keane shows is that the precultural aspects of human cognition and reasoning are a lot like that rock: necessary but insufficient components for an "ethical life." To be ethical, these impulses and intuitions require social inputs. These come in the form of parenting, schooling, Bible study, reading the *Communist Manifesto*, reading Thomas Mann, chanting the Heart Sutra mantra, listening to Bob Dylan, hearing Gloria Steinem or Naomi Klein speak, broadcasting the Ramayana epic on national television in India, and an indeterminate number of ordinary, everyday interactions and experiences one might have, from ordering a medium coffee (i.e., tall drip) at

Starbucks to jokes at a picnic. Keane's conclusion is simple but no less significant for being so: "Without its social histories, ethical life would not be ethical; without its natural histories, it would not be life."[21] Like postcolonial literature, the human story demands a contrapuntal reading.

# CONCLUSION

With so much culture on display, there is a danger of being left dazzled. We have covered a huge range of worldviews and ways of life: pious Muslims in Cairo seeking self-betterment through the advice of sheikhs; indigenous Bolivians obsessed with football but not with winning; futures traders in London for whom computer transactions promise a more perfect market; Melanesian men willing to set out across rough seas in small canoes in search of necklaces and bracelets they cannot wear; Ukrainians whose lives, and world, have been irrevocably shattered by the nuclear meltdown at Chernobyl; feisty brides and angry daughters in China, the former negotiating their nuptial haul, the latter seeking redress and honoring a mother in the medium of song.

So there is a lot of difference in the world—still. Colonialism didn't get rid of it—it didn't produce clear-cut renderings of Christianity, commerce, or civilization. It didn't make the Mashpee Americans and it didn't make Zimbabwe British; what "cricket" means in Zimbabwe is not self-evident. Globalization hasn't gotten rid of the difference either. Satellite television in Belize didn't wipe out local culture; if anything, this conduit of global flows only reinvigorated it—or, arguably, even helped make it up.

Difference for difference's sake, though, is not the point of anthropology. If it were, we would indeed be dazzled, even blinded. While anthropology wants to document difference—and often be a witness to it—it also wants to make sense of those differences. Anthropology seeks to explain. "Native points of view" are not just issues of perspective; they are matters of logic and modes of reasoning too. They reveal something of "how natives think."

Learning something about the practices of fatwaseekers in Cairo, then, we also learn about how, in Islam, freedom is defined in relation to authority, not against it. The Ese Ejja in Bolivia play down the competitive stakes of football because of their commitment to egalitarianism, a value we often find highly developed in small-scale, stateless societies that have traditionally minimized the importance of private property. Futures traders in the City of London turn to technology because they operate in a system that seeks to dehumanize the realm of market exchange. If business isn't personal, do whatever you can to get rid of the people. Men from the Trobriand Islands participate in Kula exchange because it brings them renown but also because it undergirds the very logic of sociality, in which the individual self is measured in terms of relations to others. For the victims of the Chernobyl meltdown, caught between the political and scientific regimes of a defunct Soviet empire and a sputtering postsocialist state, suffering came to define the terms of existence. Theirs is a particularly stark case of how, in many contemporary contexts, we are seeing the emergence of a biological citizenship, claims for which are based not on the human condition but on a medical one. Village brides in northeast China and mourning daughters in the Júzò valley have taken up the idiom of individualism, but it does not produce a mere echo of something Western. They are using something new to shore up, reinvigorate, and reinvent older things. These examples from China are just two of many in the book that help us understand the ways in which tradition and modernity are not fixed states but fluid and relational terms.

It is not, of course, that anthropology just "seeks to explain." After all, political science, philosophy, and sociology also offer explanations. What gives anthropology its distinctive character is the extent to which those explanations are dependent upon local knowledge. *Hau* is not just a Maori term; it has been, for nearly a century now, an anthropological term of art. It reminds us that distinctions between people and things are not nearly as clear-cut as we often assume. Perspectivism, likewise, is not just a characterization of certain Amerindian worldviews; it is a brainteaser that prompts anthropologists to wonder whether we can (and should) rethink what falls within the boundaries of humanity and humankind.

A lot of anthropological explanation, in other words, involves figure-ground reversals—switching up the foreground and the background of what you're looking at. In order to get a holistic explanation, anthropology often has to upend common sense and question what gets taken for granted. Anthropology prompts us to reconsider not only what we think we know—what it means to be affluent, why blood matters, what constitutes reason—but also the terms by which we know it. It contains elements of strangeness and surprise.

Among the people of Mount Hagen, we have learned, it makes more sense to think in terms of wild/domestic than nature/culture. Nature and culture are not hardwired, binary distinctions. They are concepts with particular histories. For the Araweté, nature and culture are more fitting and useful terms, but their ratios have to be reversed. Whereas in the West we think in terms of one nature and many cultures, in this Amerindian cosmology it is the opposite. The Iñupiaq put little store by the "blood" that Americans, Britons, and many others hold so dear in reckoning kin. Among them, it's perfectly possible to say: "he used to be my cousin." Nor is death what it used to be. In Canada and the United States, advances in medical technology, the dynamics of secularization, and a persuasive rhetoric of "the gift of life" have helped legitimize the idea of the brain-dead patient. In these contexts, organ donation is a way of giving that patient agency. If this is not a spirit acting in the world, it may be the modern equivalent—which is not to say that technological capabilities determine the boundaries of life and death. In Japan, an equally developed medical system has not given rise to the same separation of body and mind: the Japanese recognize the idea of a "living cadaver" for the oxymoron it is.

I hope that some of the specifics stay with you. Facts, social and otherwise (although perhaps not "alternative"), still count for something.* It's helpful to know a little about the Hindu caste system, what a fatwa is (and isn't), and that there is a place in the world called the Trobriand Islands—where cultural tourism and Pentecostal preachers are now just as much going concerns as the older traditions of the Kula Ring and the exchange of banana-leaf cloth at funerals.† The anthropological approach to

---

\* Donald J. Trump's advisor Kellyanne Conway coined the phrase "alternative facts" in an interview on NBC's Sunday-morning news show *Meet the Press* in January 2017. See http://www.nbcnews.com/meet-the-press/video /conway-press-secretary-gave-alternative-facts-860142147643 for a video. I don't think this will be accommodated in the anthropologist's lexicon as a term of art.

† By the time Michelle MacCarthy went to the Trobriands to conduct research for her PhD at the University of Auckland, in the 2000s, cultural tourism had become an important source of the islanders' livelihood. She discusses this at length in her thesis (MacCarthy 2012). On subsequent trips, she found

knowledge has always had an ethical dimension. We are better people for knowing more about others. And whether those others come from Zuni or London is of equal worth, equal value to the project of anthropology. What Ruth Benedict argued in 1934 is just as relevant today: "There has never been a time when civilization stood more in need of individuals who are genuinely culture-conscious, who can see objectively the socially conditioned behaviour of other peoples without fear and recrimination."[1]

More than anthropological tidbits, though, what I hope you take away is some measure of an anthropological sensibility—how to bring an anthropological approach to bear in the world around you. How to think like an anthropologist.

Some anthropological projects might seem more relevant to that world, and your concerns, than others— research on the financial markets in Chicago and London, for instance, or the ethics of organ donation and end-of-life care. These have easy applicability, perhaps even practical implications. Margaret Lock's research on organ transplants, for example, led to a key role for her in the International Forum for Transplant Ethics. Along with a philosopher and a lawyer, she worked for several years with transplant surgeons and other medical professionals in the forum to promote a more global approach to the ethical dimensions of organ procurement. This is anthropology that matters, that makes a difference. And such work is part of a broader tradition of public and

---

that some Trobriand women, drawn in by the messages of Pentecostal preachers, had stopped producing banana-leaf cloth; the Pentecostals say it's a waste of time (MacCarthy 2017).

policy-related outreach stretching back to Franz Boas's interventions in the societal debates on race.

What I have also aimed to show, however, is that the relevance of anthropology goes well beyond these instances. Knowing about the Bovine Mystique among the Basotho is just as relevant and applicable to an understanding of our world as medical ethics, financial markets, and nuclear science in the West. It is an example of how people and places remote to us are nevertheless intimately connected. The Bovine Mystique tells us about the Basotho, but it also tells us something about the global mining industry, about how people use money and other assets to negotiate gender relations, and about how traditions can be great sources of creativity and innovation. In the coming decades, a repeat study of the Bovine Mystique might well also tell us something about climate change; it was a drought, after all, that underscored its importance to begin with.

In a recent study of the 2013–15 Ebola epidemic in West Africa, anthropologist Paul Richards highlights the remark of a British politician, Norman Tebbit, who once suggested "the taxpayer could no longer afford to fund irrelevant anthropological studies of prenuptial practices in the Upper Volta."[2] Yet it is precisely in the study of many such seemingly irrelevant, esoteric, or trivial things— cultural curiosities, we might say—that we so often find things of value, things overlooked or taken for granted that actually matter quite a lot. Richards has been conducting research for over forty years in Sierra Leone, the country that saw the second-highest official death toll from the Ebola outbreak. His analysis of the epidemic is duly attentive to the epidemiological data, the facts and figures of pathology, and the strengths and weaknesses of the international response effort. But much of the middle of his book is dedicated to detailed ethnographic descriptions of burial practices in Mende and Temne villages. Why? Because preparing the corpse for burial was one of the "super-spreader events." People wanted loved ones to be properly washed and cared for, but this was also one of the most likely ways to come into contact with the bodily fluids that transmit the Ebola virus.

Knowing something about the traditions of burial in West Africa, then, and, even more important, the ways in which local people adapted what they did to accommodate public health and cultural concerns alike, was a necessary precondition to halting the epidemic. Yes, the protective body suits mattered, and rehydration fluids, and ambulances and field hospitals, and the courageous work of national and international medical experts and volunteers. But so, too, did an understanding of local techniques and traditions of care, commemoration, and common sense. So, too, in other words, did culture and a certain social science called anthropology.

## ACKNOWLEDGMENTS

If you had ever asked me in the abstract, "Have you ever given thought to writing an introduction to anthropology?" I would have said, "No way!" What a crazy thing to do. But then Casiana Ionita, who was to become my editor at Penguin, asked me to do so for one of the book world's most amazing twentieth-century legacies: the Pelican series. Well, that's a different matter. Within a few weeks of taking up the challenge, Fred Appel of Princeton University Press asked me, over lunch on a rainy September day, whether anthropology needed something akin to an introduction aimed not just at students but perhaps for a wider audience, a wider public. How's that for serendipity? I owe Casiana and Fred a huge debt of gratitude—they have been fantastic editors and interlocutors throughout.

A number of friends and colleagues have read the manuscript in whole or in part, all of whom have given helpful feedback: Jon Bialecki, Maxim Bolt, Geoffrey Hughes, Rebecca Nash, and four anonymous reviewers commissioned by Princeton University Press for the U.S. edition. In the process of writing I also asked a number of colleagues for pieces of advice, reflections on various cultural things about which they knew much more than me, favors, and so on. I can't name them all, but thank you. I'd also like to thank Hannah Cottrell for help with the bibliography and Jane Robertson and Jennifer Backer, who did the copyediting. None of these good people is responsible for any remaining errors or gaffes.

Last but not least, I'd like to thank all of the people who have ever taught me anthropology, and this has to include not only my formal teachers at the University of Chicago and the University of Virginia but my colleagues and students at the London School of Economics and Political Science, whose work and love of anthropology serves as a continual source of inspiration.

# NOTES

## INTRODUCTION

1. Cushing 1978, 46.
2. Ibid., 319.
3. Ibid., 279.
4. Zaloom, 2006, 9, 8.
5. Ibid., 10.
6. Sahlins 1972, 4.
7. Ibid., 37.
8. Ibid., 9.
9. http://www.survivalinternational.org/galleries/hadza.
10. Powdermaker 1950.
11. Parkin 2005, 169.
12. Cited in Green 1990, 12; other details from pp. 10–11.
13. Hughte 1994.
14. You can read something about this history of anthropology's role in counterinsurgency operations in a pamphlet by Roberto Gonzalez (2009).
15. Malinowski 1922, 25; emphasis (and gendered phrasings) in original.
16. Ibid., 5–6.
17. You can listen to Madsbjerg speaking to the *Harvard Business Review* at https://hbr.org/2014/03/an-anthropologist-walks-into-a-bar.
18. http://www.theguardian.com/business/2008/oct/31/credit crunch-gillian-tett-financial-times.

## CHAPTER 1

1. Mitchell 2017, 33, 34.
2. Cited in Bunzl 1996, 32.
3. Cited in Stocking 1968, 136.
4. Geertz 1973, 5.
5. Kleinman 2004.
6. Ibid., 951.
7. Cited in Handler 1988, 141.

8. Manning 2008.
9. Deetz 1995, 4.
10. Coward 2013.
11. Arnold 1932 [1869], 70.
12. Tylor 1871, 1.
13. White 2007 [1959], 12.
14. Benedict 1934, 14.
15. Baker 2011, 122. See also Baker 1998 and Stocking 1968 for fuller treatments of this history.
16. Lévi-Strauss 1966, 268.
17. Luhrmann 2012.
18. Brightman 1995.
19. Robbins 2007.
20. Fuss 1989, xi. Fuss is not an anthropologist; she's a literary critic. But she has written a really great book on the concept of essentialism.
21. Bourdieu 1977, 72, 73.
22. Appadurai 1996.
23. http://anthropology.columbia.edu/people/profile/347.
24. Abu-Lughod 1991.
25. Radcliffe-Brown 1940.
26. Firth 1951, 483.
27. Clifford 1988a, 10.
28. Malinowski cited in Brightman 1995, 534.
29. Lowie 2004 [1935], xxi–xxii.
30. Kroeber and Kluckhohn 1952, 357.

CHAPTER 2

1. Twitter post on 19 December 2016, https://twitter.com/real DonaldTrump?ref_src=twsrc%5Egoogle%7Ctwcamp%5Eserp%7 Ctwgr%5Eauthor.
2. Trautmann 1987, 10.
3. Tylor 1871, 2.
4. See Stocking 1987, 10.
5. Morgan 1877, 4–12.
6. Ibid., 16.
7. Tylor 1871, 24.
8. Morgan 1877, 169.
9. Boas 1896, 908.
10. Ferry 2012, 295.
11. Comaroff and Comaroff 1991, 1997.

12. Ibid., 213.
13. Fanon 1967 [1952], 17, 18.
14. Lepri 2006.
15. Ibid., 75.
16. Huntington 1993, 24.
17. Ibid., 25.
18. http://georgewbush-whitehouse.archives.gov/news/releases /2001/09/20010916–2.html.
19. Cited in McFate 2005, 46.
20. Fabian 1983, 41.
21. Gardner and Lewis 2015.
22. https://www.theguardian.com/katine.
23. http://www.theguardian.com/katine/2010/oct/30/story -katine-anthropologist-ben-jones.
24. https://www.theguardian.com/katine/2007/oct/20/about.
25. Wengrow 2010.
26. Ibid., xviii.
27. Ibid., 175.

## CHAPTER 3

1. Peristiany 1965, 9.
2. Cited in Pitt-Rivers 1965, 52.
3. Ibid., 41.
4. Schneider 1971, 4.
5. Ibid., 17.
6. Herzfeld 1980.
7. Abu-Lughod 1986.
8. Ben-Yehoyada 2014.
9. Candea and Da Col 2012.
10. I am quoting from the unpublished, English-language version of this essay, with kind permission of the author. The essay was published in French as Shryock 2001.
11. Dumont 1970 [1966], 35.
12. Ibid., 21.
13. Srinivas 1959.
14. Fuller 1993, 13–14. Fuller's book is an excellent anthropological introduction to Hinduism.
15. Dumont 1970 [1966], 10, 3.
16. Ibid., 6.
17. Ibid., 218.
18. Ibid., 66; emphasis in original.

19. Ibid., 20.
20. Robbins 2004.
21. Ibid., 295.

**CHAPTER 4**

1. Cited in Ferguson 1985, 652.
2. http://www.bridesmagazine.co.uk/planning/general/planning
-service/2013/01/average-cost-of-wedding.
3. http://www.ons.gov.uk/employmentandlabourmarket/people
inwork/earningsandworkinghours/bulletins/annualsurveyofhoursand
earnings/2013–12–12.
4. Malinowski 1922, 84, 86.
5. Ibid., 89.
6. Ibid., 510.
7. Ibid., 97.
8. Sahlins 1996, 398.
9. Mauss 1990 [1926], 12.
10. Ibid., 65.
11. Hart 1986.
12. Hart 2005.
13. Ibid., 4.
14. Jeske 2016.
15. Ibid., 485.
16. Ibid., 486.
17. Ibid., 490.
18. James 2015.
19. Ibid., 55.
20. Graeber 2007.
21. Graeber 2011.
22. Ibid., 103.

**CHAPTER 5**

1. Morgan 1871, 10.
2. Schneider 1968.
3. Ibid., 25.
4. Ibid., 13.
5. Stack 1976, 45–61.
6. Sussman 2015.
7. https://s3.amazonaws.com/omeka-net/3933/archive/files/
a21dd53f2a098fca5199e481433b4eb2.pdf?AWSAccessKeyId

=AKIAI3ATG3OSQLO5HGKA&Expires=1474327752&Signature
=4VgjdKhdCrZpipb4bpQkiGROVe4%3D.

8. http://www.telegraph.co.uk/news/politics/2499036/Mayor-of
-London-Boris-Johnson-is-a-distant-relative-of-the-Queen.html.

9. Schneider 1968, 23.

10. https://www.washoetribe.us/contents/images/documents
/EnrollmentDocuments/WashoeTribeEnrollmentApplication.pdf.

11. Strong and Van Winkle 1996.

12. Details on the Washoe are taken from Strong and Van Winkle 1996 and D'Azevedo 1986.

13. Bodenhorn 2000.

14. Ibid., 147n11.

15. Ibid., 136.

16. https://www.theguardian.com/books/2016/aug/27/ian
-mcewan-author-nutshell-going-get-kicking.

17. El Guindi 2012, 545.

18. This is well explored by Peter Parkes (2004).

19. Clarke 2007, 289. The material on Lebanon that follows is drawn from Clarke's research.

20. Carsten 2000.

21. Strathern 1988, 1992.

22. Carsten 2013b.

23. Saussure 1983, 67.

24. Genesis 11:7.

25. http://www.catholicherald.co.uk/news/2012/03/06/full-text
-english-and-welsh-bishops-letter-on-same-sex-marriage/.

26. Carsten 2013a.

27. Herdt 1982a.

28. Narasimhan 2011.

29. Turner 1967, 70.

30. The Chukchi example comes from Willerslev 2009.

31. Copeman 2013.

32. Herdt 1982b.

33. These details on the Nuer are drawn from Hutchinson 2000.

34. These links between blood and finance are the subject of a wonderful essay by Weston 2013.

35. Turner 1967.

## CHAPTER 6

1. Erikson 1994.

2. Erikson 1963, 138.

3. Erikson 1937.
4. Inda and Rosaldo 2002, 4.
5. This example comes from Wilk 2002.
6. http://secondlife.com.
7. Boellstorff 2008, 8.
8. https://www.youtube.com/watch?v=3-LB-FeJlc4&list =PLI0b2jAH3oFvr6J0AhWroB9lmOXRN2xLV&index=1.
9. Templeton 1998, 647. Another good source on this is Sussman 2015.
10. Benedict 1934, 13.
11. Ibid., 14.
12. Baker 2010.
13. Ibid., xi.
14. Baker 1998, 1.
15. Yudell et al. 2016, 565.
16. This example is very well-known in anthropology. It comes from a seminal essay on culture and identity by James Clifford 1988b. Clifford is an historian of ideas and a cultural critic, but he often writes about anthropology and anthropologists.
17. Schieffelin, Woolard, and Kroskrity 1998.
18. This and the following example on etymology are taken from Silverstein 1979, an essay that really launched the whole area of research.
19. http://www.telegraph.co.uk/culture/hay-festival/9308062/ Hay-Festival-2012-Tim-Minchin-breaks-taboos.html.
20. Gal and Woolard 2001.
21. Woolard 2016. Most of the details I focus on in what follows are drawn from this book.
22. Ibid., 22.
23. https://www.bnp.org.uk/news/national/video-—-pain -indigenous-community-ignored.
24. Woolard 2016, 3–7.
25. Cited in ibid., 223.
26. Ibid., 296.
27. Ibid., 254.
28. https://www.bia.gov/cs/groups/xofa/documents/text/idc -001338.pdf.
29. Merry 2001.
30. Jessie "Little Doe" Baird, http://www.wlrp.org.
31. http://www.mashpeewampanoagtribe.com/human_services.

## CHAPTER 7

1. Weiner 1992.
2. Ibid., 12.
3. Ibid., 63–64.
4. Evans-Pritchard 1931, 36.
5. Yan 2009.
6. Fong 2004.
7. Yan 2009, 170.
8. Cited in ibid., 164.
9. Stafford 2010, 204–5.
10. Mueggler 2014.
11. Ibid., 213.
12. In writing this section, I'm drawing on arguments that are often traced to the following: Bloch 1989; Rappaport 2000; Turner 1967. These are just three of the major figures in ritual theory. See also helpful reviews, especially on ritual and religious language, by Keane 1997 and Stasch 2011.
13. Bloch 1989, 37.
14. Bloch 2005.
15. A classic treatment of these points is Bloch and Parry 1982.
16. Austin 1975 [1962].
17. For this account of the inauguration gaffe, see http://www.ny times.com/2009/01/22/us/politics/22oath.html.
18. Austin 1975 [1962], 117.
19. These details on black robes are the subject of a reflection by former Supreme Court justice Sandra Day O'Connor, http://www .smithsonianmag.com/history/justice-sandra-day-oconnor-on -why-judges-wear-black-robes-4370574/?no-ist.
20. Mueggler 2014, 212–13.
21. Agrama 2010.
22. Ibid., 11.
23. Ibid., 13.
24. Evans-Pritchard and Fortes 1940, 6–7.
25. Howell 1989.
26. Ibid., 37–38.
27. Ibid., 52–53.

## CHAPTER 8

1. Whorf 1956, 137.
2. Boroditsky 2009.

3. Whorf 1956, 151.
4. See Enfield 2015 for this point, as well as for a good review of recent work on Whorfian research.
5. Whorf 1956, 151.
6. Sperber 1985.
7. Tylor 1865, 127.
8. Lévy-Bruhl 1966 [1926], 62.
9. Ibid., 61.
10. Evans-Pritchard 1976 [1937], 30.
11. Ibid., 25.
12. Ibid., 11.
13. Crocker 1977, 184.
14. Ibid., 192.
15. Turner 1991.
16. Handman 2014, 282n3.
17. Overing 1985, 154.
18. Viveiros de Castro 1992, 1998.
19. Viveiros de Castro 1998, 475.
20. Scott 2013.
21. Viveiros de Castro 1992, 271.
22. Viveiros de Castro 1998, 470.
23. Scott 2013, 865–69.
24. Viveiros de Castro 1992, 271.
25. What follows on the case of Chernobyl is drawn from Petryna 2003; the phrase "life exposed" is hers.
26. Evans-Pritchard 1976 [1937], 19.

CHAPTER 9

1. Said 1993.
2. Sahlins 1976.
3. The list is reproduced on Savage Minds, a popular anthropology blog, http://savageminds.org/2011/04/17/anthropological-keywords-2011-edition/.
4. See Lévi-Strauss 1963, 33.
5. Cited in Lévi-Strauss 1964.
6. Lévi-Strauss 1966, 268.
7. Bloch 2012, 53.
8. Lock 2002.
9. Ibid., 279.
10. Ibid., 51.

11. https://www.ipsos-mori.com/researchpublications/research archive/3685/Politicians-are-still-trusted-less-than-estate-agents-jour nalists-and-bankers.aspx#gallery[m]/0/.

12. Gallup poll from December 2015, http://www.gallup.com/poll /1654/honesty-ethics-professions.aspx.

13. Martin 1991, 490.

14. Ibid., 500.

15. The study in epigenetics in the Democratic Republic of Congo is summarized in Mulligan 2015. See that same issue of *American Anthropologist* for a set of overviews on anthropological genetics.

16. McKinnon 2005, 29–33.

17. Astuti, Solomon, and Carey 2004.

18. Astuti 1995.

19. Astuti, Solomon, and Carey 2004, 117.

20. Keane 2015.

21. Ibid., 262.

## CONCLUSION

1. Benedict 1934, 10–11.

2. Richards 2016, 8. The remark by Tebbit occasioned an interesting exchange with the director of the Royal Anthropological Institute; see Benthall 1985.

# BIBLIOGRAPHY

Abu-Lughod, Lila. 1986. *Veiled Sentiments: Honor and Poetry in a Bedouin Society.* Berkeley: University of California Press.
———. 1991. "Writing against Culture." In *Recapturing Anthropology: Working in the Present,* ed. Richard G. Fox, 137–62. Santa Fe: School of American Research Press.
Agrama, Hussein Ali. 2010. "Ethics, Tradition, Authority: Toward an Anthropology of the Fatwa." *American Ethnologist* 37 (1): 2–18.
Appadurai, Arjun. 1996. *Modernity at Large: Cultural Dimensions of Globalization.* Minneapolis: University of Minnesota Press.
Arnold, Matthew. 1932 [1869]. *Culture and Anarchy.* Ed. J. Dover Wilson. Cambridge: Cambridge University Press.
Astuti, Rita. 1995. *People of the Sea: Identity and Descent among the Vezo of Madagascar.* Cambridge: Cambridge University Press.
Astuti, Rita, Gregg Solomon, and Susan Carey. 2004. *Constraints on Conceptual Development: A Case Study of the Acquisition of Folk-biological and Folksociological Knowledge in Madagascar.* Monographs of the Society for Research in Child Development. Vol. 69, no. 3.
Austin, John L. 1975 [1962]. *How to Do Things with Words.* Cambridge, MA: Harvard University Press.
Baker, Lee D. 1998. *From Savage to Negro: Anthropology and the Construction of Race, 1896–1954.* Berkeley: University of California Press.
———. 2010. *Anthropology and the Racial Politics of Culture.* Durham, DC: Duke University Press.
———. 2011. "The Location of Franz Boas within the African-American Struggle." In *Franz Boas: Kultur, Sprache, Rasse,* ed. Friedrich Pohl and Bernhard Tilg, 111–29. Vienna: Lit Verlag.
Benedict, Ruth. 1934. *Patterns of Culture.* New York: Houghton Mifflin Harcourt.
Benthall, Jonathan. 1985. "The Utility of Anthropology: An Exchange with Norman Tebbit." *Anthropology Today* 1 (2): 18–20.
Ben-Yehoyada, Naor. 2014. "Mediterranean Modernity?" In *A Companion to Mediterranean History,* ed. Peregrine Horden and Sharon Kinoshita, 107–21. Oxford: John Wiley and Sons.

Bloch, Maurice. 1989. *Ritual, History and Power: Selected Papers in Anthropology*. London: Athlone.

———. 2005. "Ritual and Deference." In *Essays on Cultural Transmission*, 123–37. Oxford: Berg.

———. 2012. *Anthropology and the Cognitive Challenge: New Departures in Anthropology*. Cambridge: Cambridge University Press.

Bloch, Maurice, and Jonathan Parry, eds. 1982. *Death and the Regeneration of Life*. Cambridge: Cambridge University Press.

Boas, Franz. 1896. "The Limitations of the Comparative Method of Anthropology." *Science* 4 (103): 901–8.

Bodenhorn, Barbara. 2000. "'He Used to Be My Relative': Exploring the Bases of Relatedness among Iñupiat of Northern Alaska." In *Cultures of Relatedness: New Approaches to the Study of Kinship*, ed. Janet Carsten, 128–48. Cambridge: Cambridge University Press.

Boellstorff, Tom. 2008. *Coming of Age in Second Life: An Anthropologist Explores the Virtually Human*. Princeton: Princeton University Press.

Boroditsky, Lera. 2009. "How Does Our Language Shape the Way We Think?" In *What's Next? Dispatches on the Future of Science: Original Essays from a New Generation of Scientists*, ed. Max Brockman, 116–29. New York: Vintage Books.

Bourdieu, Pierre. 1977. *Outline of a Theory of Practice*. Cambridge: Cambridge University Press.

Brightman, Robert. 1995. "Forget Culture: Replacement, Transcendence, Reflexification." *Cultural Anthropology* 10 (4): 509–46.

Bunzl, Matti. 1996. "Franz Boas and the Humboldtian Tradition: From *Volksgeist* and *National charakter* to an Anthropological Concept of Culture." In *Volksgeist as Method and Ethic: Essays on Boasian Anthropology and the German Anthropological Tradition*, ed. George W. Stocking Jr., 17–78. *History of Anthropology*, vol. 8. Madison: University of Wisconsin Press.

Candea, Matei, and Giovanni Da Col, eds. 2012. *The Return to Hospitality*. Special issue, *Journal of the Royal Anthropological Institute* 18(S).

Carsten, Janet, ed. 2000. *Cultures of Relatedness: New Approaches to the Study of Kinship*. Cambridge: Cambridge University Press.

———. 2013a. "'Searching for the Truth': Tracing the Moral Properties of Blood in Malaysian Clinical Pathology Labs." *Journal of the Royal Anthropological Institute* 19(S): S130–S148.

———, ed. 2013b. *Blood Will Out: Essays on Liquid Transfers and Flows*. Special issue, *Journal of the Royal Anthropological Institute* 19(S).

Clarke, Morgan. 2007. "The Modernity of Milk Kinship." *Social Anthropology* 15 (3): 287–304.

Clifford, James. 1988a. "Introduction: The Pure Products Go Crazy." In *The Predicament of Culture: Twentieth-Century Ethnography, Literature, and Art*, 1–18. Cambridge, MA: Harvard University Press.

———. 1988b. "Identity in Mashpee." In *The Predicament of Culture: Twentieth-Century Ethnography, Literature, and Art*, 277–343. Cambridge, MA: Harvard University Press.

Comaroff, Jean, and John Comaroff. 1991. *Of Revelation and Revolution: Christianity, Colonialism, and Consciousness in South Africa*. Vol. 1. Chicago: University of Chicago Press.

———. 1997. *Of Revelation and Revolution: The Dialectics of Modernity on a South African Frontier*. Vol. 2. Chicago: University of Chicago Press.

Copeman, Jacob. 2013. "The Art of Bleeding: Memory, Martyrdom, and Portraits in Blood." *Journal of the Royal Anthropological Institute* 19(S): S149–S171.

Coward, Fiona. 2013. "Grounding the Net: Social Networks, Material Culture, and Geography in the Epipaleolithic and Early Neolithic of the Near East (~21,000–6,000 cal BCE)." In *Network Analysis in Archaeology: New Approaches to Regional Interaction*, ed. Carl Knappett, 247–80. Oxford: Oxford University Press.

Crocker, Christopher. 1977. "My Brother the Parrot." In *The Social Use of Metaphor: Essays on the Anthropology of Rhetoric*, ed. J. David Sapir and J. Christopher Crocker, 164–92. Philadelphia: University of Pennsylvania Press.

Cushing, Frank H. 1978. *Zuni: Selected Writings of Frank Hamilton Cushing*. Ed. Jesse Greene. Lincoln: University of Nebraska Press.

D'Azevedo, Warren. 1986. "Washoe." In *Handbook of North American Indians: Great Basin*, vol. 11, ed. William Sturtevant, 466–98. Washington, DC: Smithsonian Institution.

Das, Veena. 1995. *Critical Events: An Anthropological Perspective on Contemporary India*. Oxford: Oxford University Press.

Deetz, James. 1995. *In Small Things Forgotten: An Archaeology of Early American Life*. New York: Anchor Books.

Dirks, Nicholas. 2001. *Castes of Mind: Colonialism and the Making of Modern India*. Princeton: Princeton University Press.

Dumont, Louis. 1970 [1966]. *Homo Hierarchicus: The Caste System and Its Implications*. Chicago: University of Chicago Press.

El Guindi, Fadwa. 2012. "Milk and Blood: Kinship among Muslim Arabs in Qatar." *Anthropos* 107 (2): 545–55.

Enfield, Nick. 2015. "Linguistic Relativity from Reference to Agency." *Annual Review of Anthropology* 44:207–24.

Erikson, Erik H. 1937. "Observations on Sioux Education." *Journal of Psychology* 7 (1): 101–56.

———. 1963. *Childhood and Society*. London: W. W. Norton.

———. 1994. *Identity: Youth and Crisis*. London: W. W. Norton.

Evans-Pritchard, E. E. 1931. "An Alternative Term for 'Bride-price.'" *Man* 31:36–39.

———. 1976 [1937]. *Witchcraft, Oracles and Magic among the Azande*. Oxford: Oxford University Press.

Evans-Pritchard, E. E., and Meyer Fortes, eds. 1940. *African Political Systems*. Oxford: Oxford University Press.

Fabian, Johannes. 1983. *Time and the Other: How Anthropology Makes Its Object*. New York: Columbia University Press.

Fanon, Frantz. 1967 [1952]. *Black Skin, White Masks*. New York: Grove Press.

Ferguson, James. 1985. "The Bovine Mystique: Power, Property and Livestock in Rural Lesotho." *Man* 20 (4): 647–74.

Ferry, Jules. 2012. "Speech before the French National Assembly (28 July 1883)." In *The Human Record: Sources of Global History*, vol. 2, ed. Alfred Andrea and James Overfield, 295–97. Boston: Wadsworth.

Firth, Raymond. 1951. "Contemporary British Social Anthropology." *American Anthropologist* 53 (4): 474–89.

Fong, Vanessa. 2004. "Filial Nationalism among Chinese Teenagers with Global Identities." *American Ethnologist* 31 (4): 631–48.

Fuller, Christopher. 1993. *The Camphor Flame: Popular Hinduism and Society in India*. Princeton: Princeton University Press.

Fuss, Diana. 1989. *Essentially Speaking: Feminism, Nature and Difference*. New York: Routledge.

Gal, Susan, and Kathryn A. Woolard, eds. 2001. *Languages and Publics: The Making of Authority*. Manchester: St. Jerome Publishing.

Gardner, Katy, and David Lewis. 2015. *Anthropology of Development: Challenges for the Twenty-First Century*. London: Pluto Press.

Geertz, Clifford. 1973. "Thick Description: Toward an Interpretive Theory of Culture." In *The Interpretation of Cultures*, 3–30. New York: Basic Books.

Gonzalez, Roberto. 2009. *American Counterinsurgency: Human Science and the Human Terrain*. Chicago: Prickly Paradigm Press.

Graeber, David. 2007. *Lost People: Magic and the Legacy of Slavery in Madagascar*. Bloomington: Indiana University Press.

———. 2011. *Debt: The First 5,000 Years*. New York: Melville House Publishing.

Green, Jesse. 1990. *Cushing at Zuni: The Correspondence and Journals of Frank Hamilton Cushing, 1879–1884*. Albuquerque: University of New Mexico Press.

Handler, Richard. 1988. *Nationalism and the Politics of Culture in Quebec*. Madison: University of Wisconsin Press.

Handman, Courtney. 2014. *Critical Christianity: Translation and Denominational Conflict in Papua New Guinea*. Berkeley: University of California Press.

Hart, Keith. 1986. "Heads or Tails? Two Sides of the Coin." *Man* 21 (4): 637–56.

———. 2005. *The Hit Man's Dilemma: Or Business, Personal and Impersonal*. Chicago: Prickly Paradigm Press.

Herdt, Gilbert H. 1982a. "Sambia Nosebleeding Rites and Male Proximity to Women." *Ethos* 10 (3): 189–231.

———, ed. 1982b. *Rituals of Manhood: Male Initiation in Papua New Guinea*. Berkeley: University of California Press.

Herzfeld, Michael. 1980. "Honour and Shame: Some Problems in the Comparative Analysis of Moral Systems." *Man* 15 (2): 339–51.

Howell, Signe. 1989. *Society and Cosmos: Chewong of Peninsular Malaysia*. Chicago: University of Chicago Press.

Hughte, Phil. 1994. *A Zuni Artist Looks at Frank Hamilton Cushing*. Albuquerque: University of New Mexico Press.

Huntington, Samuel P. 1993. "The Clash of Civilizations?" *Foreign Affairs* 72 (3): 22–49.

Hutchinson, Sharon Elaine. 2000. "Identity and Substance: The Broadening Bases of Relatedness among Nuer of Southern Sudan." In *Cultures of Relatedness: New Approaches to the Study of Kinship*, ed. Janet Carsten, 55–72. Cambridge: Cambridge University Press.

Inda, Jonathan Xavier, and Renato Rosaldo. 2002. "Tracking Global Flows." In *The Anthropology of Globalization: A Reader*, ed. Jonathan Xavier Inda and Renato Rosaldo, 3–46. Oxford: Blackwell.

James, Deborah. 2015. *Money from Nothing: Indebtedness and Aspiration in South Africa*. Stanford: Stanford University Press.

Jeske, Christine. 2016. "Are Cars the New Cows? Changing Wealth and Goods and Moral Economies in South Africa." *American Anthropologist* 118 (3): 483–94.

Kajanus, Anni. 2015. *Chinese Student Migration, Gender and Family*. Basingstoke: Palgrave Macmillan.

Keane, Webb. 1997. "Religious Language." *Annual Review of Anthropology* 26:47–71.

———. 2015. *Ethical Life: Its Natural and Social Histories*. Princeton: Princeton University Press.

Kleinman, Arthur. 2004. "Culture and Depression." *New England Journal of Medicine* 351:951–53.

Kroeber, A. L., and Clyde Kluckhohn. 1952. *Culture: A Critical Review of Concepts and Definitions*. Cambridge, MA: Harvard University Press.

Latour, Bruno. 1991. *We Have Never Been Modern*. Cambridge, MA: Harvard University Press.

Lepri, Isabella. 2006. "Identity and Otherness among the Ese Ejja of Northern Bolivia." *Ethnos* 71 (1): 67–88.

Lévi-Strauss, Claude. 1963. *Structural Anthropology*. New York: Basic Books.

———. 1964. *Totemism*. London: Merlin Press.

———. 1966. *The Savage Mind*. Chicago: University of Chicago Press.

Lévy-Bruhl, Lucien. 1966 [1926]. *How Natives Think*. New York: Washington Square Press.

Lock, Margaret. 2002. *Twice Dead: Organ Transplants and the Reinvention of Death*. Berkeley: University of California Press.

Lowie, Robert H. 2004 [1935]. *The Crow Indians*. Lincoln: University of Nebraska Press.

Luhrmann, Tanya. 2012. *When God Talks Back: Understanding the American Evangelical Relationship with God*. New York: Vintage Books.

MacCarthy, Michelle. 2012. "Contextualizing Authenticity: Cultural Tourism in the Trobriand Islands." PhD thesis, University of Auckland.

———. 2017. "Doing away with Doba? Women's Wealth and Shifting Values in Trobriand Mortuary Distributions." In *Sinuous Objects*, ed. Anna-Karina Hermkens and Katherine Lepani. Canberra: ANU Press.

Malinowski, Bronislaw. 1922. *Argonauts of the Western Pacific: An Account of the Native Enterprise and Adventure in the Archipelagoes of Melanesian New Guinea*. London: Routledge.

———. 1930. "Kinship." *Man* 30:19–29.

Manning, Paul. 2008. "Materiality and Cosmology: Old Georgian Churches as Sacred, Sublime, and Secular Objects." *Ethnos* 73 (3): 327–60.

Martin, Emily. 1991. "The Egg and the Sperm: How Science Has Constructed a Romance Based on Stereotypical Male-Female Roles." *Signs* 16 (3): 485–501.

Mauss, Marcel. 1990 [1926]. *The Gift: The Form and Reason for Exchange in Archaic Societies*. London: W. W. Norton.

Mazzarella, William. 2003. "Very Bombay: Contending with the Global in an Indian Advertising Agency." *Cultural Anthropology* 18 (1): 33–71.

McFate, Montgomery. 2005. "The Military Utility of Understanding Adversary Culture." *Joint Force Quarterly* 38:42–48.

McKinnon, Susan. 2005. *Neo-liberal Genetics: The Myths and Moral Tales of Evolutionary Psychology*. Chicago: Prickly Paradigm Press.

Merry, Sally Engle. 2001. "Changing Rights, Changing Culture." In *Culture and Rights: Anthropological Perspectives*, ed. Jane K. Cowan, Marie-Bénédicte Dembour, and Richard A. Wilson, 31–55. Cambridge: Cambridge University Press.

Mitchell, Joseph. 2017. *"Man—With Variations": Interviews with Franz Boas and Colleagues, 1937*. Chicago: Prickly Paradigm Press.

Morgan, Lewis H. 1871. *Systems of Consanguinity and Affinity of the Human Family*. Washington, DC: Smithsonian Institution.

———. 1877. *Ancient Society, or, Researches in the Lines of Human Progress from Savagery, through Barbarism to Civilization*. Chicago: Kerr and Company.

Mueggler, Erik. 2014. "Cats Give Funerals to Rats: Making the Dead Modern with Lament in South-west China." *Journal of the Royal Anthropological Institute* 20 (2): 197–217.

Mulligan, Connie. 2015. "Social and Behavioral Epigenetics." *American Anthropologist* 117 (4): 738–39.

Munn, Nancy. 1992. "The Cultural Anthropology of Time: A Critical Essay." *Annual Review of Anthropology* 21:93–123.

Narasimhan, Haripriya. 2011. "Adjusting Distances: Menstrual Pollution among Tamil Brahmins." *Contributions to Indian Sociology* 45 (2): 243–68.

Ohnuki-Tierney, Emiko. 1984. "'Native' Anthropologists." *American Ethnologist* 11:584–86.

Overing, Joanna. 1985. "Today I Shall Call Him, 'Mummy': Multiple Worlds and Classificatory Confusion." In *Reason and Morality*, ed. Joanna Overing, 152–79. London: Routledge.

Parkes, Peter. 2004. "Fosterage, Kinship, and Legend: When Milk Was Thicker than Blood?" *Comparative Studies in Society and History* 46 (3): 587–615.

Parkin, Robert. 2005. "The French-Speaking Countries." In *One Discipline, Four Ways: British, German, French, and American Anthropology*, 155–253. Chicago: University of Chicago Press.

Peristiany, Jean, ed. 1965. *Honour and Shame: The Values of Mediterranean Society*. London: Weidenfeld and Nicolson.

Petryna, Adriana. 2003. *Life Exposed: Biological Citizenship after Chernobyl*. Princeton: Princeton University Press.

Pitt-Rivers, Julian. 1965. "Honour and Social Status." In *Honour and Shame: The Values of Mediterranean Society*, ed. Jean Peristiany, 19–77. London: Weidenfeld and Nicolson.

Popenoe, Rebecca. 2004. *Feeding Desire: Fatness, Beauty and Sexuality among a Saharan People*. London: Routledge.

Powdermaker, Hortense. 1950. *Hollywood: The Dream Factory: An Anthropologist Looks at the Movie Makers*. London: Secker and Warburg.

Radcliffe-Brown, A. R. 1940. "On Social Structure." *Journal of the Royal Anthropological Institute* 70 (1): 1–12.

Rappaport, Roy A. 2000. *Ritual and Religion in the Making of Humanity*. Cambridge: Cambridge University Press.

Richards, Paul. 2016. *Ebola: How a People's Science Helped End an Epidemic*. London: Zed Books.

Robbins, Joel. 2004. *Becoming Sinners: Christianity and Moral Torment in a Papua New Guinea Society*. Berkeley: University of California Press.

———. 2007. "Continuity Thinking and the Problem of Christian Culture: Belief, Time, and the Anthropology of Christianity." *Current Anthropology* 48 (1): 5–38.

Rogoff, Kenneth S. 2016. *The Curse of Cash*. Princeton: Princeton University Press.

Sahlins, Marshall. 1972. "The Original Affluent Society." In *Stone Age Economics*, 1–40. Chicago: Aldine Atherton.

———. 1976. *The Use and Abuse of Biology: An Anthropological Critique of Sociobiology*. Ann Arbor: University of Michigan Press.

———. 1996. "The Sadness of Sweetness: The Native Anthropology of Western Cosmology." *Current Anthropology* 37 (3): 395–428.

Said, Edward. 1993. *Culture and Imperialism*. New York: Vintage Books.

Samuels, Annemarie. 2012. "After the Tsunami: The Remaking of Everyday Life in Bana Aceh, Indonesia." PhD diss., Leiden University.

Saussure, Ferdinand de. 1983. *Course in General Linguistics*. Chicago: Open Court.

Schieffelin, Bambi B., Kathryn A. Woolard, and Paul Kroskrity, eds. 1998. *Language Ideologies: Practice and Theory.* Oxford: Oxford University Press.

Schneider, David M. 1968. *American Kinship: A Cultural Account.* Chicago: University of Chicago Press.

Schneider, Jane. 1971. "Of Vigilance and Virgins: Honor, Shame and Access to Resources in Mediterranean Societies." *Ethnology* 10 (1): 1–24.

Scott, Michael W. 2013. "The Anthropology of Ontology (Religious Science?)." *Journal of the Royal Anthropological Institute* 19 (4): 859–72.

Shryock, Andrew. 2001. "Une politique de 'maison' dans la Jordanie des tribus: Reflexions sur l'honneur, la famille et la nation dans le royaume hashemite." In *Emirs et presidents: Figures de la parente et du politique en islam,* ed. Pierre Bonte, Edouard Conte, and Paul Dresch, 331–56. Paris: CNRS.

Silverstein, Michael. 1979. "Language Structure and Linguistic Ideology." In *The Elements: A Parasession on Linguistic Units and Levels,* ed. R. Cline, W. Hanks, and C. Hofbauer, 193–247. Chicago: Chicago Linguistic Society.

Spencer, Herbert. 1972 [1858]. *On Social Evolution.* Chicago: University of Chicago Press.

Sperber, Dan. 1985. *On Anthropological Knowledge: Three Essays.* Cambridge: Cambridge University Press.

Srinivas, M. N. 1959. "The Dominant Caste in Rampura." *American Anthropologist* 61 (1): 1–16.

Stack, Carol. 1976. *All Our Kin: Strategies for Survival in a Black Community.* New York: Basic Books.

Stafford, Charles. 2010. "The Punishment of Ethical Behaviour." In *Ordinary Ethics: Anthropology, Language, and Action,* ed. Michael Lambek, 187–206. New York: Fordham University Press.

Stasch, Rupert. 2011. "Ritual and Oratory Revisited: The Semiotics of Effective Action." *Annual Review of Anthropology* 40: 159–74.

Stocking, George W., Jr. 1968. "From Physics to Ethnology." In *Race, Culture, and Evolution: Essays in the History of Anthropology,* 133–61. Chicago: University of Chicago Press.

———. 1987. *Victorian Anthropology.* New York: The Free Press.

Strathern, Marilyn. 1988. *The Gender of the Gift: Problems with Women and Problems with Society in Melanesia.* Berkeley: University of California Press.

———. 1992. *After Nature: English Kinship in the Late Twentieth Century.* Cambridge: Cambridge University Press.

Strong, Pauline Turner, and Barrik Van Winkle. 1996. "'Indian Blood': Reflections on the Reckoning and Refiguring of Native North American Identity." *Cultural Anthropology* 10 (4): 547–76.

Sussman, Robert. 2015. *The Myth of Race: The Troubling Persistence of an Unscientific Idea.* Cambridge, MA: Harvard University Press.

Templeton, Alan R. 1998. "Human Races: A Genetics and Evolutionary Perspective." *American Anthropologist* 100 (3): 632–50.

Thoreau, Henry D. 1897. *Walden.* Boston: Houghton Mifflin.

Trautmann, Thomas R. 1987. *Lewis Henry Morgan and the Invention of Kinship.* Berkeley: University of California Press.

Turner, Terence. 1991. "We Are Parrots, Twins Are Birds: Play of Tropes as Operational Structure." In *Beyond Metaphor: The Theory of Tropes in Anthropology,* ed. James W. Fernandez, 121–58. Stanford: Stanford University Press

Turner, Victor. 1967. *The Forest of Symbols: Aspects of Ndembu Ritual.* Ithaca, NY: Cornell University Press.

Tylor, Edward B. 1865. *Researches into the Early History of Mankind and the Development of Civilization.* London: John Murray.

———. 1871. *Primitive Culture: Researches into the Development of Mythology, Philosophy, Religion, Art, and Custom.* London: John Murray.

Viveiros de Castro, Eduardo. 1992. *From the Enemy's Point of View: Humanity and Divinity in an Amazonian Society.* Chicago: University of Chicago Press.

———. 1998. "Cosmological Deixis and Amerindian Perspectivism." *Journal of the Royal Anthropological Institute* 4 (3): 469–88.

Wagner, Roy. 1975. *The Invention of Culture.* Chicago: University of Chicago Press.

Weiner, Annette. 1992. *Inalienable Possessions: The Paradox of Keeping-while-Giving.* Berkeley: University of California Press.

Wengrow, David. 2010. *What Makes Civilization?: The Ancient Near East and the Future of the West.* Oxford: Oxford University Press.

Weston, Kath. 2013. "Lifeblood, Liquidity, and Cash Transfusions: Beyond Metaphor in the Cultural Study of Finance." *Journal of the Royal Anthropological Institute* 19(S):S24–S41.

White, Leslie. 2007 [1959]. *The Evolution of Culture: The Development of Civilization to the Fall of Rome.* Walnut Creek, CA: Left Coast Press.

Whorf, Benjamin Lee. 1956. "The Relation of Habitual Thought and Behaviour to Language." In *Language, Thought and Reality: Selected Writings of Benjamin Lee Whorf*, ed. John B. Carroll, 134–59. Cambridge, MA: MIT Press.

Wilk, Richard R. 2002. "Television, Time and the National Imaginary in Belize." In *Media Worlds: Anthropology on New Terrain*, ed. Faye D. Ginsburg, Lila Abu-Lughod, and Brian Larkin, 171–86. Berkeley: University of California Press

Willerslev, Rane. 2009. "The Optimal Sacrifice: A Study of Voluntary Death among the Siberian Chukchi." *American Ethnologist* 36 (4): 693–704.

Woodburn, James. 1982. "Egalitarian Societies." *Man* 17 (3): 431–51.

Woolard, Kathryn A. 2016. *Singular and Plural: Ideologies of Linguistic Authority in 21st Century Catalonia*. Oxford: Oxford University Press.

Yan, Yunxiang. 2009. *The Individualization of Chinese Society*. London: Bloomsbury.

Yudell, Michael, Dorothy Roberts, Rob DeSalle, and Sarah Tishkoff. 2016. "Taking Race out of Human Genetics: Engaging a Century-Long Debate about the Role of Race in Science." *Science* 351 (6273): 564–65.

Zaloom, Caitlin. 2006. *Out of the Pits: Traders and Technology from Chicago to London*. Chicago: University of Chicago Press.

# FURTHER READING

There is plenty of further reading in the bibliography—lots to follow up on. But I would like to offer a short list of books—just ten (a few of which are also listed in the bibliography)—that might be of particular interest and are easily accessible to non-specialists. In fact, one thing that all these books have in common is that their authors are very good writers. Half of the books are big-picture, synthetic, and often polemical works; the other half are ethnographies focused on issues of broad social and political import and interest.

Ruth Benedict, *Patterns of Culture* (New York: Houghton Mifflin Harcourt, 1934)
One of my all-time favorites, as you've probably guessed. The first two chapters in particular are still the best, most passionate, and most articulate arguments we have for the importance of culture in our makeup.

Adam Kuper, *Culture: The Anthropologist's Account* (Cambridge, MA: Harvard University Press, 1999)
It only seems fair to suggest a book by a colleague who doesn't think culture is the indispensable term I've claimed it is. Kuper is culture's skeptic-in-chief, partly for the ways in which the term gets used and abused in broader public arenas and partly because he thinks its ideational shortcomings cannot be overcome.

Daniel Miller, *Stuff* (Cambridge: Polity Press, 2009)
Stuff as in material culture. Denim jeans, houses, phones, cars, saris: Miller is interested in pretty much everything out there that can be counted as a human artifact. Miller is a leading figure in material culture studies, and this book is a condensed and easily accessible set of reflections on all the stuff that he has pored over, touched, worn, driven, observed in action, and thought about since the early 1980s.

David Graeber, *Debt: The First 5000 Years* (New York: Melville House, 2011)
Another book I've discussed already, though not as much as Benedict's. What's so great about this book is how it uses the anthropological

record to challenge some of the fundamental assumptions we hold about a range of things—not only debt and its moral loadings but the invention of money and the role of the state in modern society. Read this and you'll come away with a very distinctive take on how to understand the global credit crisis of 2008 and subsequent embrace of "austerity."

Lila Abu-Lughod, *Do Muslim Women Need Saving?* (Cambridge, MA: Harvard University Press, 2015)
No, in short: read this book to find out why. It'll give you a further appreciation of why cultural relativism is such a valuable way of approaching the thorny social and political issues of the contemporary world. It also sets out very clearly how the very question itself is tied to the colonial-era project of "civilizing" the world.

Jason De León, *The Land of Open Graves: Living and Dying on the Migrant Trail* (Berkeley: University of California Press, 2015) and Ruben Andersson, *Illegality, Inc.: Clandestine Migration and the Business of Bordering Europe* (Berkeley: University of California Press, 2014).
Two books you might want to read together. In León's case, the focus is the U.S.-Mexican border; in Andersson's, it is Africans crossing the Mediterranean into Spain. What both books show is the human side to migration. They tell stories of individuals with a depth and intimacy that helps us understand the logic and motivation behind taking such serious risks. In León's book, you'll also get a sense of how cultural anthropology can be combined with archaeology and biological anthropology, since some of his most important data come from these other subfields.

Ilana Gershon, *Down and Out in the New Economy: How People Find (or Don't Find) Work Today* (Chicago: University of Chicago Press, 2017)
Prompted in part by the concerns expressed by her students at Indiana University who were facing the job market after college, Gershon's book is a fascinating look at how applicants have to rely increasingly on new media technologies, as well as "brand" themselves not as individuals but as walking and talking mini-businesses. It's a study of the economy, but it's also a study of how ideas of personhood are changing in the twenty-first century.

Kim Tallbear, *Native American DNA: Tribal Belonging and the False Promise of Genetic Science* (Minneapolis: University of Minnesota Press, 2013)
TallBear picks up two strands that I've highlighted in different chapters: the power of blood and the power of genes in the politics of race and cultural identity. This is a book about how many Native American groups are starting to think (and, in some respects, being forced to think) in terms of DNA and genetics.

Alpa Shah, *In the Shadows of the State: Indigenous Politics, Environmentalism, and Insurgency in Jharkhand, India* (Durham, NC: Duke University Press, 2010)
There has been a major push for group rights in India over the past several decades, the noble intention of which is to lift marginalized indigenous groups out of poverty and social exclusion. As Shah documents, however, in Jharkhand these efforts have often made the situation worse, since it sets up an idealized model of how people should live in "harmony" with the nature surrounding them. A good book to read if you're interested in development and human rights.

# INDEX

Abu-Lughod, Lila, 50–51, 53, 96, 96n
adoption: among Native Americans, 145, 146; "interracial" adoption, 170, 275
Agrama, Hussein Ali, 211–14
agricultural communities, in the Mediterranean, 93–94; kinship structure and political organization of, 93; and partible inheritance, 93; and pastoralists, 93–94
*All Our Kin* (Stack), 139–40; on "personal kindreds," 140
Ambedkar, B. R., 101
*American Kinship: A Cultural Account* (D. Schneider), 137–38; absence of race in, 139
Amerindian cosmologies, 242–44, 281–82; emphasis of on "perspectivism," 243–44; "humanity" as the original condition in, 242–43
ancient Near East, 80–82; as "the birthplace of civilization," 80; the distinctiveness of Egyptian and Mesopotamian worldviews, 81–82; and the domestication of goats, 80
*Ancient Society* (Morgan), 61
Andalusians, 89–90
anthropology, 3–5, 7–8; "applied anthropology," 21–22; "armchair anthropologists," 10; background on anthropology as a discipline, 9–15; the birth of the discipline of anthropology, 16–19; the British and American branches of, 19–20; and the cliché that we make the

familiar strange and the strange familiar, 6–7; and colonialism, 13; cultural anthropology, 4–5; and the explanation of origins, 94; famous people who have anthropology in their backgrounds, 22–23; and figure-ground reversals, 281; French tradition of, 10; and international exchange, 20–21; interpretive anthropology, 96n; linguistic anthropology, 4–5, 176–77 (*see also* language ideology); and local knowledge, 281; medical anthropology, 33–34; native anthropologists, 11–12n; as points of view on points of view, 28–33; social anthropology, 4–5, 52; as a social science, not a natural science, 265; women in, 18n
"Anti Anti-Relativism" (Geertz), 14
Appadurai, Arjun, 50, 53
Araweté, 241, 281; and the claim that jaguars are people too, 227; the National Indian Foundation's naming of, 241n; self-reference of (as *bïde*), 241
archaeology, 4, 35–37; and "fieldwork," 35; focus of on material culture, 35–36
*Argonauts of the Western Pacific* (Malinowski), 17, 46; on Kula, 46, 117–19
Aristotle, 275
Arnold, Matthew, 39
Asad, Talal, 21
Astuti, Rita, 272–75